THE PAPER NAUTILUS

THE

PAPER NAUTILUS

....

A TRILOGY

Michael Jackson

OTAGO UNIVERSITY PRESS
Te Whare Tā o Te Wānanga o Ōtākou

Published by Otago University Press
Te Whare Tā o Te Wānanga o Ōtakou
Level 1, 398 Cumberland Street
Dunedin, New Zealand
university.press@otago.ac.nz
www.otago.ac.nz/press

First published 2019
Copyright © Michael Jackson
The moral rights of the author have been asserted.

ISBN 978-1-98-853179-3

Editor: Erika Bűky
Design and layout: Fiona Moffat

Front cover: Argonaut Octopus Eggcase Shell, Gilles Mermet
Science Photo Library, C019/1291

Printed in China through Asia Pacific Offset

And so a mix of truth and fiction, however unsatisfactory in philosophical terms, offered by somebody who is trying, with all the intelligence, sympathy and understanding of which they are capable, to imagine the situation of the other person from the inside out is worth far more than a pure and lonely truth. An I-and-you truth, a relational truth, is much more valuable than one more separate and more certain.

— ARABELLA KURTZ, *The Good Story*

CONTENTS

1.

THEME AND VARIATIONS

LOSING THE PLOT

I've always been drawn to two literary genres – the picaresque and the frame narrative. As a child I was entranced by the artful way in which Scheherazade's stories in *The One Thousand and One Nights* were set inside one another like matryoshka dolls. Equally intriguing to me was the way her stories were connected not by logic but by adventitious associations. In my fieldwork in Sierra Leone I was again captivated by tales whose 'chaste compactness', to use Walter Benjamin's phrase, belied their existential depth. While picaresque and frame stories bear a family resemblance to classical folktales, they are very different from the novel, a genre that emerged in the eighteenth century. Centred on individual subjects and characterised by complex plots, the novel is more akin to the academic essay than to the folktale, which was subsequently denigrated as infantile and premodern. For me, one appeal of the traditional tale is its unapologetic acceptance of the role of contingency and coincidence in human life. While the novel reflects a modernist ethos of 'possessive individualism', which foregrounds conscious purpose, complicated motivations and emotional compulsions, the unfolding of the traditional tale depends on happenstance, fate and caprice.

Although elements of the frame narrative and the picaresque find expression in modern cinema, I yearned to create a work in which variations on a theme would replace the adventures of a person. My theme is loss: the forms it takes and how we go on living in the face of it. When I reflect on the vicissitudes of my own life or my ethnographic experiences in West Africa, I am struck by the mysterious ways in which new life and new beginnings are born of brokenness. The paper nautilus provides a vivid image of this interplay of death and rebirth. A fragile shell buoys the eggs of the pelagic octopus to the surface of the sea, whereupon it is blown into inshore waters. There the angelically beautiful brood chamber breaks, the eggs hatch and the baby octopuses begin their life cycle.

But how was I to write about a theme that finds such a bewildering variety of expressions in different societies, individuals and genres? How could I do justice to this phenomenological diversity?

I took heart from David Lynch's account of wanting to create a certain kind of film but needing to let his ambition become a bait, luring ideas to him as fish are lured to a hook. By implication, ideas, images and even people come to us unbidden, and slip away from us just as unpredictably, as if obedient neither to necessity nor convention, and indifferent to whether we are worthy or unworthy of their presence. I also found inspiration in Alan Bennett's *Untold Stories*, a copy of which had been discarded on a pew near my office at the Harvard Divinity School. I read it as if it were a gift from the gods and considered keeping a commonplace book in the hope that I might be party to the kind of aperçus that seemed to fall fortuitously into Bennett's lap. In any event, I was curious to know the extent to which life itself may determine the path of one's thinking and the form of one's writing, and whether aimless wandering, daydreaming, unexpected encounters and free associations can open us up to the world in ways that conscious planning cannot.

There are times when the self splinters under the pressure of displacement and loss. One becomes multifaceted. 'I' becomes 'an-other'. Invented characters give voice to experiences one hesitates to acknowledge as one's own, and genres blur, as if none can do one's subject justice. Accordingly, this work begins discursively with a series of loosely connected essays and gradually morphs into a memoir of a marriage and a friendship, only to be reinvented as a work of fiction.

Yesterday the Dow plunged more than a thousand points. Apparently such ups and downs in the money markets are not unusual, and right now the markets are adjusting to a period of accelerated economic growth, rising inflation and a somewhat more hawkish Federal Reserve. According to one analyst, these typical late-cycle trends have generally been good for stocks.

It's not only the market that's volatile. Life too has its cycles of boom and bust, and also, perhaps, a capacity to self-correct. As for the clichés with which stockbrokers reassure their panicking clients – 'Diversify,' 'Rebalance periodically,' 'Don't try timing the market,' 'Stay focused on the long term,' 'Have a rainy-day fund on hand,' 'Talk to your financial advisor' – they are uncannily like the hackneyed phrases with which we console those whose lives are falling apart.

In life as in the marketplace, you never know when, or in what way, the rug's going to be pulled from under you – when your best efforts may come to nothing; when the things you once did without a second thought may become Herculean tasks; when you may be driven from your home by war and must cross a border to a place where you are not wanted, to await a return that may never be possible. When you lose someone you love. When age, illness and infirmity erode your hold on life, and no pleasure outweighs your pain.

Writing about neurological deficits, such as loss of speech, language, memory, vision, dexterity and identity, Oliver Sacks observes that 'a disease is never a mere loss or excess' – that 'there is always a reaction, on the part of the affected organism or individual to restore, to replace, to compensate for and to preserve its identity, however strange the means may be.' He goes on to say that the study of these curious ways in which life goes on is an essential part of a physician's vocation. This is also true of a writer's work. What interests me, however, is not how we make good our losses but how we learn to live with them. Sacks was inspired by the pioneering work of the great Russian neuropsychologist A.R. Luria, who, in *The Man with a Shattered World,* described a long-term patient who suffered massive damage to the left occipital-parietal region of his brain when hit by shell fragments in 1942. For 25 years, he painstakingly filled volume after volume of notebooks with accounts of his fragmented world. Writing, observes Luria, 'was his one link with life, his only hope of not succumbing to illness but recovering at least a part of what had been lost'. But Zazetsky was under no illusions that his scribblings would constitute a coherent narrative, help recover his memory, or be of much use to anyone else. Perhaps that is why he referred to his writing as 'morbid', despite the fact that his life depended on it. 'If I shut these notebooks, give it up, I'll be right back in the desert, in that "know-nothing" world of emptiness and amnesia.' What sustained him was a primitive existential imperative – to act rather than be acted upon. 'The point of my writing,' he said, 'is to show how I have been, and still am, struggling to recover my memory ... I had no choice but to try.'

Coping with loss is a matter not of heroically beating the odds, or triumphing in the face of adversity, but of our human capacity for new beginnings.

Hannah Arendt speaks of this capacity as natality – the faculty of countering ruin and destruction by 'beginning something new, a faculty which is inherent in action, like an ever-present reminder that [human beings], though they must die, are not born in order to die but in order to begin'. It is worth adding, I think, that we are constantly preparing ourselves for such moments in our everyday fantasies of embarking on another life somewhere else; in our search for a soul mate, a heavenly home or a panacea for all our ills; or in our nightly dreams, as we clear away the debris of our yesterdays in order to freely enter the day ahead.

In Solitary

I had been teaching at Harvard for several years, untenured and transient. Every spring I went cap in hand to the dean and asked to be given another year, like a prisoner petitioning for a stay of execution.

Yet it wasn't the insecurity of my job, nor the bitter New England winters, nor even the formality of my colleagues that drove me inward. It was an inchoate sense of loss that had accompanied me for as long as I could remember, and whose source I had never fully fathomed. Increasingly, however, I glimpsed in a half-forgotten poem, in moments of idleness or in dreams, in memories of friends who had passed away or the landscapes of my homeland, insights into the origins of my sorrow. In keeping a record of these glimmerings, I began to feel at peace with my circumstances and surer of what I wanted to write.

As the semester drew to a close, a Chinese student who was about to return to Shanghai gave me, as a parting gift, a biography of Mu Xin, the master watercolourist whose work had inspired her own. I felt an immediate affinity. It was not only Mu Xin's art that captivated me; it was his life, or, more accurately, the relationship between his art and his life.

Determined to learn more about him, I found a documentary film that chronicled his struggle to work freely in Mao's China. Incarcerated many times for counter-revolutionary activities and dissenting opinions, he endured two years in solitary confinement during the Cultural Revolution. While locked in a basement room, he was able to persuade his guards to provide him with small sheets of rice paper, ostensibly to write self-criticism and reform himself. Instead, he wrote in minuscule characters ('as tiny as rice grains'), on both sides of each sheet, recollections of his childhood and imaginary dialogues with his literary heroes. He then tightly folded the paper and secreted it in the lining of his pants. Discovery of these writings would have cost him his life, yet the act of writing kept him alive. Refusing to accept the proverbial wisdom that suffering leads to enlightenment, Mu Xin preferred not to dwell on the past, but to apply himself to the creation of something new. 'What makes me happy is creating a unique work of art. I have never dared to hope that one day my work would be seen. I just wanted to prove that I was still alive. I create so I can leave some trace of my existence.'

I reflected on this statement for a long time, wondering if we are not all in solitary – creating self-important spaces, seeking small distractions, cultivating a sense of purpose, lest we become obliterated by the darkness around us. Like the addict in search of his fix, the family just making ends meet, the young graduate hoping for a lucky break, the writer struggling to find the mot juste – how ethereal are these bubbles in which we live, and how pathetic our hope that the bubble will not burst: the bubble in which I scribble these pessimistic thoughts on a swaying train, the rising sun in my eyes, as my fellow passengers check for messages on their cellphones, scroll through Facebook, or sit absorbed in a book, all seeking similar spaces of refuge, transitory clearings in the immensity and chaos of the wider world.

In her Introduction to Walter Benjamin's *Illuminations*, Hannah Arendt celebrates her friend's 'passion for small, even minute things' and his desire to capture history in the most insignificant moments, 'its scraps, as it were'. Benjamin was particularly fascinated by two grains of wheat in the Jewish section of the Musée Cluny 'on which a kindred soul had inscribed the complete Shema Israel', and he sought to achieve something similar on the printed page. From the beginning, Arendt notes, he was less attracted to theories and ideas than to particular phenomena. His central concern was for 'directly, actually demonstrable concrete facts, with single events and occurrences whose significance was manifest' – the very phenomena that many academics would dismiss as contingent and unenlightening. Benjamin was equally fascinated by the ways in which the past carries a secret index by which it is referred to its redemption. For do we not breathe the same air that our forebears breathed? Don't the muted voices of the past echo in the voices we hear today? And is there not an unspoken agreement between past generations and our own?

Perhaps all writing is an attempt to replay reality, the better to resolve issues that were unresolved in life – a belated effort to determine the shape of events we could do nothing about.

If the history of our species and the stories of our lives comprise a series of devastating losses and creative reparations, we might conclude that art, ritual and storytelling all share a common cause – the construction of imaginary worlds and fictional characters that defy the constancies of time, space and personhood, and offer simulacra of life from which all pain has been expelled.

HUDSON REJOINS THE HERD

Hudson Rejoins the Herd is the title of a novel by Claude Houghton, purportedly a manuscript written by a certain Stephen Hudson that somehow came into the author's possession. At the beginning of the novel the 41-year-old Hudson is lying in a nursing home, recovering from a bullet wound. 'Although I am in pain, I write partly to convince myself that I am returning to life; partly to escape from an indeterminate realm where thoughts, dreams, and memories mingle in a timeless drama. I write this because, at all costs, I must return to the actual world. I cannot stay any longer in that vast interior universe in which I seem to have been wandering for centuries. By a miracle, I am alive. I *must* rediscover myself and the world.'

These lines resonated as strongly with me as they did with Henry Miller, who felt as if they had been written especially for him. 'What so startled me in reading this book,' Miller writes, 'was that it appeared to give a picture of my most intimate life during a certain crucial period. The outer circumstances were "disguised", but the inner ones were hallucinatingly real. I could not have done better myself. For a time, I thought that Claude Houghton had in some mysterious way gained access to these facts and events in my life.' Miller goes on to say that we should not be surprised that the characters we encounter in fiction correspond to real individuals, or that we can expect to meet our double one day, if not in life, then in the pages of a novel. Even before we are born, a version of each of us has walked the earth. It is not that *we* have previously existed but rather that our life story has already begun to be told, perhaps centuries ago, and that we are also destined to meet people we feel we have known already, in another life.

Do these moments of recognition mean that what is lost in one epoch or place will be inevitably found or recovered in another?

On a visit to Oxford University, where I had been invited to present a public lecture on migrant imaginaries, I was offered the use of a room in which hundreds of olive-green volumes of the *Bulletin of the Bureau of the American Ethnological Society* were shelved. These volumes contained ethnographic reports dating from 1880 onward that documented the vanishing lifeways of numerous Native American peoples. Leafing through these meticulous accounts of ritual and practical life among peoples whose lives, livelihoods and languages were lost in the course of invasion, displacement, violent assaults and pandemics, I was reminded of Claude Lévi-Strauss's comment in *Tristes Tropiques* that the world-views and ways of life that were destroyed by colonial conquest have not been lost forever, since the imaginative resourcefulness of the human mind will inevitably reinvent them. I did not regard this romantic conceit as an adequate response to the tragedy suffered by so many indigenous peoples. But Lévi-Strauss's observation reminds us, nevertheless, that the idea of absolute loss may be as much a misnomer as the idea of permanent presence. As I learned from the Warlpiri of Central Australia, everything passes away in the fullness of time, but no disappearance is forever, since everything that has ever lived reappears sooner or later, albeit slightly changed.

MUGGED

In agreeing to participate in a graduate workshop at the University of Lausanne, I hoped I might find time to make a pilgrimage to the birthplace of Blaise Cendrars, but fate had other things in store for me.

At Zurich airport I bought a train ticket to Lausanne and found my way to the platform from which my train was scheduled to depart. As I prepared to board, I was jostled by a small crowd of agitated men who vanished as quickly as they had appeared. So brief was this unsettling moment that by the time I had shoved my suitcase ahead of me into the railway carriage and readjusted my satchel on my shoulder, the disquiet was not even a memory: as I later thought, my brain had no way of comprehending what my body had felt, had no previous experience against which to assess what had occurred. When I finally found a seat, stowed my suitcase on the overhead rack and felt for my wallet, I experienced no alarm that it wasn't in my jacket pocket, and I began searching for it in my satchel. Not finding it there, I still did not panic. Despite turning out my pockets, ransacking my satchel and rummaging in my suitcase, my brain resisted the obvious conclusion that I'd been mugged. It was only when the train suddenly jerked into motion, and I stared out at the snaking, sliding rails, and soot-blackened cables slung along begrimed brick walls, that I realised what had happened. It was then that my brain went into overdrive, thinking not of how my wallet had been filched in a split second of carefully orchestrated distraction but of what I would tell the ticket collector when asked to show my ticket. I didn't have long to wait. Though I was certain my story would sound contrived, the ticket collector seemed unperturbed and promised to alert the airport police in Zurich. I should file a report online as soon as I reached Lausanne. He provided me with an internet address before moving on.

But I could not move on. I had not only been robbed of my wallet, I had been robbed of my reality or, more precisely, of my concept of what I could reasonably and realistically expect on a journey from Zurich to Lausanne. Had I been in Sierra Leone my expectations would have been very different, as would my concept of when, and with whom, I should be on my guard.

I found myself wishing I could magically turn back the clock and retrace my steps from the time I disembarked from my plane to the time I bought my train ticket. But time, like the train, rattled onward through green fields fringed with chestnuts and oaks, under a sky of broken cloud.

At Lausanne, people streamed around me while I stood transfixed, not knowing what to think or what to do. I hadn't experienced absolute penury for many years, nor the powerlessness that comes with it. It was suddenly brought home to me that life is movement, and that to be immobilised is to suffer a kind of conceptual death. Even if I knew what to do, I doubted I'd be able to do it. It was as much as I could manage to drag my suitcase to a bench at the end of the platform where I succumbed to a series of 'what if' or 'if only' ruminations that only increased my bewilderment. If only I had taken a later train. Or boarded another carriage. If only I had not accepted the invitation to this workshop. If only I owned a cellphone, like everyone else.

As I suffered this torrent of vain conjecture and second guessing, there arose a sensation that brought me back to reality. I badly needed a piss.

For this I needed two Swiss francs. But I didn't have a sou.

My appeals to the attendant at the public toilet were as unavailing as the need to relieve myself was becoming unbearable.

Leaving my suitcase behind, I dashed out onto the street, desperately looking for a blind alley, a dark corner, a deserted park.

With nowhere to go, I returned to the public toilet and repeated my appeal to use the pissoir. I even asked several passers-by if they could spare me a few francs. They looked at me as if it was inconceivable that I would be *sans ressources, sans le sou*. Perhaps they saw me as a vagrant or foreigner and for this reason alone I could expect little sympathy.

Ignoring the attendant, I clambered over the turnstile, locked myself in a cubicle and released the pent piss without thinking twice about the fly in the toilet bowl (it was painted on the porcelain), how the attendant would react to my behaviour, whether my suitcase was safe or how I was going to get to my hotel.

That evening, enjoying the company of anthropological colleagues in a chalet overlooking Lake Geneva and the Swiss Alps, I recounted my comedy of errors while sipping chilled white wine to wash down raclette, new potatoes, jambon cru and picked onions, amazed at how quickly my life had been returned to normal. Yet the disorientation and discomfort I had momentarily suffered were, I knew, the permanent condition of many migrants. Though I relished the warm atmosphere of the chalet, I did not want to forget the events of the day or dismiss them as if they had happened a lifetime ago or to someone else.

It also dawned on me that something else had changed. It wasn't only that I was now utterly indifferent to my academic future, nor even that I was more determined than ever to succeed as a creative writer. That things were suddenly different was, I think, because my recent fieldwork among African migrants in Europe had brought me face to face with the cumulative effects of my own expatriate life.

Losing Face

Dispossession can be seen in two mutually determining ways – as the loss of what one has, and the loss of who one is. Among the Kuranko people of Sierra Leone, the plural noun *mirannu* denotes both material possessions – particularly those that contain and protect, such as houses, clothes, water vessels and cooking pots – and personal attributes, such as confidence in speaking, skill in practical tasks and social adroitness. But one's *miran*, in both the material and personal senses, is always in flux. It can be bolstered by fetishes that symbolically enclose, contain and protect the vital spaces in which one lives – one's body, house, village, chiefdom – in exactly the same way that in a consumer society material possessions bolster and define a person's sense of substantiality and standing. For Kuranko, the notion of a full container is a common metaphor for being in command of oneself, and doing one's utmost to fulfil one's duty. But self-possession may be sapped or lost. Just as a person's property can be stolen, a pot broken and a house fall into disrepair, so a person can lose self-confidence, as when his or her *miran* is 'taken away' by an autocratic parent, a forceful public speaker, or a powerful bush spirit whose voice and power 'press down' with great weight, diminishing that person's *miran*. Then, it is said that 'the container has tipped over and its contents spilled out' – a metaphor for loss of self-control, or for a state of laziness or despair when one has 'let oneself go' (*nyere bila*). Ideally, a balance is struck in which everyone's voice, presence and property are accorded due recognition in relation to role, age and gender. But some people assert themselves beyond their station – as in the case of a Big Man who exploits his position to take advantage of an inferior, a senior co-wife who abuses her junior partners, a man whose jealousy overrules his better judgement, or a woman whose emotions are not held in check. A kind of intersubjective logic then comes into play, based on the principle of reciprocity, according to which one has the right to counter in kind any action that has the effect of directly nullifying or belittling one's own being.

Since *miran* blurs any hard and fast distinction between having and being, it can be augmented through taking the wherewithal of life from others – through theft, witchcraft, abuse and humiliation – or through the giving of such things as respect, food, help and protection that will later be returned in equal measure. At the same time, 'real', symbolic and fantastic calculations enter into people's notions of what constitutes their due, and Kuranko folktales, like folktales throughout the world, with their magical agencies, supernatural intercessions and miraculous transformations, attest to the vital role that wishful thinking and imaginary reworkings of everyday reality play in making life endurable.

LOST AND FOUND

I had, for some time, contemplated writing a novel called *The Museum of Unclaimed Objects* that would begin with a description of the world's first lost-and-found office, created by Napoleon in Paris in 1805 to house, in a central location on the Île de la Cité, all the miscellaneous objects picked up on the city's streets. Even today, items left in buses or the Métro – umbrellas, sunglasses, keys, wallets and handbags, cufflinks, hats, cellphones, roller skates, manuscripts, files, backpacks, motorcycle helmets and sunglasses – are catalogued and kept here, waiting to be reclaimed by their rightful owners. A truck arrives daily, laden with objects found on the Métro alone.

There are 3500 cellphones, some of which still ring, as if calling for their owners.

Coincidentally, my grandfather, who was a policeman in a New Zealand country town for 40 years, was also a custodian of found objects. The same kind of things that ended up in the warehouse on the Île de la Cité would end up in his possession and be stored in a shed behind the police station that he called his Museum of Unclaimed Objects. Abandoned suitcases, children's dolls, musical instruments, cameras, jewellery, bicycles, tack, whips, boots and shoes … all this lost treasure from people's lives, unclaimed and forgotten, was stashed away in permanent limbo. From time to time he would advertise a police auction and play the auctioneer. I attended several of these auctions when I was a boy, ruing the fact that I did not have the money to bid on the cameras and bicycles. But mostly I remember the distress my grandfather felt knowing that most of these objects would never find their way back to their owners, for he believed that the objects and their owners belonged together like close kin. He spoke of the objects as orphans. If he could reconnect them with their owners, he would redeem their lives. He may have thought of himself as a midwife of souls, thus assuaging his guilt at sending people to prison, putting them out of circulation, cutting them off from their families and from the world.

He used to entertain me with stories he composed for these lost and mislaid things. I think he was also moved to know who they belonged to, and what these objects might have experienced, witnessed, or known had they been animate and conscious – the lives that were not led, the opportunities missed, the roads not taken. I think that in telling these stories my grandfather was commenting on the regrets, missteps and misjudgements that had defined his own life – a life he had tried to lead respecting the dignity of all people, not bringing shame on those he had to arrest, incarcerate, bear witness against, or punish, and not harming those whom life had already harmed.

A Dream of My Grandfather

I am in my grandfather's house. Although he died more than half a century ago, it seems only yesterday that I visited him, as close to him as when I was a boy, hanging on his every word. As I enter the front room where he repaired after lunch to smoke his pipe and read the *Taranaki Herald*, I am surprised that he is not sitting in his favourite chair, which is nowhere to be seen. And though we speak to each other, after waking from my dream I cannot recall anything that we said.

This uncanny mix of certainty and vagueness is typical of dreams. In dream worlds, places, people and words lack the clarity we associate with everyday reality, yet we are in no doubt as to their presence, which may explain why, in recounting our dreams, we confidently flesh out and formalise what were, in fact, quite ethereal scenarios. And so, when I told my wife about this encounter with my grandfather, I explained that it was not like a dream at all, but as if I had travelled through time and space and actually been in his company.

I could not shake off this dream or the memories of migration and loss it brought to mind. Yet these were not exactly my memories but my grandfather's memories of his seven-week voyage from England to New Zealand in 1906. In the small diary his brother Arthur gave him, contingent on a promise that Fred would, in due course, return it so that Arthur might make up his own mind about the advantages and disadvantages of migration, Fred kept a daily record of the ship's progress; the changing weather; glimpses of waterspouts, albatrosses and whales; the deck games that helped break the monotony; and the seasickness to which everyone but he succumbed. Tall and athletically built, Fred took pride in his sporting prowess and leadership skills. He had been police judo champion in Yorkshire; now, on the *Turakina*, he hand-picked and captained a cricket eleven, and his team won a tug-of-war. Two weeks into the voyage, he confided that he was 'in the Pink of condition' and was 'not letting anything trouble me', though in his disappointment in some of his fellow migrants, who took one look at the bleak prospect of their new-found land and booked berths on the first ship home, one discerns some of the misgivings he may have felt at starting over in such a far-flung, isolated dominion.

Many migrants grapple with a sense of having betrayed their homeland and are haunted by guilt that they did not endure the situation into which they were born but tried to escape it. One of my grandfather's favourite stories concerned Harry Houdini's visit to a police station in West Yorkshire where my grandfather was stationed for several years before his departure from England. Houdini's routine was well known and well rehearsed. After allowing himself to be handcuffed and body-searched, he would be locked, almost naked, in a secure cell. Within a minute, Houdini would appear barefoot in the corridor, hurrying to overtake his jailers. To the delight of my grandfather, Houdini asked the chief constable if he was missing anything – his watch, perhaps. As the mystified officer dabbed at his fob pocket, Houdini produced the watch and chain out of thin air. That my grandfather enjoyed the humiliation of his superior says as much about Houdini's showmanship and skill as it reveals where my grandfather's sympathies lay and, possibly, the germ of his idea of escaping the old country.

Fred's diary was sent home, as promised, and Arthur also migrated to New Zealand. But whereas Fred tried farm work for a while before deciding to return to policing – despite his traumatic experiences in the West Yorkshire Constabulary, ordered to baton-charge workers agitating for better pay – Arthur opened a dairy in Petone.

After Arthur's death, Fred's diary came into the possession of his sister Alice, who, in 1957, bequeathed it to Fred's daughter – my mother, Emily. One hundred and eleven years after the diary had been written, it was transcribed by my sister Bronwen and in this form came to me. Reading it precipitated memories of the stories he told me when I was a boy, sitting beside him in the front room of his house on Miro Street or outside his garden shed, or at the bowling club, where his panama hat, appearing above the corrugated iron fence, would stir in me an eagerness to be with him. I felt the same anticipation when he came to our house to listen to the Ashes cricket test matches on my father's short-wave radio. We sat together in my father's radio shack as John Arlott's commentary came through the sea surge and static of the BBC broadcast, connecting my grandfather with home and me with him. Though he was retired, and perhaps in need of someone to share his interests or listen to anecdotes from his policing days, I am astonished that he tolerated my relentless questioning and confided so much to a mere child. Only now, having reached the age he was then, do I fully realise how deeply affected I was by his stories and his values. Indeed, I sometimes feel that my own life is simply an extension of his, and that I actually lived through events that unfolded years before I was born.

If my grandfather's one confessed regret was that he started work in a woollen mill when he was 10 and missed out on a decent education, my grandmother, to whom he proposed as soon as he was settled in New Zealand, never overcame the loss of her family and the gentility she associated with England. Better educated than her husband and determined, as she put it in her diary, to recreate 'an English home' in a colony where locals seemed to regard home as 'their last consideration', 'a place to go to when their pleasures are over', she found comfort in *The Pilgrim's Progress* and her Methodist faith, while Fred found consolation in his work. He took immense pride in his appearance, sending his collars to be starched by a Chinese launderer in New Plymouth and having his suits tailored from the finest English worsteds. Physically and morally strong, he gave the impression of absolute self-sufficiency. While I shrank from the shadows, fearful that the coalman would materialise out of the night and spirit me away, he patrolled the darkened streets with torch and truncheon, checking that shops were locked and stables bolted. He even outlived the RMS *Turakina*, the ship on which he had sailed from Tilbury 'in splendid weather and excellent spirits,' on 19 April 1906.

In 1940, the year I was born, the *Turakina* was sunk by a German raider off the Taranaki coast, with thirty-six crew killed and twenty-one survivors taken prisoner. Although my grandfather never mentioned the fate of the freighter that had brought him safely to New Zealand, it serves as a compelling reminder of how unpredictably the winds of history shift and fortunes founder. Indeed, his stories all touched on the vulnerability of those his policing duties obliged him to arrest and arraign. All broached the question of how to uphold the law while respecting the humanity of those who had transgressed it. Sometimes he helped a miscreant see the error of his ways or issued a stern warning. If he had to put an obstreperous drunk in the lock-up, he would see that the man got a square meal, and he would sometimes turn a blind eye to after-hours drinking in the Railway Hotel.

He had chosen to be posted to a sole-charge police station in order to preserve his autonomy, but there were times when official decrees could not be ignored, as when he was drafted to join the manhunt for Joseph John Pawelka in 1910. When captured and brought to trial, Joe Pawelka got twenty-one years' hard labour for breaking and entering, theft, arson and escape. Many people, including my grandfather, thought the sentence vengeful and unjust, and on the wintry August day in 1911 when Pawelka escaped from the Terrace Gaol in Wellington, never to be heard of again, my grandfather was happy to conclude that poetic justice had been done.

His sense of natural justice was also challenged in the aftermath of the sinking of the *Lusitania* by a German U-boat in 1915. From the moment war had been declared, patriotic fervour was intense. But most people flew the Union Jack rather than the New Zealand ensign from their balconies and porches, for they were recent migrants, and England was the home they were willing to die for. At the same time, love of country invariably goes hand in hand with hatred for whatever threatens the homeland. In the band rotunda at the centre of town the local brass band played 'Land of Hope and Glory', and a spate of knitting bees, church bazaars, fairs and fund-raising carnivals provided opportunities for people to voice their outrage at German atrocities in Western Europe and warn that the same fate awaited New

Zealand if the Hun were not defeated. Among the most vociferous were young men who had not enlisted, and on more than one occasion my grandfather was confronted by members of a self-styled 'Vigilante Committee for the Defence of King and Country', threatening violence to German-speaking tradespeople and shop owners, many of whom had migrated to New Zealand to escape persecution.

Ernst Maetzig, a watchmaker and jeweller, was my grandfather's friend and bowling partner. Not long after Ernst's shop was attacked and looted by an angry mob, my grandfather received orders to round up all German-speaking men in the district. They were sent by special train to Wellington and interned on Somes Island in Wellington Harbour. In 1918 the paranoia that had led to the policy of internment and isolation of 'enemy aliens' now determined that the island would become a quarantine, to protect the populace from the influenza pandemic.

The only clue I have as to how my grandfather felt about his role in implementing these policies, and the limits of his freedom to ensure that justice restored a lost balance in a shared world instead of simply laying down the law, is Rudyard Kipling's 'If', which he recited in front of his shaving mirror every morning. 'If you can keep your head when all about you are losing theirs and blaming it on you … if you can walk with Kings – nor lose the common touch …'

In one of my grandfather's stories, he had to arrest a troublemaker outside the post office, but he avoided taking him directly to the police station, because that would have meant going along the thronged main street. Instead, he took an alleyway into a back street so that the miscreant would not be seen and shamed.

In 1960, when my grandfather died, I went back to Inglewood for his funeral. After a Methodist service, the cortege set off for the cemetery. As our car followed the hearse toward the cemetery gates, I noticed a group of old men standing on the opposite side of the road, heads bowed, hats in their hands. Several were men whose public humiliation my grandfather had averted fifty years before.

For every story of success there's a story of failure, and for everything that shines in life there is a shadow. It is as though the law of averages demands this balance, obliging us to pay a price for every boon, so that the happiness of one person comes at the expense of another. This seems to have been the case with Fred and his brother Arthur. Loathing his job in the woollen mills, Arthur followed his brother out to New Zealand. But his business failed, and he was declared bankrupt. One night, my mother heard her father and mother whispering furtively and anxiously together before Fred hurriedly packed his bag and took a taxi to Wellington. No explanation was given. A couple of days later, Amy showed her daughter a newspaper article, holding her finger on the text Emily was to read. Arthur Longbottom of Petone had attempted to kill himself with his cutthroat razor but was recovering in hospital. In fact, he died of pneumonia before Fred's taxi reached Wellington.

Did Fred ever ask himself whether Arthur's fate could have been his own, or reflect that only luck determined the difference? And has my own migratory life not only been influenced by my grandfather's life but become a repetition of it?

SI J'ÉTAIS

When the Swiss-French writer Blaise Cendrars met Greta Garbo in Paris, he was evidently so impressed that he underlined her name in his journal entry for that day – 19 September 1951. Two weeks later he published a piece in the revue *Opéra* called 'If I were Greta Garbo' and later reprinted it in *Trop c'est trop* (1957). Meeting Garbo brought back memories of a bygone era of silent films and of his own sojourns in America making movies. Searching for a literary agent, Cendrars was told that the only honest one in America was Greta Garbo's agent, a certain Levy who had been largely responsible for inventing her mystique – the image of a secretive, silent woman of ethereal dreams, abstract and metaphysical; a kind of Ulalume, the beautiful nocturnal butterfly that singes its eyelashes in Edgar Allan Poe's burning candle.

In Garbo's heyday in the 1930s, tourists could drive by her house in Beverly Hills and glimpse the figure of Garbo on her balcony, dreamily waving to her fans or reading a book. This, however, was not the real person but a mechanical mannequin. Garbo herself was already withdrawing from the world, shunning publicity, hiding behind her famous dark glasses. In a rare interview four years before her death, she confided that she had grown weary of Hollywood long before she retired from making movies. 'I did not like my work. There were many days when I had to force myself to go to the studio ... I really wanted to live another life.'

'If I were Greta Garbo', Cendrars writes, 'I would resurrect the wax mannequin and use electronic technology to perfect it, make it speak, count, recite poetry, respond to journalists or greet the crowds.'

In Cendrars' vision of the future, the distinction between person and persona is dissolved. Humans and robots are interchangeable. Immortality is achieved through clones, look-alikes and avatars. Fiction dissolves into fact and fact into fiction. The virtual becomes the real.

But hasn't our humanity always involved prosthetic devices and fantastic scenarios? How is it possible to know ourselves except through our interactions with objects and others, whether actual or imagined? Not only do objects, animals, gods, machines and ideas mediate our understanding of who we are; human life itself is dependent on our engagements with the extra-human.

Even the dead are vital to our lives.

In the 1970s, the anthropologist Piers Vitebsky began fieldwork among the Sora of southern Orissa (now Odisha, in northeastern India), who 'held what may be the most elaborate form of communication between the living and the dead documented anywhere on earth. Almost every day in every village, living people engaged in conversations with the dead, who would speak, one after another, through the mouth of a shaman (*kuran*) in trance. Together, living and dead would chat, weep, or argue for hours at a time.' Although the Sora had cultivated the experience of communicating with the dead to an extraordinary degree, and often depended on ritual experts to put them in touch with their forebears, this practice should not be strange to us, for don't we also inhabit a social universe in which ancestors are remembered, albeit with the help of photographs, archives and family anecdotes, and without being assigned active roles in the lives of the living? During my fieldwork among the Kuranko in Sierra Leone, it became clear to me how important ancestors were to an individual's wellbeing, and how imperative it was to recognise and nourish a relationship with them through sacrificial offerings and gestures of respect. To dream of an ancestor, as I dreamt of mine (the Kuranko word *m'bimba* denotes both 'my grandfather' and 'my ancestor'), is construed not as a memory of someone who no longer exists but a glimpse of someone who continues to exist, albeit in altered form, in a parallel universe. This resonates with the way my grandfather appeared in my dream: though his house was somewhat changed, his favourite chair mysteriously absent, the words that passed between us indistinct, his features vague, I was in no doubt that this was he, that we talked as we had done in the past. He was as present to me as he had ever been.

To reify this vivid and affecting sense of his presence by claiming him to be alive, or to commit myself to a belief in an afterlife, would be to go too far. I cannot, for instance, theorise memories as the Sora do, seeing them as 'thoroughly social in character', and able to 'roam at large outside the mind of any single rememberer'. I have no idea whether my grandfather ever appears in the dreams of my siblings, or wanders a in a world of his own, jingling coins in his pocket, smoking his pipe and telling stories from his policing days, as he intermittently does in my memory. But what Vitebsky writes of the Sora also holds true for me: 'Memories fade (*masuna*) as their rememberers too change with time, recovering from their grief but also aging and finally dying themselves.'

It'll Come to Me

A couple of months after these dreams of my grandfather, and with my academic chores now completed for the semester, I received an email from an old friend to whom I had recently confided my desire to begin work on a novel. Augie was about to leave Santa Fe for a stint of fieldwork in Peru and wondered whether I would like to stay in his house while he was away. His offer was so timely and unexpected that I was inclined to see it as auspicious, confirming the Homeric view that life is a matter of placing oneself in the best possible relationship with the gods. Unlike the modernist assumption that we make our own luck, the Homeric view emphasises the wonder and gratitude we should show toward the gods for steering us through the crises of life and helping us succeed. Everything, from sleeping well to being rescued from a potential disaster to becoming a great artisan, requires an openness to the gods who govern every field of human endeavour. This view is not unlike the Kuranko view that virtue resides not in the deliberate cultivation of an inner life or the wilful creation of singular works but in a dutiful and mindful performance of your role and an acceptance of whatever life gives you or takes from you. According to one Kuranko adage, any blessings are contingent on the degree to which you have done your duty and on the fortitude and perseverance you have shown in the face of hardship. That is your portion, someone will say, as you slake your thirst or extend your hand toward a platter of rice. Whatever comes your way is your predestined lot, and the ancestors cannot be cajoled through sacrifice or petition. I like to think my books have come to me in this way, unbidden and unpremeditated, yet testifying to what it means to be open to the world, allowing me to be 'drawn from without'.

In New York City, with an afternoon to kill before catching my train to Santa Fe, I walked north for many blocks, without any idea of where I was going, and it was only when I found myself on East 82nd Street that it occurred to me to revisit the Metropolitan Museum of Art.

Hanging from the façade of the museum was an advertisement for a show called *The Theater of Appearance*. After joining the queue that stretched along the street and up the steps to the museum, and shuffling slowly forward behind a couple of middle-aged women deep in conversation, I realised that a column had blocked my view of the sign. Its subject was not 'appearance' but 'disappearance'.

'It's going to be slow going,' one woman said. 'I had my hips done a couple of months ago. I gotta be careful.'

Her companion had her own worries. 'My husband never asks me about my day. Comes home and he's immediately on the phone or Facebook.'

The first woman suddenly switched from hip replacements to bird watching. She loved it. But her husband didn't.

'You're not that old.'

'No, but with my hips the way they are I might as well be seventy.'

'Getting old's not much fun.'

In the Great Hall I bought a ticket and looked for directions to the Michael C. Rockefeller Memorial Collection, aware that in this neoclassical space, with its domes, arches and marble floors, the solitary woman in David Markson's novel *Wittgenstein's Mistress* found refuge, building a fire with artefacts and picture frames to keep herself warm. Did she burn any of the masks from Sierra Leone before she shot holes in the skylight to let the smoke out, only for the rain to come in and force her to move on, travelling the world, camping in the Tate, the National Gallery, the Uffizi and the Louvre – because she was an artist, and her parents had been artists too? Or because she was mad? Or the sole survivor of the human race? Or all of the above?

It is often difficult to know what is real.

What struck me about the display of West African masks was their alienation from the contexts in which they were carved and worn. Whatever meaning they had had in use was no longer apparent. Whatever feelings they had once evoked for those who donned them or watched them in performance had been lost. In lieu of indigenous apperceptions, you had to settle for a curator's discursive stabs in the dark.

I peered past my own reflection in the glass-fronted cabinet, struggling to read the display card inside:

'Mende or Sherbro helmet mask' from the Moyamba region of southern Sierra Leone, dated 19th–20th century.
These masks are finely carved to convey admired feminine features, an elaborate coiffure, a smooth broad forehead, narrowly slit eyes, a small composed mouth, and a sensuously ringed neck.

I resisted this Western aesthetic. It downplayed the pragmatic value that the Mende people attach to social skills and dutiful behaviour. Physical beauty is not celebrated for its own sake; rather, it is meant to inspire initiates to contemplate excellence in conduct and comportment. Virtue is a matter of what one does and how one moves through life, not what one looks like.

As I gaze at the masks, I experience a flashback to Sierra Leone. A single file of women is coming up the path from the riverside, carrying pails of water on their heads. Their arms and hands appear to be drawing them through waist-high water or long grass. As they come nearer, I see that they are not as young as I thought they were. Lithe and graceful, smiling at me as they pass, it is as though they are immune to aging, despite the slackening of their skin, their weathered faces, their wizened breasts.

The presence of a beard – a symbol synonymous with the wisdom that men achieve with age and experience – may suggest that through Sande [the women's cult association] women attain the same amount of knowledge as men.

I begged to differ. The beard did not affirm the superior wisdom of men, but only men's conviction that they are better able to control their emotions and withstand hardship than women. If men claim to be wiser than women, then women will praise that wisdom – without, however, embracing the men's assumption that they alone possess it. Women know things that men can never know.

Sande teaches neophytes what they must do to fulfil their roles as wives and mothers. Initiation prepares a girl for life as a junior wife in her husband's household. It provides her with the know-how she will need for bearing and raising children and enduring hardship without complaint. The narrowed eyes, sealed lips and covered ears of the Sande mask are all suggestive of the strict disciplining of the senses that is not only pedagogically central to female initiation but a precondition for admission into the Sande association.

We cannot take masks or customary beliefs at face value. They are images of the world as we would like it to be – magical means, perhaps, of inducing reality to be responsive to our dreams, or evidence of our attempts to combine every power we can think of – the strength of bush cows, the grace of antelopes, the fecundity of the forest, the flight of birds, the energy of youth, the charisma of great leaders – to bolster our efforts to make our lives more viable. The mask is a ritual means of affirming an ideal. We bring this ideal into focus by confronting a grotesque mélange of disparate elements: male and female, animal and human, old and young, natural and man-made.

After leaving the museum, I wandered down Fifth Avenue looking for a diner I had found on a previous visit to the city.

At 55th Street a long line of mostly African American men was waiting outside the Fifth Avenue Presbyterian Church for the soup kitchen to open. This was the same church that the twenty-five-year-old Frédéric-Louis Sauser entered on the evening of Easter Sunday, 1912, to hear Joseph Haydn's *Creation*. Penniless and famished, the aspiring writer had become accustomed to drifting around Manhattan or reading in the New York Public Library, but on April 7 the library was closed, and he was obliged to find another haven.

His thoughts were focused not on his own destitution, or on the microscope he had pawned that morning, but on the refugees from Europe, 'penned in, heaped up, like cattle, in poorhouses', or sitting in their shops under copper lamps, selling old clothes, books, arms and stamps, or hanging out on street corners – vagrants, thieves, street singers and panhandlers, all more in need of Christ's compassion than he was. Though carried away by the oratorio, Sauser was interrupted every five minutes by a succession of preachers making sanctimonious appeals for cash. When one old croaker, as pious and as tiresome as the first, entered the stall where Sauser was sitting, shook a leather pouch under his nose and tried to convert him, he left the church and trudged back to his digs on West 67th Street.

> I come back tired, alone, and utterly dejected ...
> My room is as empty as a tomb ...
>
> Lord, I'm alone and I have a fever ...
> My bed is as cold as a coffin ...
>
> Lord, I close my eyes and my teeth chatter ...
> I'm too alone. I'm cold. I call your name ...

After gnawing a hunk of dry bread and drinking a tumbler of water, Sauser fell asleep, only to wake with a start and scribble down several lines that had come to him as in a dream. Falling asleep again, he woke a second time and wrote until dawn. He slept through the following day. At five o'clock on Easter Monday he took a look at what he had written and gave it the title *Les Pâques à New-York* (Easter in New York). A few days later, he scraped together the $5.25 fare for a berth on a cattle boat back to France, and on arrival he sent a manuscript copy of his poem to his fellow poet, Guillaume Apollinaire. Published that October, *Les Pâques* was celebrated as the first modernist poem, a clean break with romanticism and symbolism. Sauser signed it with his new name:

> En cendres se transmute
> Ce que j'aime et possède
> Tout ce que j'aime et que j'étreins
> Se transmute aussitôt en Cendres.
>
> *Blaise Cendrars*

A generation before Cendrars appeared on the French literary scene, a twenty-three-old Norwegian spent the best part of two years in the United States working in a lumberyard in Wisconsin, in an auction house in Minneapolis, on a wheat farm in North Dakota, and as a streetcar conductor in Chicago. On his return to Europe, Knut Hamsun rented a cheap attic room at 18 Sankt Hans Gade in Copenhagen and began writing *Hunger*. He lived on rye bread without butter or meat, often went without food for several days at a time and chewed matchsticks to stave off hunger. Like Cendrars in New York twenty years later, Hamsun resolved not to seek work. Even though he was starving, he was bent on making a living from his writing. Indeed, for both young men, writing and living amounted to the same thing. They were also strangers to the cities where penury and loneliness had driven them inward. What was the meaning of 'belief' in these men's lives? Did they 'believe' in themselves or their potential genius? When Sauser addressed his poem to Christ, did it mean he had become a believer? Calling upon God to help one weather a difficult period in one's life hardly constitutes a 'belief' that God exists. In extremis one is wont to do and say anything that might alleviate distress.

In the winter of 1984, less than a year after the death of my wife, I found that I could no longer conjure her image in my mind's eye, hear her voice, or recall the touch of her hand. I sometimes submitted to my feeling of emptiness, not wanting to fill my head with desperate imaginings or attend to my own grieving. And so I dreamt – strange dreams in which Emma appeared to me distorted and monstrous. Then, for several successive nights, I woke from dreams that were awash with words, which I scribbled on scraps of paper by my bedside before relapsing into sleep. These intense dreams lasted no more than ten nights. I worked on what I had been given, crafting a long poem whose central figure was Mary Magdalene and whose leitmotif was a black rose. I had no idea whence these images had come. I knew the Biblical sources, of course, and was aware that Cendrars had tried for many years to write a fictional life of Mary Magdalene, 'the lover of

Jesus Christ, the only woman who made our saviour weep'. But how could I account for the fact that my poem bore, both in its length and imagery, an uncanny resemblance to Cendrars' *Les Pâques à New-York*?

I have always identified with Cendrars' and Hamsun's view that suffering is not pain but submission – a yielding to fate, an acceptance of one's lot, and faith that in one's openness to life a path will be revealed. This attitude is reminiscent of the joyous indifference that Henry Miller celebrates in *Tropic of Cancer*, a book he also wrote when down and out in a foreign city. In a preface to the original edition, Miller's friend Anaïs Nin observes that 'the book is sustained on its own axis by the pure flux and rotation of events. Just as there is no central point, so also there is no question of heroism or of struggle since there is no question of will, but only an obedience to flow.'

> *It is now the fall of my second year in Paris. I was sent here for a reason I have not yet been able to fathom.*
>
> *I have no money, no resources, no hopes. I am the happiest man alive. A year, six months ago, I thought that I was an artist. I no longer think about it, I am.*

These books are still alive and speak to me, though their authors are dead. My relationship with them resembles my relationship with my homeland, or with my grandparents, my parents, and the friends of my youth who have passed on. I think of these places and people often, though their presence is ghostly and their features indistinct. They are like the weathered lettering on old tombstones, a barely legible Braille. False memories perhaps. I have learned that we address the dead as we pray to God or bring the past to mind – groping in the dark, hoping to be given some sign that they are not illusory. But the past is another country. And the dead cannot talk back. Pale shadows of their erstwhile selves, they are at our mercy, to memorialise or forget, miss or misread. And yet, whatever *their* reality, we feel compelled to return to them, because without them we cease to exist.

LOST TO SIGHT

On my first morning in New Mexico I woke before sunup, dressed, and set off along a sandy trail that ran parallel to the paved road. Before long I was jogging through the desert, the sun rising over a distant hill, birds singing, and not a cloud in the sky. Though I did not yet know the names of the sage-green, spindly plants alongside the trail – juniper, barberry, gambel oak, banana yucca, wax currant, buffalo berry – I felt strangely at home in this arid landscape.

That afternoon, I found my way into town, passing adobe houses behind brushwood fences and tourist boutiques filled with expensive ethnic souvenirs.

In a coffee bar called Breaking New Grounds, I took a window seat and pondered which of Hannah Arendt's alternatives applied to me: solitude is being with oneself, and loneliness is being with no one. After scribbling some notes in my journal, I took a closer look at the pin board near the door. It was covered with a patchwork of flyers advertising festivals, yoga classes, salsa lessons, pre-loved electronic equipment, apartments to rent and tuition in classical guitar.

Which, if any, of these items triggered a distant memory of Aaron Friesen, I do not know. But I suddenly remembered that he had taught at Albuquerque, though so long ago that if he were still alive he certainly would not be teaching now.

My knowledge of Aaron was sketchy, if not mythical. When I was an undergraduate, he had enjoyed a reputation in New Zealand as a poet, bon vivant and raconteur. Sometime in the 1960s, he left his wife and three children for a woman twenty-five-years his junior and became persona non grata to almost all his friends. After delivering several churlish broadsides in the New Zealand press against those who had spurned him, he spent several years wandering the world with his girlfriend before settling down in New Mexico. I had always assumed he had followed D.H. Lawrence's trail to Taos, searching for the same spiritual vitality.

Getting in touch with Aaron Friesen proved to be so straightforward that I was tempted to regard it as predestined. I simply dialled 411 and asked the operator if she had a listing for Friesen. Minutes later I was telling this legendary figure that I was a New Zealand writer, staying near Santa Fe for a few weeks, and asking if we might get together. That I did not mention my career as an anthropologist or my job at Harvard suggested, perhaps, that I was searching to recover the life I had led before my academic life eclipsed it.

From Aaron's description I immediately recognised his small adobe house, set back from the road, with a cobalt-blue door and wooden trim. No sooner had I opened the gate than a grizzled individual who reminded me of the actor John Huston shambled toward me, muttering my name. I had the impression that he had been waiting years for me, or for someone who might connect him with his past, for he seized my arm and began asking fervent questions about his New Zealand contemporaries as if they were still alive, preserved forever in the amber of antipodean time. Ignoring my half-baked answers, he regaled me with an account of how he and Naomi had bought the house with money he received when he took early retirement from the University of New Mexico. It was a ruin, occupied by hippies, and it took months for the sale to go through and the squatters to be evicted. Aaron and Naomi then spent the best part of four years retiling the floors, replacing the roof, installing a new kitchen and bathroom, and filling the house with second-hand furniture. Speaking of the desert, in which Aaron said he felt utterly at home, he threw his arms wide, almost cracking me on the skull with the knobbled cane he carried, as if to embrace the rocky landscape and blinding light. 'It shames us with its silences,' he declared. 'Before it, we are stripped bare. Reduced to nothingness.'

I knew he was paraphrasing T.E. Lawrence but was happy to let Aaron blunder about among the alders, poking at saplings with his cane and periodically wondering where Naomi could have got to. 'She bikes everywhere, you know. Said she was going downtown to buy a few things for dinner. I reckon she'll be back any minute.'

'I walked into town this morning,' I said, and described the memorial I had seen in the Plaza, commemorating 'the brave victims who … perished in the various wars with the savage Indians'. 'The memorial reminded me of the one in Whanganui,' I said, 'dedicated to loyalist Māori who fought for law and order against fanaticism and barbarism. I think Mark Twain called it a monument to traitors.'

'It might interest you,' Aaron said, 'that in 1974, a young man stepped over the low fence around our monument and chiselled out the word *savage*.'

'That wasn't you, by any chance?' I asked.

But Aaron Friesen wasn't going to spoil the effect his words had had on me, and I would learn that his fondness for ambiguity and mystery debarred any attempt to establish facts or fathom the truth of anything.

We ate dinner at a pinewood table in a room filled with rustic sideboards, Welsh dressers, and sofas covered with Navajo rugs. Aaron was irrepressible, roaring appreciatively every time Naomi brought another dish to the table and repeatedly raising his glass to wish me luck with my writing.

'This is my favourite time of year,' he boomed, as if raising his voice might magically mitigate his physical unsteadiness. '"Season of mists and mellow fruitfulness. The temperate sharpness of the air." Do you know Keats wrote that ode in September 1819? All those great odes in a single year, writing at least fifty lines a day. Are you going to produce something like that, or go down like yours truly, twittering among the swallows? You know he died a year after "Autumn" was published?'

At first I was inclined to write Aaron off as all piss and wind, what with his histrionic habit of brandishing his cane, declaiming ill-remembered lines from Shakespeare or Dylan Thomas, not going gentle into that good night. But in him I found a kindred antipodean spirit – an unexpected antidote to the staidness of Harvard. And there were moments that first evening – when Aaron held a slice of apple between his thumb and the blade of his clasp knife and handed it to me with a smile, saying that it was a Gala, a hybrid developed in New Zealand – that I was won over to his cause: an old campaigner, a rogue elephant, fighting a losing battle to sustain his vision of a vanished world.

Almost as soon as dinner was over, Aaron rose from the table and stumbled toward an armchair, where he instantly fell asleep. A nearby standard lamp unflatteringly highlighted his mane of unruly hair and the broken veins on his nose and cheeks, and I was moved to ask Naomi if he was all right.

'He puts on a brave face,' she said, reaching across the table to fill my wineglass. 'Twelve years ago, an ischemic stroke left him blind in one eye. Though he could manage visually, he took it very hard, stopped writing, and sat in the dark for a year. Then he had a second stroke that robbed him of almost all his remaining vision. He said it was a punishment for having abandoned his first wife and three children and run off with me.'

'Will the damage heal?' I asked, mindful of what Oliver Sacks writes about new cells being recruited to make good what has been lost.

'The damage to his eyes or to his family?' Naomi asked.

'I was thinking about his vision.'

'Nerve cells don't replace themselves. The loss is irreversible. Aaron treats it all as a bit of a joke. A cosmic joke. Tells me there's no truth in the old adage, and that you *can* teach an old dog new tricks.'

'It must be very difficult for you.'

'It's a lot more difficult for him. He can't read. And that drives him crazy. He wanted to get rid of his library. But the books are his life. Like pieces of music that carry you back to another time and place. So they're still here. A memorial to what he's lost.'

I glanced toward the bookcase, trying to imagine what it would be like for a writer not to be able to read. Even when Naomi described how she read to Aaron every night, the pleasure Aaron found in listening to a story, and the intimacy of this nightly ritual, I had to fall back on small talk to disguise my sadness, telling Naomi that Aaron had seemed in good spirits over dinner. 'All those poems he recited by heart. His stories …'

'You brought out the best in him. He was his old self.'

I walked back to my digs along a darkened road, closing my eyes from time to time and imagining what it would be like to be sightless. I remembered Denka Marah, the blind Kuranko flautist and storyteller I had worked with in Sierra Leone. Denka had been blinded by a spitting cobra when he was a boy. Now he held one end of a stick and let himself be led around the village by his small nephew. His fabulous tales became part of my book *Allegories of the Wilderness*, and his words came back to me from his own life story. 'One day I opened my eyes on the world, and one day they closed upon it.'

In my youth, I imagined aging to be a process of slow decline and ebbing powers, a gradual slipping away into nothingness. And so undoubtedly it is for some. But in Denka, and now in Aaron, I had glimpsed the pathos of sudden loss – how one's hold on life could be lost in an instant, spirited away as if by some daemonic sleight of hand.

Now You See It, Now You Don't

I walked past a field of dilapidated corn like papyrus. A man with a crew cut was forking over a remnant garden of carrots, pumpkins, kale and marigolds. Carefully he shook soil from the carrots he had unearthed before laying them side by side on a plastic bag.

The sun was hot on my face, but in the shadows the air was chill.

Naomi was raking pine straw from the asphalt driveway. A crosshatching of bleached brown needles. The scrape of her green plastic rake. A sudden breeze scattering dead leaves from the hawthorn and apricot trees. When I asked if I could help, she said she was done for the day. I could lend a hand, though, cutting beet greens and kale from the garden, then talking to Aaron. 'He's been a bugger all day. You might cheer him up.'

I found Aaron in the living room, peering into a large computer screen. He appeared not to be reading the enlarged text of *The New York Times* so much as straining to see what lay behind it. When he asked me to fetch a glass from the kitchen and open a bottle of Rioja, I did so. Then, on a shabby sofa that Naomi's cats had ripped to shreds, I sipped my wine as Naomi washed the beet greens in the kitchen and Aaron threw questions at me about places and people in New Zealand that had figured in his past life but been peripheral to mine.

I felt the need to tread carefully – pandering to him, speaking only when spoken to. But I was curious about his poetry and sensed that the time had come to ask if he had published anything during his years in the States.

Aaron's response was to hurl my question at Naomi, still working at the kitchen sink. 'Naomi! He wants to know if I've published anything in America!'

'Why don't you tell him?' Naomi shouted back.

'The answer's no,' Aaron said.

'Do you regret leaving New Zealand?'

'The river flows one way, my boy. You lose the strength and the incentive to swim against the current.'

There was an awkward silence before Aaron pronounced the word *nostalgia* with enormous care, as if it summed up his entire life.

'A Homeric word,' he added. 'The pain of returning home.'

'I thought it was the pain of longing for home.'

'Go read your Homer.'

It did not surprise me that Aaron showed no interest in my writing. Indeed, I was relieved that he did not ask, since I was so uncertain about what I was doing and where I was going. Besides, Aaron was obviously so eager to instruct and advise, naming authors I should read and things I should know about the fraught history of New Mexico.

'When you live as long as I have, you become lost to history. An archive no one visits, filled with papers collecting dust, knowledge no one can use. But here's the rub, my boy. When you're young, you haven't got the depth of experience to write something truly great. And when you're old, with all the experience in the world, you're too far gone to put pen to paper.'

'So what's the answer?' I asked. 'Get a younger writer to ghost-write your story?'

Either to humour or to challenge me, Aaron launched into an account of how he left Denmark when he was eighteen to escape a domineering father and a bigoted community. Divorce had been his mother's way out, but rather than attend to the needs of her son, whose physical resemblance to his father was as undeniable as his personality was different, she sent Aaron to a boarding school in Aalborg and began looking for a new provider and paramour. At sixteen, Aaron absconded and went to sea. He jumped ship a couple of years later in New Zealand. His recklessness and enthusiasms had girls eating out of his hand and falling at his feet – clichés that became part of the lore that circulated in his wake – though many men took his eloquence as a sign that he was a poofter. He married for the hell of it, as he put it, and had three young children before he realised that he was, again in his own words, digging himself an early grave. What sustained him were the camaraderie of the pub and the endless parties that followed early closing. He spoke of the other young Turks he hung out with in Wellington – Jim Baxter, Denis Glover, Louis Johnson, Alistair Campbell – and hungered for news of them. Though all had passed on, he wanted me to talk about them as though they were still alive, as if he might yet return to the city he had left in ignominy twenty-five years before, all his sins forgotten.

'But there's no new land, my friend, no new sea, for the city will follow you, in the same streets you'll wander endlessly …'

I recognised the lines from Constantine Cavafy, as translated by Lawrence Durrell.

'With lines like that, why bother to write?' Aaron said.

Later, as I was helping Naomi with the dishes, I heard the distant, crumpling sound of thunder. It rumbled closer. Lightning flashed. Then torrential rain drowned out our voices.

'Don't try to walk home in this,' Naomi said. 'Stay the night.'

As Naomi helped Aaron upstairs, I found myself wondering whether it was love, loyalty, or mere habit that bound them together and in what ways their marriage was different from any other.

When Naomi returned to the living room, she switched on the standard lamp and fell into Aaron's armchair, drawing her legs up under her.

'Can I get you a drink?' I asked.

'My glass is on the table.'

After I filled it and put it into her hands, she confided that in some ways caring for Aaron was like caring for a child – the child she had never had.

'After his second stroke he felt very vulnerable. He didn't want me to leave him alone. He feared another stroke, one that would leave him completely blind or compromise his ability to speak or think. We go through life as if we've got all the time in the world. As if things will go on unchanged, day after day. You forget how precious it is. You even complain of its tedium, Then, in a split second, everything's thrown into doubt. There's no future, and even the past feels unreal.'

I wanted to commiserate, but nothing in Naomi's demeanour or tone of voice suggested she felt hard done by.

'Do you mind if I smoke?' Naomi asked. 'I don't usually. But sometimes it helps.'

'The aroma takes me back,' I said, 'to when we all smoked.'

Naomi allowed herself the glimmer of a smile. 'Our misspent youth,' she said.

'I don't think youth is ever misspent,' I said. 'Except in the eyes of the old.'

'Is that what you are writing about,' Naomi asked, 'your youth?'

'Perhaps,' I said. For I did I not yet know what my subject was. Only that I was overwhelmed by a sense of loss, for poetry, for my grandfather, for my homeland, for my late wife, or for all of the above.

I spent my last weekend in Santa Fe with Aaron and Naomi. Their company had distracted me from the false starts I had made on my novel, forays into a no-man's land from which I returned at the end of each day, dispirited and empty-handed. To put my own difficulties into perspective, I would re-read my notes of a conversation in which Aaron had spoken about his impaired vision: 'I had to decide whether I wanted to live in this eternal twilight, in which print was an indecipherable blur, and I would play solitaire for hours at a time with a deck of enlarged court cards, fighting off a desire to die. But life itself held the upper hand, and I lived on despite myself.'

As night fell, I helped Naomi prepare dinner, and later we lit a fire in the stone hearth and set out the Scrabble board on the table. We seldom completed a game, because Aaron would become frustrated at his inability to see the tiles, or dispute the scores, or get too drunk to continue. Naomi would help him upstairs to bed while I dutifully waited for her in the living room. She would reappear, blinking against the light, and ask if I wanted 'one for the road'.

We sat for some time without speaking, mesmerised by the fire.

'You must be curious to know how Aaron and I got together,' Naomi said.

'I haven't wanted to pry.'

'No, you've been very discreet.'

'You met in Wellington?'

'I was a student of his.'

I was about to say how times change, but did not want to give Naomi the impression that I saw her as a victim. In fact, I had been so moved by her devotion to the man I had been ready to write off as a has-been, that Aaron had become once more the great iconoclast that I had heard and read about in my youth. And so I asked about her childhood, and how she had become the kind of person who would throw all caution to the wind and follow a man twenty-five years her senior into the unknown.

'When I was a little girl,' Naomi said, 'my siblings used to tease me for looking Māori. I would inspect myself in the mirror, trying to see what they were seeing. But the issue wasn't my physical appearance, but my weird ways. Even my parents seemed to regard me as a stranger. And so I came to imagine that I'd been adopted. I sought out Māori friends, taught myself Māori, and imagined one day marrying a Māori. But the more I pursued this fantasy, the more confused I became about who I really was. I would never be accepted as Māori, despite appearances, but I was never going to be the person my parents wanted me to be, either.

'How can I say this? Perhaps a story will say it for me. About what's it like to be betwixt and between, never one thing or another. It's actually a true story, about a German who married a Māori girl. They lived at the northernmost tip of the North Island where he was the keeper of the Cape Reinga lighthouse. For Māori, Reinga is where two oceans collide, a leaping-off place for spirits bound for the nether world. After fifteen years in the lighthouse, the German realised a long-standing dream. He went to Stuttgart and took possession of a custom-built Mercedes-Benz. Everything was push-button – windows, sunroof, reclining seats. But this car never went out on the open road. It sat in a locked-up garage at the lighthouse, unused and seldom seen, like a symbol of what all lighthouse keepers dream about but fail to achieve – release from the solitude and confinement of their stone towers.'

THE SECOND LIFE OF ART

Naomi's email was succinct and unemotional. 'Aaron passed away on Wednesday evening. Funeral to be held in the Avista Funeral Home and Crematorium, December 15, 2:00 pm. No flowers please.'

I phoned Naomi that night to offer my condolences and try to explain why I would not be able to attend Aaron's funeral. But Naomi was too distressed to hear me out. 'He was actually talking about you,' she said, 'when he died. His voice suddenly slowed in mid-sentence, like someone dragging his feet, or a clock winding down. I thought he was drunk. That sluggish, slurred speech. Then he collapsed, like a heap of clothes from which the body has been spirited away. When I knelt and touched him, I felt as if he had been turned to stone, that I was spellbound in some terrible fable. I have lost track of time. I cannot sleep. For all I know, it *is* all a nightmare. I have been going through his things. I want to salvage something of him, to keep him alive, something that others may remember him by. His work must surely mean something. You said as much yourself, when you were here. Surely he deserves a mention in the annals of New Zealand literature, or a posthumous *Collected Poems*. Michael, will you help? You know his work. You have contacts. I can think of no one to whom he would sooner entrust his legacy. If you agree I will send copies of everything I have found. It would not take too much of your time, and it would mean the world to me, and to him. I am nothing without him. I have lost my bearings. I would welcome death myself. But I would not wish oblivion on him.'

I did not have the heart to tell Naomi how attenuated my relationship with New Zealand had become, but said I would be happy to read Aaron's poems.

The poems arrived a week later. Some were typed, some scrawled in longhand on different-sized sheets of paper, mangled, folded, stained with broken rings from wine glasses or coffee mugs. They were the careless residue of a writer who has long ago been deserted by his muse.

It was not until I began combing through the manuscript that I realised how thankless my task was going to be. The poems were all in need of revision. Most were so mediocre and maudlin that not even historical curiosity could justify their publication. I even doubted that an archive would find a place for them.

The best, I guessed, had been written about the time Aaron first met Naomi.

1

Bright sun on bridal snow
Boulders showing through the thaw
Words no more wild than we are
Beside an inlet
Hatched with reeds
A blue house with shuttered windows
A padlocked door.

This is the day I return
By train, on foot, dragging
My suitcase, my feet, footsore

This is the week I marked in my calendar
'Reading at Downstage'
This is the day I hadn't bargained for

2

I wake thinking of you
I go to sleep with you on my mind
I have before me this cameo
Of a silver ornament tying back your hair
Of your slender upper arm
Of your smile when you entered the room
These miniatures that are continents

3

I rehearse the reasons why this is impossible
I love my wife
I will do nothing to cause her pain
Or distress our children
I am too old for this
And yet my imaginings muscle their way
Through the half open door
Of my disordered house
Persuading me to buy things I do not need
Tempting, alluring, conjuring

While I for all the mantras and reasons
All the will in the world
Am powerless to keep
You from visiting me at night
Or masquerading as a stranger on the street

4

Yet this is a stale scenario
The nubile girl
The aging Lothario
Casanova crossing the Bridge of Sighs
Pinioned by arthritic limbs
Unsightly to himself, incipiently impotent
But burning in his brain for her,
Old habits dying hard
His abstract lust as lasting
As the long-remembered fire
Of an old potentate
Enthroned in fantasies
Of being born again with her
But bleeding, leaking, feeling the ebb
Of an obscene flood

I sent a selection to the editor who had published my own *Selected Poems*. Despite his evident goodwill, he made it clear that I was asking too much. Times were hard, I was told. There was little likelihood that Creative New Zealand would fund the venture. And besides, Aaron Friesen was a minor figure, and his association with more prominent writers would interest few readers now.

I wrote to Naomi, saying I had done my best, only to receive an embittered postcard in reply. She rued the day she had entrusted me with Aaron's poems. She had mistakenly thought I shared her belief in his genius. 'I am disappointed in you,' she said, 'and I can see that your parochial, moralistic little country has not changed in the slightest since Aaron and I tried to make a life for ourselves there. Aaron was too much for you to handle then, and he still unsettles you.'

I felt hurt and angry, but also relieved. I could now forget about Aaron and Naomi and turn to my own writing.

But everything conspired to bring me back to Aaron – my sense of having betrayed Naomi's trust, my fascination with Aaron's story, and something Naomi once said about writers, comparing them to ambulance-chasing lawyers, profiting from other people's losses. Above all I felt guilt at having deprived Aaron of a second life in art.

THE BOOK OF IRIS

The Book of Iris is a biography of the New Zealand writer Iris Wilkinson (1906–1939), whose pen name was Robin Hyde. Though Iris died the year Aaron was born, I felt that their lives were obliquely linked, and were, moreover, precursory to mine.

Despite being marred by unnecessarily long quotations from Iris's letters and tedious accounts of parochial bickering and literary backbiting, the biography movingly recounts the story of a passionate and gifted woman born into a morally restrictive, chauvinistic society that could not accommodate such a restive and hypersensitive soul.

When she gave birth to a child out of wedlock, Iris could not hope to keep the child and remain in work. The stigma of being an unwed mother and the struggle to earn an income from journalism undoubtedly contributed to the 'nervous breakdown' for which she was hospitalised. She was also physically handicapped by a knee injury suffered during her teens, devastated by the death of a beloved friend at the age of 25, and often immobilised by the side effects of the drugs prescribed for her pain, insomnia and depression. The one period of her life when she seems to have transcended these miseries was when she travelled to China in 1938, en route to the United Kingdom, to report on the Japanese occupation. Shocked by the atrocities she witnessed and exhausted by her own disorienting journeys in war zones, she nevertheless managed to send dispatches and letters home, some of which communicated her happiness at having discovered a country more significant than her own. 'Our country is right at the tail end of the map and has a small population; and I think we need all the restlessness and ambition we can get, even if it takes queer channels. Otherwise we may become a selfish nation, with not much interest in the world.'

It was not, however, these iterations of my own experience of growing up in New Zealand and yearning to explore the wider world that affected me deeply, but something about her brief and troubled life that I could not put into words. Was it the banality of her suicide at age 33, her life unfinished, her potential unfulfilled? Or was it the series of misfortunes she had suffered? When I considered the ill luck that had plagued her, I found it impossible to conclude that she was simply her own worst enemy, but neither could I confidently identify all the external factors – familial, social, medical or moral – that had, in combination, blighted her life. What bothered and oppressed me, I realised, was my failure to find any meaning in her story. It neither allowed an interpretation nor suggested a moral.

Other writers have been similarly troubled by the gap between reality and appearance, particularly the narrative makeovers to which we subject our raw experience. Declaring that 'the trip and the story of the trip are always two different things', Lorrie Moore fulminates against the narrator who revises life with 'kisses and mimicry and tidying up', creating her 'slow, fake song' out of the 'unsayable'. In a similar vein, Martin Amis observes that, unlike narrative, life is poorly plotted and suffers for want of good dialogue, pattern, or completeness. Though we are constantly piecing together the fragments of our everyday experience, organising them as a story, much as one periodically tidies one's house rather than live in a mess, an inner voice reminds the writer that he or she is violating the truth. The events of Iris Wilkinson's life resisted this kind of tidying up. Perhaps if I had found more to admire in her voluminous output of poetry or her journalism, I would have been able to lay down her biography, satisfied with knowing she had made a formidable contribution to New Zealand literature. But despite her productivity, I was no more attracted to her writing than I would have been attracted to her. Even her closest friends found her self-centred and difficult, looking for love but not loving herself enough to be able to give it.

As I tried to put these thoughts behind me, a comparison suddenly presented itself to me. A year ago, I had made my second visit in two years to the Holocaust Memorial Museum in Washington, DC. Before taking an elevator from the lobby to the top floor and beginning my tour, I was invited to take a small grey identification card that told 'the story of a real person who lived during the Holocaust'. On my first visit, the card summarised the life of a young Hungarian man who had worked in a *Sonderkommando* unit at Auschwitz for several months before being killed and his body incinerated in the ovens he had tended. When I returned to Boston, I kept my admission ticket and this card on my desk. I did the same with the card I received on my second visit, telling the story of a Polish boy called Shulim Saleschutz who was gassed with his mother and sister at Belzec in July 1942. He was twelve years old.

If I have kept these cards so close at hand, is it because of some atavistic need to keep these individuals in mind? Not to remember their names, or even to dwell upon their fates, but simply to feel that something of their presence has been rescued from oblivion? Perhaps this is why I could not dismiss Iris Wilkinson's life from my own. It had nothing to do with *meaning* in the intellectual sense of that word. It expressed a more primitive urge: to keep myself open to someone whose life had been shut down too early, who had glimpsed the possibility of being at home in the world without ever realising what that might entail.

How burdensome and pervasive is the search for truth – to connect the dots, identify a cause, place blame, deliver a judgement, or arrive at an explanation. It is the curse of our culture – this rabid quest for meaning at all costs, this desire to wrap things up and stow them away, safe and sound. What I seek is not a philosophy of the absurd, but a way around philosophy, morality, nationality, and all the other systematising forms we deploy to mask the complexity and chaos of existence. I think I have always been drawn to the sceptics – Pyrrho, Diogenes, Sextus Empiricus – and the aporetic method not only because I doubt the possibility of certainty but because of the liberating effect of living in uncertainty by contrast with the bondage of living in belief.

SHOAH

Holocaust: the word describes the thing. But it does not describe the way the thing is experienced, endured or remembered by those who survive it. It sometimes seems to me that for them it does not exist as a word, for what they suffered lies outside language and often calls for silence. Even when it reappears in their thoughts, begging to be named, narrated or made utterable, it remains broken, like a mosaic floor unearthed by archaeology, too damaged to be deciphered.

When I shared these thoughts with my friend Caroline Heller, she asked if I would like to meet Anna Ornstein, whom she had recently met at an event connected with the publication of *Reading Claudius* – Caroline's memoir of her parents, who survived the Holocaust, and of her own childhood, coming of age in the shadow of her parents' losses. At Anna's suggestion, Caroline and her partner, and my wife and I, met at Anna's apartment in Brookline one afternoon. Though I felt a little uneasy in the presence of someone who had survived the Nazi death camps, studied medicine at the University of Heidelberg immediately after the war, and become a well-known psychiatrist as well as the mother of three children, Anna put us all at ease, making tea, setting out snacks on the dining table, and explaining that we live twofold lives – for ourselves, and for our children. This, she said, was how she came to write her memoir *My Mother's Eyes*, for had it not been for her mother's intuitive understanding of what was going on when they arrived on the ramp at Auschwitz after days in a cattle wagon, neither mother nor daughter might have survived the initial selection. Because her mother's spectacles were taken, together with her clothing and the small bundle of belongings they had brought with them from Hungary, Anna now became her mother's eyes. They managed to stay together, surviving the dreadful winter of 1944–45 and several moves to other camps before being liberated from Parschnitz on 8 May 1945, only to learn soon afterward what had befallen Anna's father and two brothers. As Anna spoke of these events, I noticed that she involuntarily touched the sleeve of her blouse as if about to show us the tattoo on her forearm which, she later told us, had once given her hope that she would not be killed, at least not immediately; for wasn't a number better than complete anonymity, a sign that one's life was worth something rather than absolutely nothing?

In the introduction to her book, a copy of which she gave my wife and me, Anna describes how her family and friends sat around the Seder table year after year and read the familiar stories of slavery and the exodus from Egypt. Gradually, however, they began to speak of their most recent enslavement, and Anna came to regard her own biographical essays as a memorial she was creating in the minds of her children. She feared that if she stopped writing, stopped building the memorial, her children and everyone who read the stories would stop remembering the people who had been lost, and 'those who are forgotten are truly dead'. Many passages in Anna's book I read through blinding tears. Her evocation of her father's hands wrapped around her small fist to keep her warm, and his favourite song – 'Solveig's Song' from *Peer Gynt*, which I broke off my reading to listen to – filled me with sorrow, and I asked myself if Anna's loving recollections of her father could ever redeem the cruelty and brutality of the regime that had engineered the degradation and murder of millions of innocent human beings in the name of racial purity.

Two contrasting episodes in Anna's memoir are particularly powerful. Both concern her brothers, Paul and Andrew. The day after the German occupation of Budapest, seventeen-year-old Anna received a phone call from Paul, who had been inducted into a forced-labour battalion some months before. Though Paul had no time to explain his circumstances, he implored his sister to come immediately to Debrecen railway station, 120 miles away. She did so at great risk, since Jews were banned from using public transportation. At Debrecen, Anna waited on the platform for her brother. Though a uniformed official told her that she could not loiter there, she refused to leave. Before long she spotted a man in a beige woollen coat with a pail, working his way toward her under the trains in the sidings. The railway official continued to tell Anna to leave the platform, but she now recognised her brother, and they embraced. Sensing the danger they were in, they spent only a moment together before Paul disappeared back under the trains in the siding, leaving Anna with a memory of his coat and the words that immediately formed in her mind: *This is the last time I shall see you.* Before leaving the platform, she thanked the railway official for allowing her to see her brother, even though it had been only for an instant. As for Paul, he was on his way to the Eastern Front, from which he never returned. Not long afterward, Anna's younger brother Andrew was also inducted into a forced-labour battalion. On learning that his unit had been ordered to the Eastern Front, he escaped with a cousin and sought refuge in a yellow-star house in Budapest, but the janitor saw them entering the building, and for a $5 reward called the police. Andrew died in Mauthausen a day after the camp was liberated.

I could not stop thinking about the differences between the railway official who had momentarily turned a blind eye, permitting Anna and Paul to meet, and the Budapest janitor who for a derisory sum sent Anna's younger brother to his death. One might say that while neither was a free agent, each one's actions made a world of difference to the fate of the individuals who passed their way.

Rather than extol the virtue of the official and condemn the mercenary actions of the janitor, however, I felt a need not to judge, but to somehow hold these different actions in tension. It was a question neither of doing one's duty nor of dereliction of duty, but of allowing a small space in which *humanitas* could appear, like a single flickering candle in the night of Nazi-dominated Europe. And I kept returning to those moments in Anna's memoir in which the difference between life and death was decided by an unremarkable and often inexplicable gesture.

In the summer of 1944 Anna fell ill, probably with typhoid fever, and was taken comatose to the camp infirmary. She was put in a small cubicle with another girl. One of the duties of the nurse who cared for them was to identify to the SS doctors which of her charges were 'incurable' and could be gassed. Thanks to this nurse's unexplained decision to protect Anna, she survived. That such small differences exist between slavish obedience to the dictates of an inhuman regime and the exercise of one's own judgement makes the pleas of Adolf Eichmann – that he was only following orders or doing his duty, and that, in any case, war places normal moral standards in abeyance – indefensible. At the same time, it brings home to us that ethical behaviour is never a matter of conforming to unjust rules or heroically exemplifying virtue, but of making a small difference between being wholly determined and wholly free.

THE EXPATRIATES

In 2013 Martin Edmond was invited by an older writer, James McLeish, to look through some files in which he had collected, over a lifetime, the memorabilia of several New Zealanders who had achieved renown not in their homeland but abroad. Four of these individuals proved particularly interesting to Martin, and the book that grew out of this encounter, involving archival research in places as far afield as Wellington, London, Oxford, Hull, Newcastle, New York and Tenerife, was completed only a few weeks before the death of McLeish, whom Martin imagined as the controller or an operative sent into the field to add new intelligence to what was already on file.

I first met Martin in 1965 when I was teaching at Kuranui College in the Wairarapa. Martin was in form 3, and though I only once taught his class, I admired his father who, as assistant principal, became my mentor. In my spare time, I worked on poems and essays inspired by my year in the Congo, experimenting with the kinds of creative non-fiction that Martin would one day exemplify in such ground-breaking books as *Luca Antara* and *Chronicles of the Unsing*. In his memoir, *The Dreaming Land*, Martin remembers me as 'tall and bony and always [wearing] an off-white linen tropical suit, even in the depths of a Wairarapa winter, during which snow sometimes lay on the ground'. Years later, when Martin and I had become good friends, Martin said that I had always appeared cold at Kuranui, to which I replied vehemently, 'I *was* cold,' having acquired no winter clothes since my precipitate departure from Central Africa a few months before.

As expatriate writers, Martin and I were particularly fascinated by the relationship between a homeland and its colonies, which he compared to the relationship between parent and child. As the motherland sends some of its citizens to the margins of the world as settlers, missionaries, soldiers and sometimes unwanted miscreants, so the children of these outcasts, together with the children of the indigenous peoples who were subjugated by the colonising power, sooner or later resettle the original motherland as expatriates. But for many migrants, the effort to reconcile competing bonds of sentiment and citizenship is exhausting, and expatriates, like exiles and orphans, seldom fully overcome the sense of loss of the land of their birth or feel entirely at home in their country of adoption.

Crossing class lines, Martin observed in the course of our correspondence, was also a kind of migration, to which I agreed, mentioning my book on the figure of the limitrophe – the ambiguous zone where one loses one's way or risks one's life but which is potentially a place of nourishment and new growth. Although the subjects of Martin's book all entered the middle class, they were sons of coal miners, bootmakers, grocery warehousemen and garment workers, leading me to wonder whether a social conscience formed in a world of egalitarian values could be reconciled with the ambitions and entitlements one associates with the bourgeoisie. When Martin described his forthcoming book to me, I was aware that he was recounting an allegory of his own ambivalent feelings toward his homeland, having lived outside New Zealand for many years while preserving a sentimental attachment to his natal town of Ohakune, and to the city of Wellington, which he described as his 'first city, if not my last. Past, present and future are so mixed here that I am unable to say what is actual, as opposed to what may be imagined or remembered. This,' he goes on to say, 'could of course be a life condition.'

Not long ago, knowing that I was a fan of David Markson's *Wittgenstein's Mistress*, Martin made me a gift of one of Markson's last books, titled *This Is Not a Novel*. When I read it, I was both enthralled and fascinated by its often cryptic or morbid lines. As I reluctantly turned the last pages, I realised that when Markson was writing this book, his body was packing it in, and death was at his shoulder. For some reason I fell into a reverie of my first days in Kabala, in northern Sierra Leone, in the dry season of 1969, recalling the repetitive piping of a suluku in the tawny elephant grass, the granite inselberg looming over the town, smoke drifting skyward from cooking fires, the patter of drums, the thrilling sense of being embarked on a life-transforming journey. I do not know how to interpret such transitional moments – how to decide whether we are on the threshold of rebirth or death.

When I first left New Zealand, it was in the vague expectation that the world beyond the place in which I had come of age would somehow fill the void I had felt within me from early childhood. I did not know whether this irrepressible sense of loss reflected something I had once possessed that had slipped through my fingers, or something that had been promised but withheld. And so I embarked on a quest for a country where I belonged, or some material windfall or spiritual awakening, though all the while doubting what I really wanted, even when I thought I had found it. Perhaps this uncertainty sprang from the troubling thought that life is not a possession but a gift that is meant to be passed on. Like the hau that inheres in taonga, breathing life into objects and compelling their exchange, yet constantly yearning to be returned to its original source, so I pined for places

I had left long ago and people with whom I had lost touch, as if in receipt of a daemonic summons it would be perilous to ignore.

Lost to the World

On my night flight to New Zealand I watched a documentary about an Australian kayaker's attempt to cross 1600 kilometres of the Tasman Sea from Fortescue Bay, Tasmania, to Milford Sound, New Zealand – a voyage many considered impossible – only to drown a month after setting out. His wife, Vicki, described the day her husband paddled away as the most emotionally intense day of their married life. 'But,' she said, 'I would never have asked him to not go. I couldn't have done that to him. I knew the risks. I knew it was an enormously challenging undertaking, but I had no other choice than to just believe in him and believe that nothing would go wrong.'

The final preparations had allowed the couple little time together. When the moment of Andrew's departure arrived and he embraced his wife and small son on the beach, 'it was,' Vicki said later, 'like our hearts were being wrenched out of each other's chests. It was as if we weren't going to see each other again.' As Andrew paddled out into the bay, Vicki sprinted along a path that followed the coastline, trying to catch a last glimpse of him and wave, 'but he couldn't hear,' she said, 'and I was hysterical because I didn't want him to go.' As for Andrew, he stopped paddling, half turned and waved at the headland. Struggling to catch his breath, he said, 'I love you, beautiful boy,' before holding his head in his hands and sobbing uncontrollably. Then he paddled some more, and against the splashing of his paddle, he addressed the camera mounted on the kayak. 'I'm really worried I'm not going to see my wife again, or my little boy. I'm very scared. I've got a boy that needs a father, and a wife that needs a husband, and I'm wondering what I'm doing. I'm wondering why I'm doing this. I really am. And I don't have an answer.'

At this point, I could not watch any more. I was overwhelmed by a grief I had not felt so intensely since the death of my first wife, who had elected to defeat cancer through diet, acceptance and meditation. Though I turned off the video, it possessed me in the same way that Emma's vision of inner purity had possessed her. It was as if a daemon were taking her from me, obliging me to watch as it assumed control of her body and mind, and she lost her hold on life as a mariner loses sight of land.

Unable to sleep, I switched on the screen and returned to the video.

It showed a close friend of Andrew's, also an adventurer, trying to answer the question of why some of us risk our lives and the happiness of those we love in dangerous undertakings. 'Some adventurers are extremely emotionally hardened,' he said. 'And to feel alive, to get that high, requires them to put themselves into a higher level of risk than someone with greater emotional sensitivity. For many people, to experience that intense feeling of being alive you need to touch that potential to die, and in realising you might lose your life some people get a sense of how special life is. So, I think this passion he had for adventure was very much in … conflict with the love he had for his family.'

'His fear factor was zilch,' Vicki said. 'He pushed it beyond the recreational and enjoyable level to the totally out there.'

For me, it was like watching a scene from a classical tragedy – Penelope beside herself with anguish as Odysseus sails away to war, possibly never to return. I could not understand why someone would risk everything they loved on such a banal venture. Even if Andrew succeeded in crossing the Tasman in his fragile craft, braving gales and high seas and surviving exposure and insomnia, what joy could it bring? What would it add to what he already had? He had been a climber and high-risk athlete all his life, going where angels fear to tread, pushing himself beyond the limits of endurance or safety. What adrenalin or dopamine rush could override what he himself acknowledged to be central to his life – his wife and son?

2.

Significant others

....

THE ALBEMARLE

Jet-lagged after my thirteen-hour flight across the Pacific and the connecting flight from Auckland to Wellington, I was in two minds as to whether the city was real or a figment of my imagination. At four in the morning, unable to sleep and unwilling to lie in bed counting the hours until daybreak, I dressed and headed out into the pitch-dark city, hoping to find a café where I could buy a coffee and something to eat. A stiff wind was blowing from the north, and there wasn't a soul in sight. Walking along Oriental Bay, I felt like a relict or revenant. Rather than continue to Point Jerningham, I climbed the steps to St Gerard's and doubled back to the city where, as if obeying some atavistic urge, I found myself in Ghuznee Street, facing the now-derelict Albemarle Hotel.

I lived in the Albemarle in 1961. At that time it offered cheap lodgings to pensioners, many of whom had spent their working lives on the waterfront. As a twenty-one-year-old would-be writer who spent my evenings banging away on an Olivetti typewriter and waging a war of attrition against the legions of fleas that emerged from the torn wallpaper of my shabby cell, I was as anomalous as I was alone. My sole consolation was that my literary heroes had spent time in similar circumstances: Blaise Cendrars in New York, Knut Hamsun in Copenhagen, and Henry Miller in Paris. My identification with Miller was lent some weight when I discovered that prostitutes were using several rooms on my floor for their trysts.

Years later I learned that the Albemarle opened as a hotel in 1905, only months before my grandfather arrived in Wellington as a migrant from England. I have no idea whether he stayed in the Albemarle or even whether he would have been able to afford a room there, but the hotel became the unofficial headquarters of militant leaders of the General Strike in 1913, including Peter Fraser, who became prime minister in 1940. Its subsequent decline from hotel to boarding house cum knocking shop was, I also discovered, about to be reversed. A Wellington developer had bought the 'grand old lady' and planned to make it earthquake-proof before refurbishing it as apartments with a ground-floor restaurant.

During the year I lived in the Albemarle and explored its neighbourhood, I happened on a deserted bungalow that had been occupied by wharfies during the waterfront strike of 1951. The floors of every room were ankle deep in trade union leaflets and flyers, personal letters to wives and girlfriends, and family photographs. Battered leather suitcases disgorged memorabilia that appeared to have lain undisturbed for a decade. Although I had been persuaded by an old Auckland friend, Herman Gladwin, to find a house where we could install equipment for making Herman's patented floor polish, I was loath to desecrate what I felt was a historic site, and for several days I rummaged through this midden of personal effects and historical documents, filling a suitcase that I later deposited in the Alexander Turnbull Library. There, I imagine, it remains to this day. The house, with all its memorabilia, was long ago demolished to make way for a high-rise commercial building.

As the dawn light infiltrated the streets, I strolled back along Cuba Street to see whether the old Communist Party headquarters was still standing on the corner of Marion and Vivian Streets. Much to my surprise, the building was as I remembered it, its rusticated yellow-painted weatherboard and bay windows catching the early morning light. A locksmith's premises now occupied the ground floor, and 'KEYS CUT' was advertised in large letters. But what was key for me?

When I had gazed up at the façade of the Albemarle I had seen my own aging face, as if in a mirror. Or perhaps I was recapturing an image of who I was when I lived there fifty years ago, for it suddenly occurred to me that I had lived my life à rebours, much older then, but younger than that now.

This experience was not unconnected with the experience of being an expatriate, for inasmuch as you are born into a second life in another country, your previous incarnation becomes part of a bygone age. In this respect, my feelings echoed those of the Sierra Leonean migrants I had been working with in London, who had discovered to their chagrin the bitter truth of Thomas Wolfe's famous line, 'You can't go home again.' If you try, not only do you find that the environment has changed in your absence; you also discover that you have become a different person. Yet much remains the same, in the landscape as well as within yourself, and this sense of constancy and continuity may be reinforced when old friends greet you as if you had not changed, and relate to you solely in terms of what you once had in common.

This uncanny sense of being at once familiar with and a stranger to a place preoccupied me as I retraced my steps to my motel, where, succumbing to jet lag, I lapsed into a reverie in which I was an undergraduate again, reading Albert Camus' *The Fall* for the first time and pondering the connections between Jean-Baptiste Clamence's fall from grace, the fall of man in the Garden of Eden, and Heidegger's notion of *Verfallensein* (the inauthenticity and bad faith into which Heidegger himself fell when he embraced National Socialism). The metaphorical relationship between physical and philosophical fallenness had never ceased to intrigue me, and it set me to remembering my months in the Albemarle and the depressing sense I suffered there of being old before my time. Perhaps this came from hanging out with old codgers – those tattered coats upon sticks that Yeats contrasted with 'sages standing in God's holy fire' and 'singing-masters' of his soul. Perhaps it came from my dead-end job, proofreading the classifieds in *Truth* five hours a day, five days a week.

As if the sleaze, scandal and domestic violence that filled the pages of *Truth* were not enough, I spent my days off in the Roxy Cinema in Manners Street watching B-grade horror films and westerns. One of these movies, *Jack Slade*, left a lasting impression on me. Based on the life of Joseph Alfred Slade (1831–1864), it opens with a homesteader and his wife being gunned down by outlaws in front of their twelve-year-old son, Joey. Adopted by foster parents, Joey vows to avenge the murders of his father and mother. He changes his name from Joseph to Jack, acquires a revolver, and finds work as a division agent on the Overland Stage Line out of Julesburg, Colorado. In the imaginings of Jack Slade's contemporaries – including Mark Twain, who met the desperado in the course of a journey through the West in 1861 – Slade was not only a respected and efficient servant of the Overland but also an outlaw among outlaws, scouring the Rocky Mountains for the men who killed his parents in cold blood. Twain presents a farfetched account in *Roughing It* of encountering the fearsome gunslinger in a stage station, only to find him 'so friendly and gentle-spoken that I warmed to him in spite of his awful history'.

In the movie, Slade finally tracks down his quarries, but killing them brings neither closure nor peace of mind, for vengeance is the only code he knows, and he is fated to die as he has lived – by the gun. What held my interest in the movie was not only that it blurred the line between fact and fiction, but also that it broached the theme of fate and free will. Despite everything Jack Slade attempts in the course of his brief life, he remains in thrall to the childhood trauma of losing his parents. And as my recollections of this movie flooded back to me, I realised that it presaged my friendship with Leon Donnelly and spoke directly to what became of him.

LEON

Leon had been working as a proofreader on *Truth* for at least a year before I was taken on. Ten years older than me, he helped me master the British Standards Institution's marks for proof correction and gave me tips on how to detect typos. When, in a fit of boredom, I repaid his tutelage by creating typos rather than correcting them, he applauded my irreverence and said it was exactly the kind of treatment *Truth* deserved.

For Sale
Generously sized home with large lot, family room with fireplace,
huge dick for entertaining and enjoying the view.

It wasn't long before I was spending most of my free time in Leon's company. Instead of sitting through B-grade movies at the Roxy or hammering out short stories in my dingy room, I joined him in the pub most afternoons from five to six and repaired to his Hawker Street flat every Friday and Saturday night for impromptu parties. Though I still identified with the Beats (a hangover from my student days in Auckland, when my uniform was a black turtleneck sweater, beret and duffle coat), Leon's blackness was at once more stygian and stylish. He was a Goth six years before Goth was invented, with black stovepipe trousers and bovver boots, a skull painted on his T-shirt, and dark unkempt hair. Tattooed roses and ravens covered his forearms, and posters of Edgar Allan Poe, Friedrich Nietzsche, Salvador Dali and Charles Baudelaire adorned the walls of his basement flat. In his bookcase, *The Viking Portable Nietzsche* kept company with the *I Ching*, Ezra Pound's translation of *The Four Books of Confucius*, Jack Kerouac's *The Dharma Bums* and Marco Polo's *Travels*. This unembarrassed eclecticism was so new to me that had I not been so desperate for intellectual companionship, I might have taken one look at Leon's underground life and fled. But his idiosyncratic preoccupations offered an alternative to the narcissistic literary circles that I'd reconnoitred but never been invited to join, and Leon knew a lot of girls, who were attracted by his charisma and his seemingly endless supply of marijuana. He would regale them with the macabre stories we read in *Truth*, embellishing them in ways I could not have imagined doing myself and citing some of my most outrageous typos, hoping these might arouse the girls' interest in me.

For several months Leon's dark energy brought me back to life. I had a brief affair with a ballerina who'd quit dancing because of a meniscus tear (or was it posterior tibial tendinitis?). Unfortunately, these injuries had depressed her spirits and compromised her sex life, though I suspect that my social and sexual gaucherie was the real reason for our difficulties. I smoked a lot of weed while listening to Miles Davis and John Coltrane. Yet this wasn't the life I craved. Most of Leon's crowd seemed bent not on making something of themselves but on unmaking themselves. And while I pounded away at my typewriter, as if this manic activity would produce publishable writing, Leon adopted an attitude of studied indifference, apparently happy to go with the flow.

I instinctively recoiled from such self-immolation, longing 'to move away / From the hissing of the spent lie / And the old terrors' continual cry / Growing more terrible as the day goes over the hill into the deep sea.' Whereas most of the writers I met seemed to believe that creativity required getting high and avoiding the snares of marriage, I longed to travel. I wanted to rough it, like Mark Twain. I dreamed of exotic places in which I would be reborn. Creative writing would follow naturally from the metamorphosis I would undergo *in myself*.

Leon liked to quote T.S. Eliot: 'Human kind / Cannot bear very much reality.' Perhaps this was why he was so evasive when I pried into his personal life. He fobbed me off with witticisms, like the time I asked him about his parents and he told me that he had brought himself into the world, or the time I asked if he had gone to university and he answered, 'I went, but it was closed.' In fact, he had completed an honours degree in classics at Victoria University, where he had been hailed as the most brilliant student who'd ever graduated from the programme. Why he had gone from such promise to the ignominious and underpaid position of proofreader on a tabloid newspaper remained a mystery that he refused to help me fathom. When I learned from a mutual acquaintance in the pub that Leon had working-class roots, I wondered if this was the reason he'd shied away from the prospect of Oxbridge, guilt-racked at betraying his own kind. But his Gothic and literary predilections surely put paid to that idea, unless the crucifixes and contorted Messiahs that figured among his bric-a-brac suggested a masochistic streak in his character. For, despite appearances, Leon struggled even more than I did with self-esteem. He put himself down before anyone else could. He sold himself short before someone else pointed out his limitations. The man who I believed to be a genius thought of himself as doomed to serve penance for a crime he had not committed.

Something of this was revealed one rain-lashed afternoon as we were walking past the former Communist Party headquarters in Marion Street. Though not yet leased to a locksmith, the building held the key to one of Leon's best-kept secrets.

'My father was in the CP,' he muttered, so matter-of-factly that it took a few seconds for this to sink in.

'Your father?'

We turned the corner into Vivian Street and took shelter in the doorway of the Trades Hall. The rain was pelting down as I waited for Leon to say more.

Leon confided that one of his earliest memories was going with his mother to meet his father, who had just been released from detention with other CP activists. The Auckland railway station had opened in 1930, the same year Leon was born, and he remembered, as if it was yesterday, the crowded platform and his mother pulling him into a niche in the brick and granite wall as raised voices echoed under the roof. When the great K locomotive pulled in, clanking and panting at the head of its train of dark red carriages, the crowd pressed forward, and shouts rang out as men recognised and cheered their returning comrades. Leon's mother was shouting too, shouting her husband's name as he was borne aloft on the shoulders of his mates, a homecoming hero. But her shouts were drowned out, and Leon could not tell which of the heroes he should wave to. Nor did he know what to think in the aftermath of this tumultuous day when the man who was his father sat drinking beer in the sitting room, as oblivious to his son as he was to his wife, or of the day his mother took him to the Salvation Army Home and tearfully gave him into the care of a woman dressed like a soldier. 'I can still remember the pillow shams,' Leon said, 'embossed with the words "God is Love", and a woman whose name was Sally, who told me that my mother was finding it hard to cope and that I should not think that my parents did not love me. "God loves you," she said. But I did not know who God was, even though Sally explained, "He is your heavenly father." As for my sister, it would be three years before we were reunited and reclaimed by our remorseful mother. By then,' Leon added, 'our father was history.'

My most desolate days before meeting Leon and throwing in my lot with him had been Sundays, when the Wellington Citadel Brass Band of the Salvation Army marched down Cuba Street to Courtney Place, playing tunes like 'Onward Christian Soldiers', handing out copies of *War Cry*, addressing each other as 'Comrade', 'Brother', and 'Sister' in an uncanny echo of Communist Party usage, while deploying a militarist hierarchy in which soldiers were ranked as majors, brigadiers and lieutenant-colonels wearing 'the armour of God' (or did they mean the amour of God?). I would follow them, just as I had followed brass bands and circus processions through the streets of my hometown in the hope that they would lead me to somewhere or something that would transform my life. On those depressing Wellington Sundays, I would fantasise romance with one of the young bonneted women in black stockings beating a timbrel against her skirted thigh in time to the brassy music, and when Leon told me that he had spent three years in a Salvation Army home and that his father had sacrificed the happiness of his own family in pursuing his utopian vision of a just society I was deeply touched, and I thought it was nothing short of miraculous that he had survived this primal storm seemingly unscathed.

The Paper Nautilus

In Leon's company, I gave no thought to the morrow, certain that he would dream up some scheme to astonish and entertain me. He was the hare; I was the tortoise. While I plodded along, eyes to the ground and self-absorbed, Leon raced ahead, drawing me along in his wake, like the time we went to Mayor Island in search of argonauts.

The only Argonauts I had heard of were Greek, but Leon explained that the ones he had in mind were equally fascinating. He showed me a pencil drawing he had made of the delicate shell-like brood chamber, and described its function and its fate. 'It is rare to find unbroken specimens,' Leon said. 'If the gulls don't destroy them, the rocks will.'

It was New Year's Eve, and Leon had rented a car for our journey north. The idea was to drive to the Bay of Plenty, stay overnight in a motel, and take a boat to the island early the following day. I presumed it would be just the two of us, but Leon had asked his girlfriend to join us, and she in turn brought her roommate along for the ride. I hid my disappointment, finding it hard to share Barbara's exuberance as she threw herself across the bonnet of the car and made faces at Leon while I loaded rucksacks in the boot and made a space for Penny beside me on the back seat.

Of our night in the motel, all I remember is being prodded awake several times by Leon and called a party pooper. I heard the noise of spluttering fireworks, someone drunkenly singing 'Auld Lang Syne' and the door slamming shut as Leon and the girls headed out into the night. As I sank back into sleep, I wondered how people could attach such significance to New Year's Eve, allowing themselves to believe it was a magical threshold to a new life.

Late the following morning we drove to Whangamata and joined a small crowd waiting for the midday boat to Mayor Island. Leon and Barbara were so wrapped up in each other that Penny and I were left to lug our gear from the car and attempt some sort of conversation.

'So, are you a lawyer like Barbara?' I asked.

'I sit my bar exams in June.'

After a long pause, I ventured to say that when Barbara said we were going to Mayor Island I had confused it with White Island.

'White Island's an active volcano. Mayor Island isn't.'

'Let's hope it stays that way,' I said, 'at least for today.'

'But there are hot springs,' Penny said.

The crossing took two hours, during which the wind picked up and the sea became increasingly choppy. On arrival, as we left the jetty, Leon and Barbara announced they were going to find the crater lakes and would meet us on the beach in a couple of hours.

'Which beach?' I called after them, but they were already out of earshot.

'Looks like it's just us,' Penny said.

There was nothing for it but to resume our stilted conversation and pretend we were having a good time.

I was reluctant to undress and go swimming, but Penny had no qualms. She was wearing her bikini under her clothes. Quickly unbuttoning her blouse and stepping out of her cotton skirt, she teased me into joining her in looking for an argonaut.

I was warmed by the ironic way she said *argonaut* and by her carefree attitude to what I already decided was a misadventure.

As we waded into the sea, I wondered how we were going to find a paper nautilus in this wind-whipped water. But maybe that wasn't what this trip was all about.

When Penny plunged into a breaking wave, I followed. She was obviously a strong swimmer. Though I could not keep pace with her, I was surprised at how quickly we passed beyond the first line of breakers and how far away the beach now seemed. Then I realised we were in a rip and were being carried out to sea.

I focused on keeping my wits about me and not attempting to swim straight back to the beach. But to my dismay, Penny was determined to do just this. Before I could warn her against wearing herself out fighting the rip, she had disappeared in the trough of a swell.

Suddenly Leon appeared on the beach. He had seen the danger

and was shouting at Barbara to go for help. Then he plunged in, just as I began swimming parallel to the shore, finally free of the rip. Battered by waves, I could see neither Leon nor Penny, and by the time I reached the shallows and could plant my feet on firm sand, my legs were buckling under me.

By the time Leon reached Penny, her body could no longer answer to her will. I watched helplessly as they appeared and disappeared in the surf. When they finally staggered ashore, they were utterly spent. Penny fell onto her hands and knees, coughing up sea water. Leon was gasping for air. 'Got to get her warm,' he stammered. We had all brought a change of clothes, but Leon, now joined by a distressed Barbara, said it would be better if we walked to the hot pools.

Even after the four of us had lowered ourselves into the pool, we were still in shock. Penny kept muttering about how she could have drowned. I felt ashamed at my powerlessness. That Leon had come to Penny's rescue was a bitter reminder of my ineffectuality. I tried to apologise to Penny for what had happened and asked her how I could help. But she kept whimpering about how close she had come to drowning.

It was already dark when we crossed back to the mainland, the boat thudding and breasting the sea, a stench of diesel oil and salt spray in our nostrils. Penny huddled in the wheelhouse, still in shock, with Barbara comforting her. Leon kept his eyes on the horizon and his thoughts to himself.

At Whangamata we bought fish and chips and crammed into the car. The windows misted up. Though cut off from the sea, I could smell the salt in Penny's hair. When Leon passed a bottle of vodka back to us, Penny said, 'So now you want me to drown my sorrows too?' I wanted to be close to her, though I did not want to risk speaking in case she was still brooding on my failure to rescue her from the rip. Besides, she was now focused on the paper nautilus that Barbara had found washed up on the beach.

'I'm amazed it survived that rough sea,' I said.

'That I survived is what amazes me,' Penny said.

'I'm sorry I was so useless.'

'You weren't to know.'

But I did know. I had been raised by the sea. I knew that rips weren't very wide, and that it was easy to swim across them or tread water and allow the undertow to carry you back to shore.

'So where to?' Leon said.

'Home,' Barbara said.

I turned to Penny. 'What about you?'

'I'm happy to drive back tomorrow.'

'And in the meantime?' Barbara said.

'We could drive up the peninsula,' Leon said.

Which is what we did, parking by the sea and dozing fitfully until first light, when we climbed out of the car, cramped and bleary-eyed. While Penny and I gathered driftwood for a fire, Barbara and Leon got back into the car and began arguing. We could hear their voices above the wind, but not their words.

'What's got into them?' I asked.

'I'm surprised things have been as calm as they have,' Penny said.

'Why?'

'Don't you know?'

'Know what?'

'I only know what Barbara tells me.'

'What does she tell you?'

'Maybe he's different with women than with men.'

'Different how?'

I didn't really want to know and headed back to the car, where I kindled a fire while Penny, clearly irked by my withdrawal, returned to the foreshore to gather kai moana.

She came back in her bra, having removed her blouse to hold the sea urchins she'd plucked from the rocky shallows.

'Sounds like the lovers have made up,' she said, nodding toward the car.

I would have made love to Penny had she showed the slightest interest in me. But as with everything else at that time, I was held in check by a self-defeating force I could not name or change. Even when, several weeks later, Penny and I did become lovers, it was not something we decided or that our passions swept us into; it was another accident, like entering the sea at Mayor Island on a day when a rip tide was running or finding a perfect paper nautilus.

That we wound up living together for half a year was equally unplanned. So too the series of coincidences after Penny passed her bar exams: Barbara moving to Auckland and Penny inviting me to take Barbara's place.

'You're not serious!' Leon exclaimed when I told him I was leaving the Albemarle.

'Why not? We get on okay. We don't argue.'

'That's the problem! You *never* argue!'

Leon and I had got into the habit of playing chess together, and rather than respond to his accusation I began setting up the chessboard on the coffee table between us.

'Which hand?' I said.

'Chess isn't life, you know,' Leon said, tapping my right hand, which held a black pawn.

'Tell that to the Persians. They invented it.'

'It was invented in India.'

'Tell that to the Persians then.'

I opened with the Ruy Lopez. Before long I was in a quandary over my knights. I moved my queen to threaten Leon's king's pawn. Naturally, it was the wrong move.

In my journal, I wrote that our defences are paper thin, our lives as fragile and beautiful as the paper nautilus. It was prescient. When it came time for Penny and me to go our separate ways, I was devastated, though I selfishly assumed that it was worse for me than for her. As I detached myself from Penny, I unburdened myself of the things I had accumulated during our time together – a Roy Orbison album

(*Dreams*), a fragment of black obsidian, a pebble from the Poor Knights Islands, a chunk of kauri gum, a postcard from Spirits Bay, and Leon's pencil drawing of a broken paper nautilus – a drawing to which I attached no significance at the time, though it might have been my first inkling of his true vocation.

A TALE OF TWO CITIES

Nine months of trial and error passed between the ending of my affair with Penny and my departure from New Zealand. In Australia, I worked a night shift in a printing press before landing a job in Aboriginal welfare. Within a year I moved on to Paris, then to London, where I found employment in a welfare office for the homeless. It seemed I was doomed to wind up in the company of bums and misfits, though penury made any other social life impossible; I simply couldn't afford to go to the pub or a movie, and even scraping together a meal was a daily challenge.

When I received an aerogramme from Leon saying he'd been awarded a scholarship to Oxford and asking if I could offer him a place to crash for a few days before he went up, I responded with enthusiasm and surprise. 'My old professor twisted my arm,' he said, when I asked what had changed his mind about academe. That he refused to elaborate suggested that he was deeply ambivalent about the whole thing.

Leon dossed on the floor of my bedsit in a sleeping bag. I would wake in the dead of night to find him hunched over the dining table, dressed in a grubby T-shirt and torn jeans, and scribbling (or sketching) in a large hardbound notebook. I'd told him to help himself to anything he could find in the fridge, but after forcing himself to eat the stew I served on his first night, concocted from cabbage leaves and carrots scavenged from the Hammersmith Markets, he insisted on stocking the fridge with what he called 'human comestibles' and cooking for us both. He also bought wine. He could not understand my straitened circumstances, even when I told him how little I earned and how much

I gave away to the tramps I worked with. 'Plus ça change, plus c'est la même chose,' he declared. 'You travel half way around the world and manage to find yourself the English equivalent of the Albemarle and *Truth*. I admire your consistency, if not your choices!'

For ten days I accepted Leon's generosity as if my privations had earned me the right to eat decent meals, drink wine, enjoy conversation about books and share my experiences of hanging out with Aborigines in Australia, of being down and out in Paris and of fraternising with the homeless in London. When Leon left to go up to Oxford I was bereft, and as summer turned to fall, I felt increasingly desperate to change my circumstances as he appeared to have changed his.

I have a distant memory of a snowbound house in Oxford, a Christmas tree in the living room, Leon's college friends drinking and singing, and the overwhelming sense that I had no place in their company. I saw myself as one of the derelicts that haunted the precincts of Hungerford Bridge or the transport café under the Arches that advertised 'Chips with Everything, Including God' (actually 'Cod', badly written). With hindsight, however, Leon was even more anomalous than I was. It wasn't just his garb, made even more Gothic when he donned the borrowed bat-winged gown he was obliged to wear to hall. Nor was it his tattoos. He was manifestly older than the other students, in years as well as demeanour, though I now think it was his antipodean awkwardness and colonial accent that made him an object of disdain, even as it drew us closer in our common contempt for class snobbery.

In the new year, Leon came down to London more frequently. He was disenchanted with Oxford and drinking heavily, though whenever I asked what exactly it was that had disappointed him – his research, his college life, or his short-lived liaisons – he would evade my questions by urging me to amuse him with what he called 'anecdotes from the abyss' or my 'notes from Underground' – by which he meant my experiences of staying overnight in a spike, my meetings with men and women who had stumbled into homelessness after their marriages had gone on the rocks, or my own perennial struggle to find sixpences for the gas meter or avoid buying tickets for the Underground. The Artful Dodger, he called me. I objected to the sobriquet partly because I resented him foisting on to me *his* idea of who I was, partly because I lacked any identity I might claim as my own. How could I call myself a writer if I hadn't published anything? How could I think of myself as a student of life if I hadn't really lived?

A couple of weeks before Easter, Leon wrote to say that his mother had passed away and that his sister, Molly, was coming to England to visit him. But he did not want her to come to Oxford, and it would be tiresome showing her around London. He thought it might be a good idea to go to France for a while. What did I think of Paris? The three of us could go together. Money was no object: Molly would pay our way. These slap-happy proposals struck me as odd considering that his mother had recently died, though not having suffered bereavement myself, I did not know what a 'normal' response might be. But wouldn't you be manifestly distressed? Wouldn't you want to talk about something like that? My clumsy attempts to broach the matter proved fruitless, and I concluded that Leon's unwillingness to talk about his mother's death had the same source as his reluctance to talk about his parents when I first met him.

In any event, I said yes. I was about to quit my job anyway and fly to the Congo as a volunteer community-development worker with the United Nations. Returning to Paris, albeit briefly, would give me a chance to acquire more books by Blaise Cendrars and explore his haunts in the Latin Quarter. I even fantasised an affair with Leon's sister, though that dream was shattered, I am ashamed to say, when I met her. Dressed in a shapeless black tracksuit and afflicted with a broad New Zealand accent, she fell foul of my own incipient snobbery. It also seemed that Leon and his sister had little in common. They bickered over who would queue for the ferry tickets, where and when and what we would eat and whether we could fit in some sightseeing in London before we headed off to Paris (Molly declared that she wanted to see Buckingham Palace and the Mall 'if it's the last thing I do'). I should have realised then that this venture would turn out badly.

We arrived in a city overrun with visitors and with no vacancies in any pension – at least in the Latin Quarter, where Leon insisted we stay. We walked for hours through anonymous neighbourhoods, along boulevards and into blind alleys, becoming hopelessly lost. When it came on to rain, we took shelter in a corner café, bought a carafe of wine and some French fries, and weighed our options. Since we couldn't find accommodation in Paris, we decided to head out of town. Surely it would be a simple matter to take a train to Normandy or Brittany, where there were no tourists, and find a hotel? Despondently, we made our way to the Gare d'Ouest, none of us on speaking terms, each silently blaming the others for our plight.

After discovering that the last trains had departed and there was no way of leaving Paris until morning, we had no choice but to spend the night in the station. The waiting room was filled with clochards, and there was barely room for one more person on the wooden benches. Leon and I decided that Molly should have the seat while we slept on the floor, using our rucksacks for pillows. But I did not sleep. I spent five days of the week among derelicts, and here I was, on my first trip away from London, spending a night among them! Worse, they gave off a suffocating, sickly-sweet odour that I imagined to be the smell of leprosy or gangrene. Disgusted, Leon said he was going for a walk. 'I may be some time,' he said. Molly was not amused. She crossed her arms, let her head fall forward and feigned sleep. I punched my rucksack and threw myself down as if Morpheus could be bullied into possessing me.

It was dawn when Leon returned. Molly was dead to the world, her body rigid, head tilted back and mouth wide open. Leon crouched beside me and confessed his sins. He had gone to Pigalle. Badly in need of a drink, he ordered a Pernod in the first bar he came to, and then another. The oppression of the night began to lift. He watched the whores coming and going, the gawking tourists, the local touts, downed a third Pernod, and began to feel that Molly and I no longer existed, that he had passed into another world on which the miserable day would never dawn and from which he would never have to return. In a blur of neon and noise, he bought a beer for the girl who approached him and blithely accepted her offer and her price. 'I don't know what possessed me', Leon said. 'The worst of it is that Molly entrusted her money to me, and I shelled it out without a second thought, buying a bottle of champagne, paying for the room the girl took me to, giving her what she demanded.'

It turned out that he had blown half Molly's money. I couldn't have cared less. I thought of those lines from Cendrars' *Prose on the Trans-Siberian Railway* about the need to push oneself to the limit, though I could not take this train of thought any further. Perhaps I envied Leon's crazy profligacy.

When we were sitting in the station café with croissants and bowls of coffee, Molly seemed to regard her brother's ill-considered actions as confirmation that our trip had been doomed from the start. She was ready to go back to London anyway, she said. She wanted a hot bath and some time to herself. Leon accused her of abandoning ship and begged her to reconsider. 'Find me somewhere I can have a hot bath and I might,' she said.

We decided to split up. While I bought tickets for the ten o'clock train to Rouen, Molly went looking for a public bathroom, and Leon set off to buy a *Herald Tribune*. We agreed to rendezvous at the café in an hour.

None of us had anticipated the labyrinthine vastness of the station. After buying our tickets, I couldn't find my way back to the café. I'd been simply too tired and disoriented to make a mental note of its name or location. Molly's search for a bathroom took her out of the station, and she did not return for more than an hour. Only Leon found his way back to our rendezvous at the agreed time. I was frantically wandering down long tiled tunnels, trying to get my bearings from the echoing chords of an accordioniste or from the exit signs. I kept anxiously checking my watch. Ten o'clock came and went. I wondered whether our tickets would be valid for a later train, though I was rapidly getting to the point where I didn't give a shit what happened. And during this exasperating time, Leon was wandering around the same labyrinth, hoping to bump into one of us. He'd got fed up waiting at the café. We later reckoned the three of us were all in the station for over an hour, passing like ships in the night, cursing one another and in half a mind to give up the search – except that I had no money, and Leon, filled with remorse about his night at Pigalle, was determined not to give Molly a reason for detesting him more than she already did.

After seeing Molly onto the boat train to London, Leon and I took a train to Rouen and checked into the first hotel we found. We took turns to shower, then slept. It was mid-afternoon by the time we ventured out to find a place to eat. On a narrow street, rue Guy de Maupassant, we found a small café where the plat du jour was jambon de campagne, petits pois and frîtes. The proprietor's wife wished us bon appétit, then busied herself clearing adjacent tables and setting out clean ashtrays. Her husband stood behind the bar, polishing glasses, observing us with an air of great satisfaction. He asked if we were from England. La Nouvelle-Zélande, I said, and explained how we had come to Paris for Easter but hadn't been able to find a hotel room. Madame assured us we could have done worse than come to Rouen. This was the birthplace of Corneille and Boieldieu, not to mention Flaubert. And did we know that Jeanne d'Arc was burned as a witch in the market square? When I expressed an interest in all this, the proprietor said he would be pleased to draw a map for us, so we could make 'un petit tour'.

So we took in the tower and the cathedral, with its shrapnel-scarred masonry and windows of plain glass, and stood at the spot where Joan of Arc was burned alive, and walked down long avenues of pollarded plane trees in the blustery spring afternoon.

Leon was lagging a few metres behind me. I was impatient to get on, though to where I could not say.

I heard a small cry. When I turned, I saw him crumple like a burst balloon on the sandy path.

'What is it?' I said anxiously.

Leon's face was contorted with pain.

'I think it's my ulcer,' he said.

'What ulcer?'

He couldn't talk. I bent down, got my arm behind his back and asked if he could make it to the nearby bench. He seized my coat and tried to get to his feet, but his legs buckled and he fell back onto the path.

My feelings had changed from irritation to concern. In desperation, I looked up and down the long avenue. Miraculously a bus was approaching. I waved wildly at the driver, and the bus drew into the curb only metres away.

I urged Leon to stand up. This time he succeeded. Dragging one leg, he let me half carry him onto the bus where he collapsed into a seat reserved for 'femmes enceintes, aveugles, personnes agées and les mutilés de la guerre'.

I was confused and out of breath but managed to ask the driver if he went anywhere near the hospital.

'C'est tout près,' he said, and assured me he would let me know when we reached it.

I sat beside Leon, who was bent double, clutching his stomach and moaning.

The other passengers, I noticed, were looking away.

In the emergency room, two orderlies got Leon onto a gurney. A doctor bent over him with a clipboard. He had a checklist of diagnostic terms in four European languages. Using a one-word method of interrogation, he established the source and possible cause of Leon's distress.

As the doctor gently prodded at Leon's abdomen, he asked me questions in French. Had my friend been drinking heavily? Was he married? Where did his parents live?

I waited a couple of hours after Leon was wheeled away. Then a nurse came and said my friend's condition was serious but stable. He had suffered the rupture of a gastric ulcer. They were operating at that very moment.

I did not see Leon until the following morning. He was dressed in a green gown, propped up on a heap of pillows, his face deathly pale. He relayed to me what the doctors had told him. He would have to remain under observation for a week. 'If I were you, I would go back to Paris or London,' Leon said. 'I'll be fine. In a way, I'm glad this has happened. It's been on the cards for a long time. I know that now. I won't go back to Oxford, I'm sure of that. I don't know what I'll do, but I won't be going back to Oxford.'

A couple of days later I returned to Paris, and with the money Leon had given me (and Molly had given him) I bought a notebook and several Livre de Poche editions of Cendrars' novels.

In London, I hoped to hear from Leon before I left for the Congo. But several weeks passed before his postcard reached me, forwarded from my former London address.

It was from Athens.

All's well that ends well. Leon.

I sent him a letter in care of American Express, Syntagma, Athens, describing the flaming sunsets over the Congo River, the Livingstone Rapids, the rusting riverboats at the Brazzaville ferry landing that reminded me of Joseph Conrad, and the orphanage to which I'd been assigned. My inquiry about what Leon was doing in Athens was appended as an afterthought.

Two months passed before I heard back from him. In Rouen he had arranged for his scholarship money to be transferred from Oxford to Paris. He then travelled to Greece by train, arriving in Athens on what he called the morning of the first day of his life. Having given all his money away to beggars in Omonoia Square, he had found work teaching English to college students and begun learning modern Greek.

'I have burned my bridges,' he wrote.

Every morning I walk up to the Byzantine Chapel on Lykavittós. From the top of the hill I am above the city, which is smothered in smog. The Parthenon emerges from this sea of mist and murk, catching the light. Sometimes I go into the chapel, light a candle, and pray. Not asking for anything. Not even believing in the gods to whom I vaguely address my thoughts. More to acknowledge the fates that brought me here. How often in your life do you realise you are happy at the very moment you are, instead of later, looking back, when what you thought of as happiness was probably an illusion? It's incredible how our lives unfold. We think we are masters of our fate, but in fact very few people actually determine the course of their lives. We never take the reins between our hands, never really control the horses; we let them, and the road, decide our destiny and destination. Liberation is seldom a heroic act; it usually begins in cowardice, as we abnegate responsibility for ourselves, and allow happenstance to carry us along. I suppose this explains why certain things in Athens have struck me with such force. The peddlers on every street corner, with lottery tickets lodged in slotted sticks. The blind banjo player on the steps of the Plaka, whose monotonous songs have been passed down, or so I imagine, through generations of seers, perhaps from Tiresias himself.

Leon's life was so absorbed in augury and myth that from my vantage point in the Congo I found it difficult to relate to his Mediterranean meditations. It is only now, many years later, that I can see that it was not the distance between Greece and the Congo that prevented me appreciating his happiness but the fact that I had still not reached the point where I could say, as Leon had, *I have found my path.*

ATHENS

It may be impossible or illusory to claim that a particular moment in our lives constituted a turning point when we saw the light, found ourselves, or discovered our vocation. Yet, in recounting the story of our lives, we often make such claims in order to give coherence and a retrospective sense of purpose to events that were, in reality, arbitrary and indefinite.

I like to think that I first glimpsed my future as an anthropologist in the midst of a violent insurgency in the Eastern Congo. I had taken refuge at a coffee plantation, abandoned by its Belgian owners two years before and brought back into production by a group of Franciscan monks working with young Congolese men, many of whom had lost their homes and families in the fighting that brought the secession of Kasai Province to an end.

At night I went down to the river to watch the hippos come ashore and browse. The grasslands glittered with the light of fireflies, as if entire galaxies had disintegrated and fallen from the sky. Other evenings I listened with growing fascination as a Bena Lulua boy explained to me the meaning of his initiation scars, the purpose of the statuettes I'd seen among the manioc, and the reason why mourning women covered their faces with kaolin. Or I skimmed a dog-eared copy of Claude Lévi-Strauss's monumental study of kinship (*Les structures élémentaires de la parenté*) that I'd found in a bookcase in the main house, my imagination captured by the idea that beneath the empirical diversity of social life lay universal structuring principles of reciprocity and exchange.

Though I was increasingly disenchanted with aid and development work, and fantasised about living in an African village and learning its lifeways at first hand, there was no single moment at which two roads diverged in a narrow wood and I chose one over the other. Nor can I pinpoint any one event that led me to reject the idealism of Claude Lévi-Strauss's structuralism and explore the negative side of reciprocity – our propensity for exploiting or exterminating our fellows, denying their humanity simply because they do not look, speak, or act exactly as we do.

After leaving the Congo I went to Paris, expecting to revise the novel I'd written in Léopoldville during the rains, but I failed to find work teaching English with Berlitz, and rather than wind up stranded in Paris without a sou, I accepted Leon's long-standing invitation to join him in Greece.

Leon seemed completely at home in Athens. Although he had shed his Gothic accoutrements, his shabby apartment near Omonoia Square seemed completely in character. As we climbed the wooden steps to the third floor, Leon carrying my battered suitcase like a child in his arms, I felt immense relief. For a short time, at least, I had a roof over my head and a friend on whom I could rely.

A large studio easel stood in the middle of the living room. Propped on it was a large painting of an olive tree. I might have dismissed the thought that this was Leon's handiwork had it not been for the smell of turpentine and linseed oil permeating the room, and had he not already mentioned that he lived alone. The painting literally took my breath away. As Leon lowered my suitcase to the floor, I stared at this ancient tree, its knotted and contorted trunk resembling tensed sinews, its drab foliage haloed by light.

'How long have you been painting?' I asked.

'I used to paint when I was a kid. We all do, I guess. But I lost the knack, or the incentive …'

'You never mentioned anything about painting in your letters.'

'I would have, if I had accomplished something.'

I gazed at the painting on the easel. 'I would call this an accomplishment,' I said. 'It's brilliant.'

Leon was determined to dismiss both the painting and my praise. 'Painting olive trees is more profitable than growing them,' he said. 'A chic gallery in Kolonaki sells them to rich Americans. My real work doesn't sell at all.'

When I observed that this had always been the case with great art, Leon disputed the notion of greatness, though he admitted that he at least knew what was real.

I had never seen this side of Leon before – so serious, focused and uncompromising.

Over the next few days Leon introduced me to his Greek friends and found me a job teaching English at the Polytechneion. His fluency in Greek, like his artistic gifts, made me realise how little I had to show for myself. I had come back from the Congo with a sheaf of poems, the rough first draft of a novel, a smattering of Lingala and Swahili, and a fading memory of events that had once seemed momentous but now seemed hardly worth remarking.

We established a routine. While Leon painted, I found a café in a quiet side street and pored over the dog-eared pages of my novel. If Leon could put in long hours painting, surely I could do the same with my writing? I was determined to apply myself until a breakthrough came. As for the teaching, I was surprised to discover that I had a talent for it, and that students seemed to like me.

At least once a week Leon took me sightseeing, retracing the steps he had taken during his own first weeks in the city. In Syntagma he showed me the ornamental orange trees whose fruit he had hoped would assuage his hunger. But the oranges were inedible. At Sounion he showed me Byron's name, carved at the base of one of the columns of the Temple of Poseidon, in all likelihood the work of a fan. And we visited the Acropolis.

After Turkish coffees in the Plaka, we made our way to the Beule Gate. The sky was cloudless, a stiff wind was blowing, and the air was filled with the odours of cedars and diesel fumes. Despite the early hour, the place was already swarming with tourists, picking their way over the broken ground, talking in a score of languages, and so relentlessly photographing everything in sight that I was tempted to conclude that they saw nothing with their own eyes and that the only meaning attaching to these images was that they would, at some later date, prove to their families and friends that they had indeed been there.

Leon wanted to show me the Erechtheion. He returned there periodically to celebrate the moment he realised that Greece was his spiritual home. As he described his first visit to the Acropolis, he gave the impression that no one else had ever seen it in the same light. That morning the temple was also surrounded by tourists. It had been impossible to see anything, so Leon eavesdropped on the guide who was explaining that Poseidon left his trident marks in the stone and that centuries later, a Turkish commander accommodated his harem there during the war of independence. When the tourist party moved on, Leon said, it was blissfully quiet for a while, and he had stepped back from the temple to take in the caryatids that supported the architrave. The figure at the left end of the porch fascinated him. Her arms and feet had been amputated, perhaps when a Turkish shell almost destroyed the building in 1827, and her face was ruined. But the erosion that had scarred her nose and upper lip had imparted to her a beauty more compelling than had she remained unblemished. Her marmoreal loveliness – her supple shoulders, her relaxed stance, the left knee slightly bent, breasts and belly sensuous beneath the folds of an Ionian tunic – transcended the rubble at her feet, which is why, Leon said, he had fallen in love with her.

Gazing up at the subject of Leon's infatuation, I was at first amused by his confession and was about to counter it by telling him about my sordid affairs with prostitutes in the Congo when I stopped myself, as guilty about my dalliances as I was envious of his. That evening, Leon showed me some of his 'real' work: charcoal drawings of hands; sidewalks slicked with rain; smoky, cloud-smudged Athenian skies; watercolour sketches of peasant clothing and artefacts in the National Archaeological Museum; and, most memorable, a series of small oils, each one the face of his beloved caryatid from a slightly different angle or in a slightly different light. Only one of these beautiful paintings would survive, and though I can recall them all as they were revealed to me that long-ago afternoon, it pains me to look at the one that graces the wall of the room where I write this memoir, separated from its other iterations, its other selves, singled out by happenchance.

When we travelled by bus to Delphi that weekend, Leon was so eager to show me the site of the Castalian Spring that I anticipated a revelation as marvellous as the one he'd had on the Acropolis.

A trickle of water issued from a fissure in the red rock, but not enough to fill the ancient cistern, which had been pissed in by recent visitors and reeked of urine. I looked up at the sheer cliffs and thought of Aesop, thrown to his death. I imagined others who had made this pilgrimage to slake their thirst and hear the Sybil's wild utterances, telling them what they should do. But when I asked Leon if this, too, had been a place of illumination for him, he laughed.

Leon wanted to make some charcoal drawings of the omphalos in the museum, and though I was moved by some of the archaic statuary, I was less interested in fragments of the past than in the pinewoods behind the museum, where the air was warm and resinous, and where I sat in silence, thinking of the Congolese coffee plantation in which I had found sanctuary only a few months before.

Leon left the museum only when it closed. He found me sitting on a stone wall, scribbling in my journal.

It was evening by the time our bus deposited us in the main street of Itea on the Gulf of Corinth. After booking into a one-star hotel, we ate dinner in a backstreet taverna – baby octopus, tzatziki, Greek salad, fresh baked bread and retsina – and talked about myths and landscapes. Perhaps it was because Leon told me about Oedipus on the road to Delphi that I asked if he believed in fate, or perhaps my question arose from my own difficulties in seeing the road ahead.

'I mean,' I said, 'your medical crisis in Rouen. It seemed so dire at the time, yet it turned out to be your salvation.'

'My day of reckoning,' Leon said, and laughed.

'But do you think we are destined for certain things? Like you were destined to become a painter?'

'I don't know that I'd call it destiny. They say all roads lead to Rome, but in my case they led to Athens. Why did I do classics at university, why did I become fascinated by the Greeks? What led me to my caryatid and inspired me to paint again? It's as if I was on my way to Greece before I knew where Greece was, and that my early life was a preparation for this one.'

'You mean your childhood?'

'I don't think you can explain a person in terms of a single event,' Leon said, 'or even a single lifetime. You'd have to go back centuries to grasp the concatenations that produced any moment in present time. Oedipus was not fated to murder his father or marry his mother because of any one thing *he* did, or even that his father did before him. Sophocles makes everything appear inevitable, because this is what most people want from a play or a story. They want it to be morally coherent, to satisfy their need for justice and closure. But is life really like that?'

'Mine certainly isn't.'

'Then you're lucky. You have a future.'

'But what kind of future could Oedipus hope to have? He seems to have been doomed from the start.'

'He wasn't doomed. He had to be punished.'

'What's the difference?'

'To be doomed is not to be free. But Oedipus *was* free. He chose his own death.'

If I have difficulties in reconstructing this conversation (which I recorded all too hurriedly in my journal), it is because to this day I'm not completely sure I understand what Leon was driving at. Perhaps he was talking about Socrates, not Oedipus. Perhaps he was struggling to understand his own parentage. Perhaps he was indulging his gift for casuistry. Since I hung on his every word and regarded him as both older and wiser than I was, it is possible that he was playfully chiding me for taking him too seriously. Perhaps he was improvising an allegory of his own life, and I was too dim to see it.

THE ORDINANCE OF TIME

When I left Greece, having borrowed from my parents the price of the airfare home, I wanted to explore the possibility of working in Māori welfare or, failing that, going to Vietnam as a war correspondent. Instead I found myself back in Wellington, working as a builder's labourer and falling into the funk that had defined my life in the Albemarle four years before.

But then I met Emma, and for the first time in my life everything became clear. Emma was my caryatid, the column that held me up, a figure that filled my heart with such love and longing that when we were apart, I felt as though my soul had suffered a partial eclipse. In a memoir I published forty years after our first meeting, I wrote,

> *I have never believed in miracles. The very idea irritates me. It belongs to the vocabulary of those irksome individuals who answer your phone calls by confiding in awed tones that they'd been thinking of you at the very same moment you rang. People who believe that every coincidence is evidence of some hidden hand benignly steering them through life. People who pepper their stories with words like karma and synchronicity.*

Despite this, I was no more immune to superstition than any other human being; in meeting Emma I felt that a miracle had happened.

Though Leon and I had exchanged letters since my precipitous departure from Athens in early 1965, he did not respond to my account of meeting Emma, my success in publishing some of the poetry and prose pieces I had drafted in Congo, or my decision to return to university and complete an MA in anthropology, but in a sidelong allusion to my change of fortune (or was it a series of happy accidents?) he mentioned that he was researching a politically ill-advised biography of a Greek friend and activist, adding, mysteriously, that he was also thinking about coming back to New Zealand.

Though I was immersed in my studies and passionately in love, my own political life centred on protests against the American war in Vietnam and keeping a file of newspaper clippings concerning the worsening situation in the Congo. I was therefore slow to connect Leon's grim missives from Athens with the military coup d'état of April 1967. It was only when his battered package arrived, plastered with Greek stamps, and I read the typescript inside that I began to grasp the seriousness of his situation.

This typescript, now lying on my desk, its pages tattered and time-stained, was a portion of a longer manuscript about a certain Takis Harissiadis, presumably the activist Leon had mentioned in his letters. What strikes me now, however, reading between the typed lines, is how deeply Leon identified with the Left, as if in some oblique way he was honouring the legacy of his father. I also wonder whether it was his increasing involvement in politics that brought about his disenchantment with painting.

'When the Colonels came to power in 1967', Leon wrote,

> *almost all Takis's acquaintances despised the junta, though discussions raged long into the night over what to do – civil disobedience or violent resistance, remaining at university, going underground, or leaving the country. There were arrests every day, but with no discernible pattern. A curfew was imposed, rebetiko music was banned, and the only reliable news came from short-wave BBC radio broadcasts. People avoided the roadblocks, heard rumours of* khafiés *(police informers) and of pre-dawn raids, arrests and torture, but no one knew how long the regime would last or what would happen next. Even the police seemed not to know what was going on.* We have orders, but we do not know who is giving them. *Even within families, silence seemed the best defence against treachery.*

> *This silence made Takis irascible. He lost his temper with friends, exacerbating the ideological rifts that were opening up between them. And though starved for information, no one dared seek it. In Piraeus, a mother and her small child were detained and the child tortured in front of the mother until she divulged the hiding place of her husband. Arrests were commonplace. But even as Takis and his friends protested these outrages, they also laughed to relieve the tension, poking fun at the mangled sentences uttered by Georgias Papadopoulos, the ridiculous hats worn by his wife, the oafish appearance of Stylianos Patakos, the lackey Nicolaos Makarezos, and the anti-communist ravings of Ionnis Ladas, as if mockery could do as much damage as grenades.*

> *On Takis's last evening with his 'little group', they gathered at Demetrius's home at Kifisiá, drinking retsina and listening to*

Mikis Theodorakis's Kaïmós, which would soon be banned. The following morning, Takis awoke from a premonitory dream, the words of Kaïmós running through his head: 'Barren rock, barren rock, my grief, I measure it, and am filled with pain. And it is my plaint: "Mother, when will I see you again?"'

An hour later, Takis was crossing a street near Kolonaki when a police officer accosted him and demanded to see his identity card. Takis explained as politely as he could that his apartment was only a few meters away. He had stepped out to buy some pasta and forgotten to bring his ID with him. He must have phrased his explanation clumsily or given the impression of questioning the policeman's right to stop and interrogate him on the street. Enraged, the policeman shouted at him, spitting into his face: 'Why? You ask why? There is no why in Greece!' Minutes later Takis was bundled into a car and taken to the Plaka police station. He foolishly presumed that he would simply have to sign some kind of document, then be sent or taken back to his apartment to get his papers. But when he asked the police officer who had detained him whether it would not be easier for them to pass by his apartment so he could pick up his ID, the officer shouted, 'No why!' as if Takis were a stranger on the other side of the street.

The police station was crowded with women in black, sitting in silence with their hands upturned on their laps. Were they waiting for news of a loved one arrested in the night and disappeared? Takis began to fear for his own safety. He remembered stories he had heard as a boy, of the civil war, of the persecution of members of the Left, of the concentration camps on Makronisos and Yaros, and he understood how quickly, and with what terrible finality, a person could pass from the light of day into darkness and be swallowed up. He was taken to an interrogation room where he sat waiting for someone to come, increasingly prey to his worst fears, too frightened to admit hunger or thirst, or even wonder what his friends would think or do when he did not turn up for their evening meeting. When, after an hour or two, a plain-clothes police officer finally entered the room, it was not to ask questions but to take him down to the basement and lock him in an isolation cell.

Next morning he was led upstairs. An ultimatum was delivered. No one was in a mood to waste time with him. They knew he was a communist. He must provide a list of names of his comrades and contacts. Takis was aware that his story would echo the stories of a million other Greeks whose lives had been erased like chalked names on a pavement as the hard rain of civil war swept over them. What should he say? What could he do? He said nothing. It was not a conscious decision, let alone an act of courage: he was so terrified and confused he could not formulate a response. Whose names would he write down? How much of this interrogation could he endure before he fell apart?

Reprieve came improbably when another detainee was shoved into the room, his hands manacled behind his back and a blood-stained mail sack covering his head and shoulders. Takis was told that this man was a communist. Hurling abuse at the shrouded head, one of the policemen beat him across the lower back with a mahogany truncheon. Takis was astonished that the victim did not cry out. Then the man was pushed and shoved from the room. Minutes later, another was led in and given the same treatment. Takis was invited to participate. If he wasn't a communist, he would have no hesitation in showing these traitors the contempt they deserved. This, Takis said, he could not do. The officer in charge then stunned him by saying he was free to go. Convinced this was a ruse and that as soon as he walked toward the door he would be hit from behind, he did not move. 'Go,' he was told, the word screamed into his ear. 'Get the hell out of here. Get lost. Scram!'

He stumbled into the street. It was as if he had been carried a thousand miles from Athens and dumped in an unknown country at an indeterminate time. It was night, the street deserted. Already an exile, he resolved to become the person he had been forced to be. There was no question of meeting his 'little group'. He felt that he had betrayed it. Even though he had not given the police any names, he believed he would have done so to save his skin. As for his family, would they understand? His father, who had fought with the Partisans, might be proud that he had escaped and survived, and would work from abroad for Greece's liberation *from this new fascist gang. But to return home might incriminate his family. He walked to his ransacked apartment, stuffed a suitcase full of clothes, a few books and papers, and detoured down back streets to the bus station. That evening, he arrived in Thessaloniki, where he got on a train to Belgrade, hoping to rendezvous with other exiles and make his way to Moscow.*

> *Whence things have their origin, there they must*
> *also pass away according to necessity; for they*
> *must pay the penalty and be judged for their injustice,*
> *according to the ordinance of time …*

I could not be sure why Leon had sent me this manuscript (there was no covering note), though the fragment of Anaximander with which it abruptly ended perhaps provides a clue. Leon would also leave Greece under cover of darkness, though in a cryptic postcard from Belgrade he suggested that it was not because he feared for his life, but because, despite the depth of his feeling for Greece, he had realised that he was not Greek.

Years would pass before I realised how well Leon had kept the truth from me. Or was it that I was so gullible, always taking him at his word? For all I know, Leon *was* Takis.

Envois

In 1968 Emma and I won doctoral scholarships to Cambridge. To qualify for a married students' flat at Churchill College, we got married. It took us several weeks to muster the courage to do so. We were so deeply committed to each other – or was it because we were unconsciously so uncommitted? – that we felt no need to formalise our relationship. Treating the event as farce enabled us to dodge this question. We tied the knot on Friday the 13th, Emma wore black, and when the Registry Office informed me that I would need a ring and the licence would have to be witnessed, I dashed out into the street, bought a second-hand gold band in the first jeweller's I came across, and then, as luck would have it, ran into a couple of friends who agreed to witness our signatures and help us laugh off the event over whiskey sours in the upstairs bar of the George Hotel.

That Leon and I lost touch with each other after his postcard from Belgrade had as much to do with his peripatetic life and impermanent addresses as it did with my new life with Emma. I had assumed that our love for each other would be perfectly compatible with our affection for old friends. But I found myself jealous of Emma's friends, while she could not understand why I spent so much time in the pub, hobnobbing with journalists and 'losers'.

'I don't know what you see in them,' she said.

I persuaded her to join me one evening and meet them. Her prejudices were confirmed. 'All you do is get drunk together. You shout into each other's faces. Either you don't hear what the other person is saying or you don't care. You shout back. It's ridiculous.'

She was right, of course, but only now do I realise that, despite my devotion to Emma, I still harboured a vestigial sense of myself as a loner and a loser. Among the regulars in the back bar of the Duke of Edinburgh I could revert to that old identity, perversely recoiling from the homely existence I shared with Emma, and at the same time resisting, like Leon, the academic life that lay ahead of me.

When I travelled to England that August, Emma remained in Wellington to prepare for her final exams. Though I sensed that we both needed time apart, to take stock of the relationship into which we had fallen so precipitously and passionately, it took me only a week to discover that I could not live without her. Whether I could live *with* her was another matter.

My darling Emma,

A bleak day – overcast, rainy, bad light. The flat is very austere, with a view over playing fields and an avenue of elms – already shedding their leaves. I've thrown myself into work, spending most afternoons in the Haddon Museum, studying the pare there – handling them, sketching them, getting a feel for how they were made in order to guess at why. I draw my inspiration from Lévi-Strauss's theory of split-representation, and I'm also looking at moko patterns and waka huia, exploring the way profiles of a face or left and right sides of a figure are separated, transposed, and then rejoined. It seems to me that the energy of the pare springs from this tension between the separated halves – polarised and flung to the perimeters as manaia – and the recomposed central figures. The chaotic interstices hold us in suspense – the movement being at once towards dismemberment and splitting, and towards wholeness and healing. The dynamic self-containment of the central figures is born, therefore, of a union of forms which, in other contexts, oppose each other. And the imagery of the pare condenses into itself, processes both natural and cultural – the waxing and waning of the moon, the unfurling of fern fronds, the onrush and retreat of waves on a beach, and the coming together on ceremonial occasions of several whānau in a single ancestral house and their inevitable separations and schisms.

I'm acutely aware of the curious kinship between my ideas about the pare and my own emotional preoccupations – my own divided self, my sense of being incomplete and immobilised without you. I suppose the intellectual life is always grounded in the personal life. Wasn't it Nietzsche who said that all philosophy is disguised autobiography? And undoubtedly the reverse is equally true.

Had a marvellous letter from Leon, who is living in a city called Split on the Dalmatian coast. He mourns his exile from Greece as I mourn my exile from you. He's been reading William Blake and sent me a quotation that I did not know whether to read as a reflection on his own situation or mine. For man has closed himself up, till he sees all things thro' narrow chinks in his cavern. Perhaps he is undergoing some kind of religious conversion, or painting again, for his letter was filled with descriptions of prophets mantled in flame, of God's calipers, and light's free energy coursing through the world.

As for me, all my free energy flows toward you. I read into the small hours, in coarse-grained cloying darkness, then glimpse your photo on my table and become hot and cold as if with fever at the sight of your bare shoulder, your smile, at the thought of your perfect body, your dark hair. A wild goat-cry rises in my throat, choking me with joy. I love you with my whole being. You fill me with life.

My darling Michael,

Reading your letter was like reading The Politics of Experience. It made me feel as if I was truly myself and not a figment of someone else's imagination. It made me feel good in another way, too, as I will try to explain as truthfully as I can. This causes me great travail and pain, but because I feel that you are as separate from me as you are attached to me, it is easier to speak my mind.

Some of this you already know. I hope you won't dismiss it as mere sentimentalism or regard it as a confession.

You know my parents lived apart when I was young, and that for a summer I lived with my father, to whom I was terribly attached. When school started again, I was forced to go and live with my mother – and you know of my feelings for her. I was overjoyed to go to boarding school, though it turned out to be just another confinement – like her place. I slept with Christopher literally the day school finished – my 17th birthday in fact. When he left the country, I was miserable, of course, but the earlier severances from my father made it seem facile. The anaesthesia I've told you about is a reflex action with me now. When David Gilchrist left to take up his scholarship at Reading, I felt nothing. And you also know about my nymphomania between that parting and meeting you. I even slept with my best friend's husband. There was a complete blanket over my mind and emotions – a complete physical abandonment. To what I don't know. I suppose I wanted to be a child again – to be subjected to and loved by men. I can't tell you of the intensity of feeling that came over me when I met you. But this was coupled with an equally strong desire not to become attached to anyone in particular. I wanted to be burnt out, to be exhausted by surfeit, rather than have a healthy focused love. I didn't want intensity, I wanted diffusion. You know full well of the times I tried to wrench myself away. You did too, for your own reasons. And I went back to Waiongona that time to try and do just that. You probably thought nothing of this, but I hadn't actually seen my mother and father for years. They were back together – had been for some time. I couldn't see my father the way I had as a child. I suppose we are as completely estranged now as I am from my mother. But during that time away from you I found myself overcome with a sense of your physical presence – and the rest you know. That summer in Auckland when you were oppressed by the future – was I to go to training college, and how could you manage to write your thesis – and I went and stayed for a while with the Southalls, I felt nothing. I know that I am strong, and that this strength is diabolical. You are not as strong, but you are more human, more fallible, more susceptible. All this is hard to say. It is the first time in my life I have really thought about my life or myself. Anyway, with my characteristic strength of will, I have made a decision – intellectually – to have only you, though everything else – my admiration for your brains, your physical beauty, your strangeness, my great and abiding love for you, backs up my resolve. All this has, however, thrust me into a region of weakness and doubt. Of course, I resented you, and resented myself even more. My dependence on you, you may not realise, was far greater than yours on me. When you and Stella flitted off at that party I was terribly hurt, though of course I had only to remove myself from the scene to become a tabula rasa again. It was an excuse, nicely provided for me; this, coupled with the knowledge that I should never lack for men, the soft quilt of sex. But because I was so alive to other people's pain, because I believed that I should see those closest to me through their travail, I went back to you, even though I knew I would lose the regard of people who meant a lot to me. When everything was OK with us again (and how good it was, and always has been, between us) I could let myself become as one with you. Sometimes during our years together, I have been sexually attracted to other men – but again the decision not to compromise myself, because I conveniently separated sex from love. But there were times – like at Murphy's party when you kissed that Polish girl – and I felt you were making the very compromises I'd decided against. I felt rejected and angry. I couldn't wait for you to leave the country, and that first week I thought little of our separation, try as I did, because there seemed nothing at the end of it. When your plane took off I felt immeasurably free. Free of all *the restrictions – though not, of course, of you. I had no desire to salvage anything. That is not me at all. Then your letters started coming and I felt your misery as I would feel anyone's (the Biblical 'bear ye another's burdens' is a life-principle with me). I knew your misery and thought about that more than I thought about my love for you.*

Where is all this leading?

Let me tell you. These past few weeks, I have been terribly happy. I have snatched at every freedom that has come my way. I've said what I liked to whom I liked. I feel that I have become so fully integrated that I am a goddess – the thing Conrad talks about, 'the feeling that I could last forever, outlast the sea, the earth, and all men'. The feeling that I could control my destiny – vain, perhaps, but very real. The feeling that I am what I am – myself in my own right. That everything touches me because nothing touches me. The complete negation of the ego, the complete submergence in everything that is not me, the loss of pride and selfness – the feeling that I have outstripped myself to become myself. Is all this true? I am very conscious that all this is written to you, Michael, and not for my own gratification. It does not gratify me at all to write it. It is an effort that is tearing me apart. I don't know even how you will feel about it. It might be your means of repudiating me, for all I know. I have had to dissociate myself from the part of me that is you to write it. That is why I have no intimations at all of how you will react. I write it as honestly and unembellished as I can, hoping you will see in it the core that is me, and accept or reject that core, not the clothing upon it which you think of as me.

Let me tell you something else. When you grew cold toward me I felt dashed to pieces. This may help you understand why I glory in the effect I have on other men. Casual sex has become easy for me and pleasures me deeply. Not with the idiots we know mutually. I am far too conscious of 'us' for that, but with young boys you and I shall never know. It is a freedom and womanliness I glory in.

Both of us love that poem by Edna St. Vincent Millay:

What lips my lips have kissed, and where, and why,
I have forgotten, and what arms have lain
Under my head till morning ...

One day there will only be vague memories of the sweetness and tenderness of it all – 'For unremembered lads that not again / Will turn to me at midnight with a cry.' I feel no sense of betrayal. I just feel very beautiful. There is no line any more between what I can and cannot have. But there is some vindictiveness – though by writing this tortured letter to you I feel I can alleviate some of that too. I will never want to be divided again.

I reacted to Emma's letter like a wounded child. Kicking my way through dead leaves along an autumn lane, eyes blinded by tears, my feelings lagging far behind my thoughts, I was torn between returning to Wellington and using my scholarship to follow Leon's example and forge a new life on a Mediterranean shore. It took me days before I could compose my thoughts and write back.

Dearest Emma,

When I first read your letter, I was so stunned that I hardly registered a thing. Now, two days later, though still devastated, I am beginning to experience a strange sense of release. It's like the feeling that overwhelmed me at Albertville when I walked those ghastly streets filled with the bloated and stinking bodies of the dead. That other purgatory. Today, as then, something has died in me, or been killed off. I see you afresh, almost as a stranger, and the clarity with which you appear before me is more than I can bear.

When we said goodbye in Auckland, our future was so uncertain that I suppose it was inevitable that we would not be faithful to each other. My sole affair – with a morose girl I met at a party in London – was embarrassing, not pleasurable, and left me depressed because I felt that sooner or later you would reciprocate the infidelity. In fact, you anticipated it, and found fulfilment where I found only a waste of shame. I suppose this is partly why I have been so deeply hurt – my male pride requiring that I am the one who calls the shots. Such poetic justice now. I see the sway of Eros in your life, of Thanatos in mine – in you the urge to return to some primal unity, sensually merged with others without moral or intellectual discrimination; in me the death instinct – a craving for order, division, and possession. My puritanical self! Yet Eros rules me, too, making me crave union with you, the blissful blurring of sex, the marriage of true minds. Although I have wanted you to be truly independent, I allowed myself to become dependent on you, usurping your right to determine your own life. In my confusion now, I wonder who I am. You wrote about your childhood and tried to fathom things from that perspective. Perhaps I can do the same.

When I was two or three, my mother sometimes left me with my grandparents while she and my father travelled far and wide, seeking a cure for her rheumatoid arthritis. I was also hospitalised for a tonsillectomy and did not see my mother for several days. I lay stranded and caged in a green cot, forced to wear nappies, surrounded by a mural of rabbits and toadstools and listening to the sticky sound of shoe soles on linoleum. I was startled by strange routines – a stainless steel meal trolley and the smell of boiled cabbage, a wooden spatula depressing my tongue while I gargled drily aaarh, nurses with watches attached to the fronts of their starched white uniforms. I lost my grounding. I lapsed into a melancholia from which I have never really recovered. When I went home from the hospital (my parents told me years later), I would go to the front gate every day at the same time and cry inconsolably. When I started school, I huddled under the trees at playtime, too fearful to join the other kids. Like a hermit crab, I shrank from the world. I confided my heartache to no one, and accepted loneliness as my lot. I found happiness in constructing machines and vehicles with Meccano, or playing with Hornby trains. I associated both with England, the country my grandparents still called home. A sense of exile pervaded my consciousness. I mourned some lost security, a perished kingdom where life had been entire and untroubled. I pined for the absent part of me (the mother, the rock?), but it wasn't until I read Thomas Wolfe's Look Homeward, Angel that I saw that others, too, had known that forlorn yearning for a vanished Eden – a stone, a leaf, an unfound door ...

At sixteen I became fascinated with prehistory and missing links. I studied anthropology in the vain hope that some other society might give me a glimpse of what I had not found in my own. This attraction to exotic places was presaged by my boyhood reading of Conan Doyle's The Lost World and Rider Haggard's King Solomon's Mines. I fantasised some magical regeneration on a tropical plateau or beyond the Mountains of the Moon. My world was filled with surrogates and substitutions. I found companionship with trees, and union with rivers. When Taranaki was cloud covered, I really did believe the mountain was grieving. I was a poet before I wrote a line of poetry – at home with landscapes as others feel at home with family or friends. This was my day-world. My night-world was the movies. I went whenever I could and imagined I would one day share the heroic and quicksilver life of Tyrone Power or Alan Ladd, meet Jean Simmons or Elizabeth Taylor, and live happily ever after. With you, dear Emma, I found my rock, my river, my mother, my Hollywood ending, my lost world, myself. But having found you I found myself at a loss to know what was necessary if our life together was to flourish. I took you for granted.

Perhaps we are all doomed to reenact the scripts we are handed in our early lives – your parents' estrangement from each other and your gradual estrangement from them, my foolish fantasising. How can we change, be reborn, escape our karma – all these habits inscribed in us, these compulsions to repeat? And if we do gain some insight into ourselves, how in God's name can we put this into effect? What control can we really have over our destinies? You quote Youth, dear Emma, but there is a semicolon where you put a full stop, and that passage about outlasting all things continues by saying how deceitful that feeling is, and how it lures us on 'to joys, to perils, to love, to vain effort – to death'.

I have just got back from a long walk to Coton. It is already dusk, with cold, stippled cloud over the water-meadows, dead leaves underfoot. I have wept, wounded, unable to overcome the feelings that surge through me. It is the child in me, I know, crying out for

false comfort. But while one part of me is inconsolable, another
celebrates your freedom. I am honoured by your confidences, your
openness. I do not feel betrayed. But my heart is broken, and it
will take time for our new understanding to emerge, of who we
both are and how we can be together.

SIERRA LEONE

Arriving in the far north of Sierra Leone after a long day negotiating degraded laterite roads without a map was like coming to the threshold of a new life. Although darkness was falling as we drove into Kabala, we found our way to the district commissioner's bungalow on a hill overlooking the town where, at the DC's invitation, we parked our Land Rover, unrolled our mattress in the back of the vehicle, and slept.

I woke at dawn in a place I had first dreamed of in the Congo five years before. Everything enchanted me – the scattered acacia trees on the slopes of the hill, with their wizened seedpods littering the ground, the dusty streets along which we picked our way. Women with basins of cassava leaf or bundles of firewood on their heads, kids trundling hoops or skeletal trucks along the road ahead of us, the persistent patter of distant drums. The thronged market where we bought bananas, oranges, bread and Pickwick teabags before following a path worn by bare feet across a dry paddy field, where three cows, with white egrets at their feet, grazed the stubble. Even the name of the town boded well, though I would later learn that it had nothing to do with occult doctrine; it simply meant 'Kabba's place'.

If arriving in Athens had been the first day of Leon's life, coming to Kabala was mine. So many events, planned and unplanned, had conspired to bring me here. Years in the wilderness had culminated in this moment of sublime clarity, equal only to the day I met Emma. What could possibly break this spell?

My fieldwork began with a fortuitous meeting with a young schoolteacher, Noah Marah, who took me to his natal village that Christmas and subsequently agreed to become my research assistant.

Over the next twelve months I made the long trek from Kabala to Firawa many times, becoming familiar with the great inselberg of Senekonke (Gold Mountain), its granite flanks gouged by centuries of rain, and the uncanny way it seemed to recede as I approached it, as if to remind me of the hubris of thinking that I was doing more than scratch the surface of the lifeworld into which I had been magically transported.

Although my fieldwork was adventitious, it yielded hundreds of stories, recorded and transcribed with Noah's help, as well as reams of notes on clan histories, family life, death and initiatory rebirth, divination, djinn and shape-shifting, from which I drew inspiration on our return to Cambridge. Named for the Barawa chiefdom in which Firawa was the main town, and fusing ethnographic reportage with prose narrative, my book would take several years to complete and would not find a publisher for another decade. Though I would become painfully aware of its faults, it gave me a sense that I was finding my own voice and bringing literature and social science together in ways that made the former more real and the latter more readable.

Despite wanting to pour all my energies into *Barawa*, I first had to complete a doctoral thesis that demonstrated my ability to do fieldwork and engage with current anthropological debates. My time was, however, no longer my own. Emma had deferred her own doctoral work on the Icelandic sagas in order to accompany me to Sierra Leone, and our daughter, born in Freetown during our year in the field, demanded our time and attention. We therefore divided our day into three portions: one for Emma, one for me, and one for doing things as a family.

I remember sitting down to my first day of writing, surrounded by uncollated field notes and leather-bound tomes from the university library, only to reach an impasse. How could my Herculean task possibly be done by working three hours a day, five days a week? My initial efforts to draft a thesis outline brought me to the brink of despair. Writing *Barawa* had been a joy; this was a chore. Had my year in Sierra Leone led to a disenchantment with anthropology, or was it that I needed to keep faith with my experiences in the field rather than pay lip service to the theoretical fashions of the discipline?

Emma fared little better with her three hours, but rather than throw up her hands and declare the task impossible, she quoted her favourite mantra from cybernetics, a mantra I would come to adopt as my own: *No advantage without limitation.* Instead of imagining how I might gain more time, I should accept the limits imposed upon me *and work within them.* Within a couple of days, I had learned to ignore the impulse to take a break or think ahead to the finished product and to concentrate solely on the matter at hand, even if all I had to show for a day's work was a single well-made sentence. Time was annulled. I did my daily stint and left it at that. In fact, I had created the routine I would stick to for the rest of my writing life, long after my children had left home, my academic commitments were less onerous and I had all the time in the world to write.

That New Year's Eve, Emma and I went to a party in London hosted by our daughter's godmother, Fleur Adcock. Most of those crammed into the four rooms of Fleur's terrace house were expatriate New Zealanders. That so many were unknown to me caused me to recall Kurt Vonnegut's *Cat's Cradle*, in which his fictional prophet, Bokonon, refers to a group of people that presumes a connection that does not really exist as a *granfalloon* or 'false karass'. Feeling like a foreigner among my fellow Kiwis, I was also concerned that our eight-month-old daughter might be having difficulty sleeping through the uproar or, worse, might suffocate under the pile of coats carelessly thrown on the bed where she was lying. I suggested to Emma that we try to catch a late train back to Cambridge and forget about seeing in the new year. She was about to agree when I spotted an apparition on the far side of the smoke-filled room. Surely it wasn't. It couldn't be. He was in Split. Or the Balkans somewhere. But it was, and in a trice I was introducing Emma to Leon, and he was introducing the raven-haired woman standing tongue-tied at his side as Antigone, his wife – though he used four crooked fingers to place the word *wife* in scare quotes, a gesture Emma would later declare to have been all too revealing of the place the poor woman actually occupied in Leon's life.

With the Rolling Stones singing 'You Can't Always Get What You Want' and the party noise making it almost impossible to talk, I urged Leon to give me his address, thinking we might meet the following day before Emma and I headed back to Cambridge.

'We don't have an address,' Leon shouted.

'No address?'

'We only arrived a couple of days ago. We're still looking for a place.'

Emma excused herself and went off to check on Aisha.

'Are you working?' I shouted.

'No!'

When I suggested to Leon that he and Antigone could stay with us in Girton until they found somewhere to live, I instantly regretted it. We had a large enough house, to be sure, but with our domestic routines so newly established, the presence of Leon and Antigone might prove disruptive. Besides, what was I thinking of, issuing this invitation without asking Emma what she felt?

'I will have to check with Emma,' I shouted.

Leon nodded. Antigone showed no signs of having understood anything.

When I did put the proposition to Emma, I argued that the arrangement would be temporary. It was only until they found a place of their own. 'It doesn't have to be an imposition,' I said. 'And Antigone might be able to babysit Aisha.'

'So, it's a fait accompli?'

'Not unless you agree.'

'He's your friend. You've been singing his praises for years. I'm not going to say no. But let's not make the arrangement a permanent one.'

But it did become permanent. Or, as Emma put it, it redefined the meaning of temporary.

Within weeks of our refugees installing themselves in our house,

I fell into the habit of keeping Leon company every evening, playing bar billiards and drinking beer in the Old Crown. As a result, I woke every morning with a hangover. Blearily, I would lift Aisha from her crib and make my way downstairs to the kitchen, where I changed her nappy, heated a jar of puréed vegetables and fed her. Still half asleep, I took her back to bed and settled her down with a warm bottle of milk before collapsing into bed beside Emma, hoping for another hour of shut-eye. Not only was this routine exhausting; it was damaging my relationship with Emma. Antigone tried to help around the house, but her English was minimal, and Emma and I were wary of entrusting our baby daughter to someone with whom we could not communicate. As for Leon, he lay abed until lunch time, then ensconced himself in an armchair where he whiled away the day chain-smoking, sipping whiskey, and reading Greek tragedies. That our scholarships were about to run out only added to our woes. And though we did not expect our impecunious guests to buy groceries or even cook the Greek meals they had promised us when they first moved in, we began to resent their presence in the house.

Strolling home from the pub one evening, I told Leon that I would have to forgo our nightly drinking sessions. Getting up at six in the morning with a hangover was making it impossible to write. It was also affecting my marriage.

'Surely Antigone finds it difficult, too?' I said.

'She's Greek. She puts up with me.'

'What about your painting?'

'What painting?'

'That memoir you sent me, then.'

'It came to nothing. Like the resistance. The Colonels came to power. They're still in power. My friends went underground or scattered to the four winds, and when I saw no future for myself without them, I also abandoned ship.'

I suddenly realised that Leon was not simply homeless. Fortune had deserted him, just as, long ago, his parents had given him away.

Not knowing how to respond, I fell back on empty gestures, acting as if moral encouragement could lift his spirits.

'Have you ever considered going back to Oxford?'

Leon laughed. 'You must be joking.'

'But why not?'

'Because I had my chance and blew it. That's why.'

'But it's never too late,' I said, still on my naïve tack to some utopian shore.

'I'm forty-three. No longer promising and past my prime. I missed my moment, and that's all there is to it.'

'I refuse to believe that. Say you live for another thirty, forty, years? Why make *this* the end when the end is so far off? Why not do something *now*, so that in forty years' time you can look back and say "I almost missed my second chance but didn't. I seized it when I had it"?'

Leon laughed in my face and told me that casuistry was not my strong suit.

'I am what I am,' he said. 'I accept this, why can't you?'

'What about Antigone?'

'Oh, she accepts me. Warts and all. But unlike you, she doesn't moralise.'

'So that's what you think I'm doing?'

'I'm not you, Mike, and you're not me. We're opposites. That's the key to our friendship. If everything begets its own negation, isn't it possible that we have created each other? I can paint, when I have a mind to. You've got the gift of the gab. You apply yourself to hard work and sobriety, being a good father to Aisha and a loving husband to Emma. That's why you exaggerate my sloth, my scepticism, my indifference to Antigone, my drinking. But aren't these traits born of your own, just as mine are born of yours? Isn't that what binds us? Isn't that the core of our friendship? The mystery of *enantiodromia*, the play of opposites that Heraclitus saw as the reality of all things?'

The Interview

Within days of Leon and Antigone's abrupt departure for New Zealand, where Leon confidently presumed they could live on the dole, I redoubled my efforts to complete my dissertation and find work. To husband our dwindling resources, we also gave up the house at Girton and moved to a Cambridge flat adjoining Trinity College, where Emma was tutoring in Old Icelandic. Just as the billboard eyes of Dr T.J. Eckleburg gazed over the Valley of Ashes in *The Great Gatsby*, so a pair of bespectacled eyes on a painted shingle hung over the doorway of an optician's shop below our flat, surveying Magdalene Bridge and the Cam. Perhaps they were also watching over us, for finding a job proved relatively straightforward.

In the summer of 1971 I was interviewed for a lectureship in social anthropology at Edinburgh University. I was among the last applicants to be ushered into a dark wood-panelled room where the faculty were seated at a long table, with copies of my dossier in front of them. Given their world-weary demeanour and careless introductions, I concluded that a decision had already been made and that nothing I might say in response to their offhand questions would change their minds. When I left the interview, I gave the departmental secretary the address of the bed and breakfast where Emma, Aisha and I would be staying for the next few days and breathed a sigh of relief that the charade was over.

But it was not. Three days later, after enjoying unseasonably warm weather on the Fifeshire coast, we returned to Cambridge to find several telegrams lying on the floor inside our front door. The first informed me that I had got the job. The second and third appealed to me, with increasing urgency, to let the department know whether or not I accepted its offer. The fourth informed me that the salary was negotiable, if this was the issue that was delaying my response. After a quick conversation with Emma, I called Professor Littlejohn from the public phone box near Magdalene Bridge and thanked him for the offer – which had completely taken me aback – before politely declining it. When asked if the salary was the sticking point, I said no, that was not it. Then what? To my own surprise I said that I had been unimpressed by the interview. Neither the questions asked, nor the attitude of the appointment committee, had inspired me.

To this day, memories of my churlishness oppress me, and though neither Emma nor I had warmed to the idea of living in Scotland, I still cannot understand the alacrity with which I turned down this job – unless it was because of my deep ambivalence toward academic life and my fear of an ivory-tower existence that would cut me off from the real world. That I at once determined to find funds for a return trip to Sierra Leone suggests that I was also desperate not to lose the connection with Africa that I had sought when I was in the Congo and finally found in northern Sierra Leone.

One afternoon I ran into Meyer Fortes on King's Parade. Meyer headed the Department of Anthropology at Cambridge, and though Jack Goody had been my supervisor and Edmund Leach my role model, I had no more than a passing acquaintance with Meyer. He was, however, eager to know of my plans and prospects. I told him that I was teaching anthropology for the Board of Extramural Studies, tutoring a few students at St John's and applying for research grants. He immediately invited me to come and see him. He managed a small fund and might be able to help.

Thanks to Meyer, I made my second field trip to Sierra Leone, and though the months away from Emma and Aisha were emotionally difficult, the data I gathered helped me develop the event-centred, experience-near anthropology to which I was now intellectually committed.

A few weeks after my return to Cambridge I received a letter from Hugh Kawharu, who had supervised my master's research at the University of Auckland. He had just been appointed head of the new Social Anthropology and Māori Studies Department at Massey University and wanted to know if I would consider taking up a senior lectureship in the department and helping him develop an undergraduate programme in social anthropology. It took Emma and me less than a day to realise that New Zealand was where we wanted to be. The Manawatu would be a healthy environment for Aisha, and we would be home, close to family and old friends.

Manawatu

I cannot remember how, or from whom, I heard of Leon's whereabouts. But in the waning summer of 1973, Emma, Aisha and I climbed into our vintage Citroën and drove north into the Rangitikei country in search of the farmstead where Leon and Antigone had come to roost. I had been told that the farmstead was more like a hay barn than a house, and when we found the mailbox on which 'DONNELLY' was scrawled in ungainly black letters and took the gravel track into the valley, we were astonished to come upon a white weatherboard bungalow with a broad veranda, shaded on one side by two enormous macrocarpa trees.

The air was still. Magpies gurgled coldly in the paddocks. And Emma expressed surprise at the north-facing English garden, choked with withered roses, delphiniums and foxgloves.

No sooner had I stopped the car than Leon and Antigone appeared on the veranda, shading their eyes with their hands and clearly mystified about who could possibly be visiting them. Leon was wearing gumboots and a Swanndri and had a bottle of beer in his hand. Antigone warily drew back into the doorway.

While Emma helped Aisha out of her car seat, I climbed the wooden steps to the veranda where Leon and I embraced in bemused silence.

It was Emma who broke the ice. 'We should have told you we were coming,' she said, 'but we didn't have a phone number.'

'That's because we haven't got a phone,' Leon said.

At the sight of Aisha, Antigone moved out of the shadows. She spoke English with a strong Kiwi accent. 'Remember me?' she cooed, placing her hand on the side of Aisha's head, and simultaneously kissing Emma on both cheeks.

Neither Leon nor I knew what questions to ask, what explanation to offer.

We followed our wives into the house.

'You're the last person I thought I'd see in these parts,' Leon said.

'I could say the same about you.'

'You still on the wagon?' Leon asked.

Was this an allusion to Girton, when I gave up drinking with him at the Old Crown?

'I wouldn't say no to a beer,' I said.

Leon went to the fridge in the kitchen while I loitered in the middle of a large, carpeted but barely furnished living room.

There was a shadow over Leon, a darkness I could not penetrate. He had not smiled once. He handed me the uncapped bottle of beer, and cheerlessly knocked his bottle against mine. 'Here's to fortuity, then,' he said. 'And by the way, I don't own this house. A local farmer does. I dig drains and help out with the shearing and crutching. It pays the rent.'

I noticed that Leon's hair, as ill-kempt as ever, was greying above his temples. His face was weather-beaten, crow's feet etched at the corner of his eyes and trouble written all over his furrowed brow.

'No children?' I said, casting my eyes back to the front door where Antigone and Emma were deep in conversation.

'You obviously don't know the etymology of Antigone,' Leon said.

'Which is?'

'Against birth.'

Everything I witnessed that day was all of a piece. When Leon put a record on the turntable, it was Leonard Cohen singing 'Bird on the Wire'. When he asked if I was still writing poetry, he immediately answered his own question by quoting something of Dylan Thomas's about the lovely gift of the gab banging back against a blind shaft. And when I asked what had happened to his friend Takis, whose surname I had forgotten, Leon's response forbade further inquiries.

'He's back in Greece.'

Leon led me out onto the veranda, down four wooden steps, and away from the house. 'Yep, back in Greece,' he said as we crossed a paddock toward a distant fence.

It seemed that Takis had returned home to discover that his close friend Stratis had died in a quarry accident on Yaros and that his younger brother, Dimitriou, had been shot at point-blank range by members of the personal guard of the minister of public safety while transporting wounded demonstrators during the polytechnic uprising.

'Takis is living on Aegina,' Leon said. 'If he leaves his house, he goes to a kafeneion on the seafront to drink coffee, talk politics or play dominoes. But much of the time he sits alone in a shuttered room with his father's German Luger on the table beside him, trying to summon the courage to shoot himself and finally join those he abandoned to their fates all those years ago.'

It was too morbid for me – Leon's gloom, the change I saw in him, the gap between us. He had not even asked what had brought me back to New Zealand.

When we came to the fence, Leon wrenched the barbed wire strands apart, bent over, and eased his body through the gap. I tried to do the same, but my parka snagged on the wire, and Leon had to free me. He led me into a paddock where he had planted a thousand native trees.

'This whole area was once covered in tōtara forest,' he said. 'You wouldn't have been able to hear your own voice for the sound of birds. Our so-called pioneers felled and burned as much as they could. They say smoke from the fires blotted out the sun and left people temporarily blind. All to make their pretty English farms and destroy the menace of something they could not live with.'

I now saw the landscape through Leon's eyes – its dark history, its dubious sanctuary, a place that he might yet make his own. Circling back to the house, we stopped by a fenced-in vegetable garden where Leon plucked snails off the lettuces and uprooted random weeds.

After tugging open the door to a nearby henhouse, he gathered four eggs from a straw-covered shelf and transferred them to my hands. I was dismayed to see that the door was decorated with a weather-worn painting of an olive tree. Not daring to ask if he was painting again, I followed him back toward the house, clutching the eggs awkwardly in my cupped hands. Leon pointed out the three olive trees he had planted and spoke of his self-sufficiency, but I felt that we had become strangers. So deeply did I sense his desire to be left alone that when Antigone said we must stay for dinner, I drew Emma aside and whispered that we should go.

'But she expects us to stay the night. She's already prepared a room for us and found a cot for Aisha.'

'Not tonight,' I said. 'Some other time perhaps. Find an excuse. I want to leave.'

Our sudden departure dismayed Antigone but did not seem to faze Leon, who confessed he wasn't very good company these days. But he would be driving down to Palmerston North in a few weeks' time to deliver firewood. If we needed any, he was the go-to guy.

'Firewood?'

'That's my line. Or one of them.'

I forced myself to say that it would good to see him and climbed into the car, where Emma had already strapped Aisha into her booster seat.

'Antigone suggested we go home via Apiti,' Emma said, as the Citroën laboured up the steep gravel track. 'She says it's quicker.'

The sun was low in the sky, illuminating the great papa bluffs of the Oroua River. The clay seemed to be sweating from its effort to hold itself together. Huge slabs had already broken off and collapsed into the river below.

Loose gravel ricocheted against the chassis of the car. Dust churned in our wake. I was going over the afternoon in my mind. Leon's taciturnity; the tension between him and Antigone; the appalling pass he had come to, working as a farm labourer in that isolated valley of shadow where the only sounds were a dog barking, magpies gargling and lost lambs bleating for their mothers.

'You're very quiet,' Emma said.

'I was thinking of Leon,' I said.

'I hope you're not feeling sorry for him. It's not as if he hasn't chosen to live in the back of beyond. Though how Antigone can endure it doesn't bear thinking about.'

'I don't pity him. But I used to envy him. Now that I don't, I feel as if I have lost something essential to my own wellbeing.'

'You've always said that he's the shadow side of yourself.'

'Did I say that?'

'Darling, you say it almost every time you mention him!'

BLUE COLD ROUGH WATER

Our flaws are invisible to us. They resemble fault lines in stone. A stone is hit hard by another stone and breaks cleanly along this hitherto hidden fissure. Shakespeare observed that 'the fault … is not in our stars / But in ourselves'. But it is not always in ourselves. It is in the nature of things, and unfathomable, like the shadow that suddenly sweeps across a distant sunlit hill, or dark clouds that appear like stacked anvils in a summer sky.

Such thoughts would not have occurred to me before Emma's illness. Afterward, I could not see life otherwise.

We had a bought a house. It stood on an ancient river terrace with a view of the Ruahine Range. Aisha was happily installed in kindergarten. Emma was teaching English in a local high school. And I was writing.

That autumn we often went mushrooming in the hills above the Pohangina Valley, returning home with brimming buckets of champignons, their delicate pink gills going dark brown as they aged, their white caps veined with grass, our hands stained with their black spores. In Emma, a more sinister burgeoning had begun. She was easily fatigued and often feverish. When she discovered that her lymph nodes were swollen, she consulted our doctor. A biopsy was followed by a shocking diagnosis: Hodgkin's disease. Cancer.

Treatment began immediately. The radiotherapy scarred her lower face and neck. As if adding insult to injury, her doctors refused to discuss her condition with her. As one oncologist put it, 'You may have attended medical school for a year, Mrs Jackson, but that doesn't mean you can advise us on how to do our job.' When scheduled to undergo a splenectomy, Emma wanted to know why. 'It's for your own good,' the doctor said. We subsequently discovered that the sole reason for this surgery was to prevent metastasis of the disease below the diaphragm, thereby arresting it at 'stage 2'. This had no therapeutic value but simply created a more palatable medical statistic. Emma decided to discontinue treatment.

It was around this time that Antigone left Leon and returned to Greece. The Regime of the Colonels was over, democracy had returned and she saw no point in prolonging her exile.

Leon called to see me on his way back from dropping Antigone off at Wellington airport. We met in the pub, rather than at home. Emma did not want visitors.

I found it difficult to respond to Leon's news or imagine the impact of Antigone's departure on his already reclusive life. Perhaps I resisted the thought, struggling subliminally with the awful possibility that Emma might die.

That she survived cancer may have been the result of the timely intervention of a maverick Czech cancer therapist called Milan Brych, who administered a yearlong course of chemotherapy that brought the disease into remission. Brych was removed from the register of New Zealand medical practitioners just as Emma was completing her treatment. After relocating to the Cook Islands, he was subsequently convicted, in California, of practising medicine without a licence and sent to prison. I don't think Emma or I ever gave much thought to whether Milan Brych was a doctor or a charlatan. He treated Emma with compassion and gentleness at a time when she was losing her hold on life and being upbraided by her GP for taking her health into her own hands. As far as I was concerned, it did not matter what toxins were being dripped into her veins, or whether Brych's confidence in her recovery was feigned or genuine. He had accompanied her on the most gruelling journey of her life and helped her come through.

Although in remission, Emma no longer took anything for granted. And this contrast between what it is like to live in the certainty that one has all the time in the world, and what it is like to live as if every day might be one's last, found expression in a children's novel she began to write, called *Back of Beyond*. Ostensibly it is the story of two children, brought together one summer on a high-country station, who become involved in unravelling the mystery of an attempted murder. The two very different protagonists – a rough, high-spirited New Zealand girl and a gauche and timid English boy – echo the change in Emma's personality before and after her ordeal. In the solution of the crime lies the resolution of an existential mystery – how we may live with a sense of our vulnerability while drawing on our strengths, neither succumbing to our fear that the world is too much for us nor retrospectively seeing ourselves as heroic and virtuous, simply because we survive.

As Emma worked on her novel, I worked on my Kuranko tales, giving shape to my own book *Allegories of the Wilderness*. Whatever the season, we took a morning coffee break together, sitting under a gnarled plum tree on our back lawn. These were halcyon days, with both of us deeply immersed in our individual projects yet unshakably together.

That we now lived so cautiously – vegetarian diet, practising yoga, eschewing cigarettes and alcohol – made it difficult for our hedonistic friends to accommodate what they viewed as joyless asceticism. Leon was particularly mystified, if not outraged. He had lost Antigone, and now he had lost his drinking partner.

I had no answer to his anger. How could I explain what it was like to be stone-cold sober yet obliged to suffer the tautologous raillery of someone living life to the lees? How could I expect Leon, or anyone else in my small circle of acquaintances, to share my passion for Sierra Leone, or anthropological ideas? And how could I claim to be lonely, when his aloneness was so much greater than mine?

Yet we did stumble onto common ground.

It began with Emma's intolerance of Leon's boorishness, was given momentum by his childlike belief that cancer was contagious (which meant he avoided our house like the plague), and reached a happy climax when Emma's purchase of a hack coincided with Leon's request that I help him cut mānuka on a block to which a local farmer had given him free access. 'Take all the fuckin' firewood you want, mate, so long as you don't cherry-pick. I want that land for pasture.'

Most weekends, while Emma and Aisha went riding near Stoney Creek, I drove to Leon's now-squalid bungalow. From there we took his battered Land Rover and utility trailer into the foothills of the range.

At first I found it hard going, or 'hard yacker', as Leon put it. One day, as we were slipping and staggering up a rain-sodden slope, lugging our heavy chainsaws, Leon confided that he felt an atavistic loyalty to the working class, but as individuals they appalled him.

I limbed the logs; Leon cut them into lengths, and together we toted them to the trailer. Even now I can recall the staccato idling of Leon's chainsaw, the way it worked itself up into a frenzied snarl before biting into a hapless log, then backed off with an exasperated series of unsyncopated coughs. I remember struggling with a loose chain; the smell of oil, sawdust and trampled earth; and the deep satisfaction of being physically toughened by toil. Within weeks I was fitter than Leon, whose laboured breathing and constant cursing were ominous signs of things to come. He was always finding excuses to take a smoko and crack open a cold one. And as I too picked up the local argot, I felt increasingly confident in my ability to pull off the unlikely feat of being seen as a good bloke, and not a fucking wowser, by Leon's beer-bellied neighbours. Leon saw it happening to me as it had happened to him – the ineluctable sloughing off of our educated selves, clearing our language of its Latinate implantations and cultivating a cluster of four-letter words and choice images that could convey every thought and feeling worth sharing.

But there was a difference. I was acting my part. Leon was fighting for his life.

I did not see it then as I see it now, but what was on the line for him was as critical as that life-or-death moment when Emma consulted Milan Brych in Auckland. The difference was that Leon had learned to disguise his woes in the same way that he had learned to censor his speech. And because he was usually pissed by the time I took my leave of him every Saturday and headed home in the gathering dusk, it took me a while to see that beer and whiskey were his chosen blunt instruments, the means of dulling his inner pain, silencing his inner voices, shutting down his memories of Antigone, of Takis, of Greece and of Oxford. By the time I understood the depth of his unhappiness, I felt powerless to do anything about it. Perhaps I had become emotionally exhausted by Emma's needs. In any event, I blamed the victim, appalled that he should squander the experience of abject misery, wallowing in it rather than painting his way back into the light.

WALLS

I lived an oddly compartmentalised life. Mornings, I repaired to the washhouse that I had converted into a study and travelled in my imagination to Sierra Leone, writing the ethnographic essays that would, I hoped, one day secure me a job in a more intellectually congenial environment. After lunch with Emma, I would cycle or drive (depending on the weather) to the university, deliver my lectures and see my students before picking Aisha up outside her school.

To conserve her energy, Emma had given up full-time teaching and begun working in the school library for a few hours every afternoon. She was also studying Zen, seeking immunity to illness in a transformed attitude to life. One day Aisha was interviewed, along with other kids, by a local radio reporter. When asked what her father did, she said, 'He reads books and works at the Unibersity.'

'And your mother?'

'She lies in bed all day and reads comics.'

Nothing could have been further from the truth, but seen through Aisha's eyes, our house resembled Sleeping Beauty's castle, spellbound and suspended between life and death. Perhaps this is why Emma took such pleasure in riding, merging her body with the lithe and muscular body of her beloved Rosie, galloping beyond boundaries she could not have crossed alone. As she rode, I laboured beside Leon, who had given up selling firewood ('fuck that for a joke') and gone into the business of building stone walls. In the wintry dawns we would load his ute with ice-cold greywacke stones from a local riverbed then drive to the house, usually in Marton or Feilding, where Leon had, during the week, erected wooden shoring or trench boxing. While I started the generator and got the concrete mixer going, he ensured that all the struts and spacers were in place before we began dropping stones into the shored-up space. It sometimes occurred to me that this was his sublimated art. He had an uncanny ability to find stones that seemed to belong together, as if rebuilding some Cyclopean structure that had been dismembered and scattered, or resurrecting one of the archaic temples we had seen on our visit to Delphi. We worked together, shovelling concrete on top of each layer of stones and ensuring that it filled all the gaps. But as the winter wore on, I came to believe that we were only shoring ourselves up against some further ruin.

DRYING OUT

Twelve years after Leon's mother's death, his sister Molly, now living alone on the Coromandel Peninsula, finally found the time (or plucked up the courage) to sort through their mother's belongings. In a leather Gladstone bag with rusty fittings she came across a bundle of letters from their father, all postmarked Katherine, NT, where, it appeared, he had lived from 1937 onward. Reading these letters made it increasingly clear that Leon and Molly's father, with whom they had had no contact growing up and whose very existence remained a mystery to them, had regularly sent postal orders to support his estranged wife and children.

On one of Leon's infrequent forays into Palmerston North we met in the public bar of the Café de Paris to shoot pool. But the triangle of coloured balls remained unbroken as Leon told me what these letters had revealed and what their mother had hidden from her children. He compared this experience to the moment in *Great Expectations* when Pip learns that his benefactor is not Miss Havisham but the convict Abel Magwitch. Leon had always made allowances for his mother who, deserted by her husband, had supposedly been forced to place her children in a Salvation Army home, from which she later heroically recovered them and raised them alone. Now it seemed his father had been the hero and his mother the betrayer.

'Where is he now?' I asked.

'I'm going to Australia,' Leon said, 'to bloody well find out.'

He was away for several weeks. He discovered that his father had passed away in 1974 and been buried in the Knotts Crossing Cemetery in Katherine. A square cast-iron plaque bolted into a stone read 'Frank "Cobber" Donnelly, died 1974 aged 75 years'.

Leon searched for someone who had known his father. 'He liked to hang out with Abos,' a barman told him. 'Sold 'em sly grog.' The Katherine police corroborated this story but refused to allow Leon access to their records. He returned to the bar and asked why Frank Donnelly had been called Cobber. 'Prob'ly a good bloke,' the barman said, 'despite his weird ideas. You get a lot of 'em up 'ere. Runnin' from somethingorother. Or searchin'.'

When Leon recounted his fruitless researches in the Australian Outback, I asked what on earth his father had been running from.

'From us, I suppose. Looking for his socialist utopia. I rented a car and drove south to Wave Hill where he'd worked as a jackaroo. The Aboriginal stockmen went on strike there in 1966. Two hundred men, with their wives and children, picked up their swags and billies and walked ten miles to Wattie Creek and camped there. A few months later they petitioned the governor general of Australia for help in getting back 500 acres of their traditional land so they could run their own cattle station. I wouldn't be surprised if my father was involved in that, organising, agitating, fighting the good fight.'

'What happened to the petition?'

'The Aboriginals' claim was dismissed. Rather than pay Aboriginal workers the same money as whites earned, station owners stopped hiring Aboriginal stockmen and advertised in eastern cities for white jackaroos. The Aboriginal stockmen lost their livelihoods, just as they'd lost access to their land.'

The thought crossed my mind that Leon's father might have played no role in organising the strike but instead gone to Wave Hill to pick up one of the jobs that had fallen vacant there. But the thought of the old communist becoming a scab unsettled me, as did the possibility that the money he'd sent back to New Zealand to support his family had been ill-gotten. Though I didn't share this thought with Leon, it may have also occurred to him.

'I still blame him. you know. Sending us money but not being there for us. Refusing to be a part of our lives growing up. You can't ever forgive that.'

'Wasn't it punishment enough that he languished and died in exile?'

'What the fuck would you know about punishment?'

This sour note initiated a period of estrangement. It wasn't that I took offence at Leon's remark. But I think it gave me an excuse not to spend my weekends toiling on wall building or scrub cutting, especially since all the money Leon earned was squandered on hard liquor and weed.

Leon may also have sensed that our friendship had reached a point of no return, for the next time I saw him, when he delivered a cord of firewood to our house one Saturday morning, he confided that he was going on the wagon, or at least prepared to give it a go. 'I'm driving to Hanmer Springs to dry out.'

When Emma heard this news, she laughed. 'Don't you have to acknowledge that you are powerless, and that you must place yourself in the hands of a higher power?'

'That's AA, but I guess that's part of the treatment.'

'I can't see Leon acknowledging any power higher than the proof number of his whiskey.'

Emma's cynicism was justified. In a postcard from Hanmer Leon crowed about his ability to avoid therapy. 'The psychiatrist tells me I'm too clever for my own good. Cheers, Leon.'

'I don't want to psychoanalyse him,' Emma said, 'but the bottom line is that Leon has never been loved, and doesn't know how to love. He doesn't even love himself.'

'Clearly, he loves his liquor.'

'Yes, but does the liquor love him?'

Emma's comments came back to me when, weeks later, Leon turned up at our back door one evening. He had been on a three-day bender in Wellington and looked like shit. Dishevelled, unshaven, bleary-eyed and hardly able to speak for coughing, he recounted how he'd met up with his AA buddy in Wellington and persuaded this vulnerable young man to share a drink with him in the Thistle Hotel. From there it had been downhill all the way.

Both Emma and I listened to this appalling tale in disbelief. Why had he submitted to a treatment plan only to subvert it? And not only that, but also wittingly, almost gleefully, shove his so-called buddy off the wagon?

For Emma it was the last straw. 'With friends like that, who needs enemies?'

'He needs my friendship,' I said, thinking, *just as I once needed his*.

As it happened, Emma did not have to suffer the sight of Leon any longer. He left Rangiwahia a few weeks after returning from Hanmer. We met one last time in the Café de Paris, where he told me he was heading to the winterless north, where the whiskey wasn't so cheap, but weed was readily available. I'd shared joints and eaten weed brownies with Leon, listened to music with him when we were high, and even attempted to drive home from Rangiwahia one night in a state of complete intoxication. The experience itself meant little to me, but it had become, for a while, a substitute for drinking together, and when I desisted it was like a Native American refusing an offered pipe of sweetgrass – an insult, a declaration of war.

RETURN TO SIERRA LEONE

For six years I had been sustained by the prospect of returning to Sierra Leone with Emma and Aisha. My old friend S.B.(Sewa Bokarie Marah) wrote from Freetown, assuring us of a warm welcome. Aisha would be back in the 'land of her birth', and the Kuranko people, who had used my recently published book in campaigns to secure government funding for the building of roads, bridges, schools and dispensaries in the neglected north, were eager to collaborate in my ongoing research.

From the outset, the journey was exhausting. Our first leg took us from Auckland to Singapore, now radically transformed under Lee Kuan Yew from the third-world city I had visited in 1963, with its thronged kampongs, narrow lanes and wooden houses, into a 'garden city' and an international financial capital with laws against littering, loitering and long hair. Although our hotel had been built for budget travellers, we stole a taste of finer things by passing a languid afternoon in the courtyard of Raffles Hotel, sipping Singapore slings under the fan palms while Aisha swam in the pool. Replenished, we anticipated an easy onward flight, but we were delayed at Mumbai and had to spend the night in a dimly lit transit lounge, drinking tea with other stranded passengers, including a Ugandan flight instructor who explained that the military situation on the Uganda–Tanzania border had delayed our flight. By the time we reached Nairobi we were dreaming of another Raffles, which we were fortunate enough to find in the form of a colonial-era bungalow, converted into a guesthouse, on a hill overlooking the city. Though our luggage had gone missing, a young man called Peter Kuguru, who had done his degree in New Zealand, took us in hand, filing our complaint and offering to take us sightseeing.

G.K. Chesterton quipped that an inconvenience is only an adventure misconstrued. We, however, were constantly veering between adventure and inconvenience, and never in one state for long enough to construe it as one thing or another. While our stopover in Nairobi and our visit to a tourist village might be considered an adventure, we found it impossible to consider our night in the Avenida Hotel, Accra, as anything but an ordeal. For me, it was like being back in the Albemarle. A single malfunctioning neon light imparted a ghoulish aura to the grey concrete walls of our room, and we hardly slept, bitten by mosquitoes and uncertain how we could get back to the airport in the morning to catch our flight to Freetown. As it happened we were early for our flight, though not canny enough to realise it had been overbooked. We had to fight our way through the small crowd on the tarmac, board the aircraft and claim our seats. From our place at the rear, we watched an airport worker using a long wooden pole to batter the rear stairs into place. For the duration of our flight I had visions of the stairs dropping open and my family being sucked from the aircraft into thin air.

We returned to earth without mishap, only to be drawn into a social whirl from which we could not escape. After driving us to our bungalow at Fourah Bay College, S.B. insisted on taking us out to dinner at the Bintumani Hotel. We could not plead tiredness or the need to sleep. This was Sierra Leone. Sociability was all that mattered. If our personal thoughts and feelings were inimical to conviviality, they had to be suppressed. So we sat with S.B. and his wife, Rose, at a table under the stars, staving off sleep as the balmy night and hilife music conspired with our jet lag to render our efforts at conversation dull and dissociated. Aisha was exempt from these strictures. She crawled onto the grass under our table and fell into a deep slumber. Within days, however, we had recovered our equilibrium and begun to renew old friendships.

If I single out Lansana Suma at this point in my narrative, it is because, in retrospect, he had a lot in common with Leon Donnelly. Moreover, my friendship with Lansana, like my friendship with Leon, began and ended in a barroom.

I first met Lansana in 1970 at the City Hotel in Freetown, made famous by Graham Greene, who frequented the hotel during the Second World War. He set the opening of *The Heart of the Matter* on its balcony, with Wilson very slowly sipping his gin 'because he had nothing else to do except return to his hot and squalid room and read a novel – or a poem'. Lansana was also an anthropologist, though he gave the impression of caring more about the exploitation of Sierra Leone's mineral wealth by multinational corporations than about the Susu community into which he had been born and where he was now doing his fieldwork. When Aisha was born on May 15, Lansana and I had gone on a nightlong bender, drinking omole – distilled palm wine. And at the end of my second period of fieldwork in 1972, I stayed with Lansana and his wife in their house on the Fourah Bay College campus.

Though Lansana now held a lectureship in sociology and invited me to speak to his class about my fieldwork in Koinadugu, it quickly became clear that the high point of his day was drinking with friends at the City Hotel. I accompanied him a couple of times. Not fluent in Krio, I felt out of place. And besides, I had lost my appetite for booze and bars and their heady commingling of belligerence and bonhomie. Most evenings I found myself keeping his wife Mary company and listening to her complaints. 'He's a lecher, not a lecturer,' she pronounced one evening, in a room decorated with fly-specked paper flowers and Guinness calendars.

Nine years later Lansana's chosen watering hole was no longer the City Hotel but the Fourah Bay College Guest House bar. Again, my social skills deserted me. When Emma pleaded tiredness one evening, and I told Lansana I was going to accompany her back to our apartment, he pursued us, shouting, 'Aisha is a proper Sierra Leonean. Michael, you are one by adoption. But Emma, you are only 50 per cent. Now shape up and don't let these people down. This is Sierra Leone!' I ignored him and followed Emma up the terrazzo steps to our top-floor apartment.

When I ran into Lansana the following morning he was filled with remorse. 'I have to carouse and carry on,' he lamented. 'If I spend the evenings with my wife, or my weekends at my mother's place at Bullom [a village north of Freetown], my compin gets resentful.'

Mindful of my falling-out with Leon when I stopped going to the pub in order to focus on my writing and support Emma, I told Lansana it was different for me and asked for his understanding.

Later, I shared Lansana's apology with Emma. 'Once people are on the carousel it's hard to get off,' she said. 'They get swept into a stream where everything happens through chance and accident, and they're at the mercy of whatever's going on around them. They feel free, but they are dead to the world.'

The stream in which Lansana was drowning was not social but historical. And that history was *now*. Which was why he railed against the privileges of expatriate whites and their sordid adulteries, and cursed anthropology, which he regarded as the bastard child of slavery, along with colonialism and the extractive economies that were destroying his country's future.

If the Colonels' coup in Greece had been the undoing of Leon, Lansana's nemesis was Siaka Stevens. A few years after our altercation at Fourah Bay College, Lansana was persuaded to join Stevens' All People's Congress government as minister for education and accept kickbacks in return for his loyalty. When the APC was driven into the political wilderness after the National Provisional Ruling Council coup in April 1992, Lansana, along with S.B., was among the politicians detained in Pademba Road Prison. Following his release, Lansana committed himself to the promulgation of Islam and wrote several tracts before dying of undiagnosed causes in his mid-fifties.

EMERGENCY

Within hours of our arrival in Firawa, the old medicine master Saran Salia Sanoh insisted we occupy his house for as long as we stayed in the village. He even recruited his nieces and nephews to replaster the walls and repair the porch.

While Emma home-schooled Aisha I threw myself into fieldwork, and for a month everything went well. But despite daily doses of Maloprim, I was laid low with malaria. My recovery was shaky and slow, and no sooner had I got back on my feet than Emma fell ill. Feverish and complaining of swollen lymph nodes, she feared her lymphoma had returned. For several days we waited, hoping for an amelioration of her condition. But she did not get better. Nor could she sleep. We needed medical help.

Late one night we made the decision to leave. By the light of hurricane lanterns, I hastily distributed our few possessions among friends and neighbours and bade farewell to Saran Salia, who, like me, was fighting back tears. Then, with the help of several young men, I constructed a litter on which Emma could be carried the ten miles to the Seli River crossing. The nearest clinic was a further twenty-five miles away, but if we were lucky we might hitch a ride in a vehicle returning to Kabala from the riverside.

The journey was a nightmare – the bearers stumbling over exposed roots or stones, Emma febrile and retching on the makeshift litter, Aisha holding my hand and asking if her mother would be all right, and me racked with guilt at having badgered my family into accompanying me into the field.

It took us six hours to reach the Seli where we made ourselves as comfortable as we could on a stretch of shaded river sand. After paying the bearers, we were alone.

Hours passed. The sun burned through the mist. Flies buzzed. I assured Aisha and Emma that a vehicle would come, sooner or later, though we might have to wait for days.

Toward noon a young man arrived on a moped. He was dropping

off a friend who was on his way to Barawa Komoia. I greeted the young man, asked his name and explained our predicament. Would he deliver a message to the hospital in Kabala, saying that my wife was gravely ill and in urgent need of medical care? I would tip him generously for his help. When he agreed, I gave him the note I had scribbled and watched him disappear down the rutted clay track.

Utterly spent, Emma could not be convinced that help was on the way. I gathered some driftwood, made a fire and boiled some water for tea. Aisha and I chewed on pieces of grilled meat that a friend's wives had wrapped in brown paper and thrust into my hands as we left the village. Emma could eat nothing.

The ambulance ride to Kabala was worse than our trek in pitch darkness from Firawa. When the vehicle arrived I thanked God for our deliverance, but within minutes I was arguing with the Russian-trained paramedic, who wanted to inject Emma with a used hypodermic and a solution he refused to identify. Emma was too far gone to argue, but Aisha was now aware that something terrible was happening and was begging me not to raise my voice. In desperation, I continued to protest, while the paramedic, outraged at this white man's arrogance, argued back.

Only when Emma was safely in a hospital bed, attended by a doctor and senior nurse who administered pain medication and assured us that Emma would be all right, did Aisha recover her composure. Leaving Emma to sleep, I took Aisha to the market to buy bread and fresh fruit.

Two days later we were back at the Fourah Bay College Guest House in Freetown, eating English food, spending our days on Lumley Beach and our evenings listening to the Debussy and Schubert tapes we had brought with us from New Zealand. It was hard to believe that we had passed from despair to hopefulness in such a short space of time and that I, who had applied myself so ferociously to my ethnographic work, questioned the price I was paying for pursuing it. Was I not like the musicians and dancers I had heard about, who owed their abilities to bargains struck with djinns, and had to forfeit the life of a loved one in repayment?

THE TWO MOMORIS

Though I returned to Sierra Leone alone that October, we spent the remainder of my sabbatical in England, where Aisha attended a local school, Emma worked on *Back of Beyond*, and I drew on my recent fieldwork to complete *Allegories of the Wilderness*. Just as Emma's book was an allegory of her experience of a life-threatening illness, so my book, despite its academic pretensions, was informed by a new sensitivity to life's everyday struggles and ethical dilemmas. In Kuranko stories, people risk their lives on hazardous journeys into the bush where they hope to gain, from a djinn or supernatural agent, the wherewithal for a richer life. My own ethnographic forays could be understood in similar terms, except that I had risked my wife's health and my daughter's happiness by taking them into a wilderness from which they stood to gain nothing. I had momentarily lost all sense of the balance that must be struck between what is necessary for oneself and what is necessary for those one loves.

One Kuranko story affected me deeply. The two protagonists are close friends who bear the same name and conscientiously share the profits from their common trade. When it comes time for them to marry, they discover they have only enough bridewealth for one wife. They therefore decide to share the same woman. When this arrangement proves untenable, the first friend, whose name is Pure-Hearted Momori, generously gives the woman to the other Momori, declaring that if their trading is successful, they will soon have enough money for a second wife. But the second Momori schemes with his wife to kill Pure-Hearted Momori and steal the money they have made. One day, travelling far from their village, they ambush Pure-Hearted Momori, pin him to the ground, gouge out his eyes, and leave him for dead among the rocks.

Despite being blinded, Pure-Hearted Momori manages to drag

himself into the shade of a great cotton tree where an old hyena and an old vulture meet each evening to share their news of the day. Pure-Hearted Momori overhears their conversation, in which the vulture confides to the hyena that it has laid a sixth egg in its nest, and that whoever breaks any of these eggs will have his wishes fulfilled. In turn, the hyena describes how, earlier that day, a young man was beaten and blinded beneath the tree and left to die. 'Too bad that young man is not here now,' he says, 'because if he were, I could tell him that if he washed his eyes in the sap of this tree, he would recover his sight.'

The following morning, as soon as the hyena and the vulture have gone on their way, Pure-Hearted Momori takes a stone, dashes it against the tree, and washes his eyes with the sap from the cut. He then climbs the tree and takes three of the vulture's eggs. After a long journey into an unfamiliar land, Pure-Hearted Momori breaks one of the eggs and wishes for a large town to appear. He breaks the second egg and wishes to be made chief of the town. Breaking the third egg, he wishes to become the wealthiest man in that land. In the years that follow he marries many wives, has many children and prospers.

The other Momori and his wife fall on hard times. Their luck runs out and their ventures fail. But one day, hearing of a great chief who rules a distant town and possesses immense wealth, they decide to beg him for help. It takes them two days to reach the town, and two more days before the chief grants them an audience. Despite their ragged clothes and woeful appearance, the chief thinks he recognises the couple. He gives them lodgings in the house next to his own and orders that they be fed and given new clothes.

That night, the chief goes to the house in which he has lodged his visitors. The man and his wife are afraid of the chief, and their fear only increases when he asks them to recount the story of their misfortunes. In telling their story, they pretend that Pure-Hearted Momori died of natural causes. The chief then retells their story, describing what actually happened. Realising the true identity of the chief, the man falls to the ground in terror. As he and his wife prostrate themselves before the chief and plead for forgiveness, Pure-Hearted Momori says, 'I never showed you anything but goodwill. That is the nature of friendship. And so, tomorrow, I will divide my chiefdom into two. I will rule one half, and you the other. We will share everything, just as we once vowed we would do.'

No sooner has the chief returned to his house than the man and his wife begin wondering how Pure-Hearted Momori became so wealthy and powerful, and as dawn breaks they go to his house and ask him. When the chief tells them about the hyena and the vulture, they waste no time in going to the place where they ambushed and blinded him so many years ago. The man finds the three remaining vulture's eggs and asks his wife what he should wish for. She tells him to use the first egg to get a large town in which to live. With the second egg, she says he should wish for a great river to appear, since one cannot live without water. With the third egg, she says he should wish for her family to become wealthy, since a man with rich in-laws will want for nothing. What happens, however, is that the man's family becomes impoverished, the wife's family takes her away from him and he is left with nothing.

It wasn't that I reconsidered my friendship with Leon in the light of this story, though the theme of reversed fortunes would come to preoccupy me. Rather, the tale of the two Momoris brought me to ponder, perhaps for the first time in my life, the possibility that stories about significant others are symbolic explorations of divisions within ourselves. The duplicity and doubling in the Kuranko narrative make explicit the fault lines that lie within each and every one of us. We shape-shift from moment to moment, depending on who we are with, the situation in which we find ourselves, or the goal we are pursuing. The characters in our fictions, like the figures in our daydreams, are submerged aspects of ourselves, brought fitfully into the light. 'Each of us is several, is many,' wrote Fernando Pessoa. 'In the vast colony of our being there are many species of people who think and feel in different ways.'

If this perspective meant that I saw the self as always implicating another, it also changed my understanding of the creative process, and I now yearned to be back in the Manawatu, settled in our house with its view of the distant range and in my writing routine. I no longer nursed an ambition to leave New Zealand or further my academic career. And though both Emma and I soon found ourselves embroiled in demonstrations and protests against the 1981 Springbok tour of New Zealand, our lives were deliberately low-key.

During our first winter back, we drove to a country pub once a week for lunch in front of a roaring fire and went walking across windblown hills under lowering skies. We made new friends, Dutch, Norwegian and Hungarian, and spent a weekend each month with them at a lodge in the Ruahine foothills, not far from where I had wielded a chainsaw with Leon during his days as a firewood dealer.

Though Leon and I had been out of touch for two years, I thought of him often. One such memory was prompted when our friend Joost recounted how he had survived the Japanese occupation of Java during World War II. As a medic, Joost knew that everyone's chances of survival would depend on a collective understanding that the healthy would care for the sick and would expect to receive care when, as was inevitable, they fell ill themselves. Several prisoners rejected Joost's counsel. But as he had predicted, those who decided to take their lives into their own hands, confident in their individual stamina and will, were those who perished. The ones who were prepared to help others in need were in turn helped in their own hour of need, and lived. But even those who helped others and died could be said to have lived, Joost said, because they had retained their humanity to the last.

I think it was Joost's story, more than anything else, that made me resolve to visit Leon in Northland.

NORTHLAND

It was dusk by the time I located Leon's shack near Paihia, though I lost my footing several times as I stumbled down the clay track between the coast road and the boathouse. Groping my way toward the glimmering light of a storm lantern in the boathouse window and sensing the silence of the falling night, I felt as if I were being drawn against my will into a tale from the Brothers Grimm.

My qualms were partly confirmed by the young woman who opened the door and scrutinised me for a disconcertingly long time before declaring, 'You must be Mike!' Even then, I remained disoriented. It had been a long time since anyone called me Mike. But then Leon's voice boomed from the shadows, asking if it was me, and I stepped into a room of unpolished floorboards where a fire was roaring in a pot-bellied stove. Leon was ensconced in an armchair, his familiar glass of whiskey on one side and a gold packet of Benson and Hedges on the other, grinning at me as if my presence had confirmed some secret suspicion.

'So, you made it?'

'Not without difficulties.'

'Everyone gets lost,' the young woman said. 'I'm Alison, by the way.'

'I won't get up,' Leon said, stretching out his hand. Was I to shake it, or help him to his feet?

'Oh, come on!' Alison sneered. 'Aren't you guys going to embrace?' We did as we were told, Leon leaning forward in his chair, me stooped over him, our hands awkwardly patting each other's back.

'You must be hungry,' Alison said.

'I am a bit.'

'It's pretty basic here. It'll be herrings on toast, with a fried egg, if that's all right.'

'Sounds good to me,' I said.

'Ally,' Leon shouted. 'Give him a glass, for Christ's sake!'

Alison dutifully handed me a jam jar. I poured myself a thimbleful of Leon's Johnny Walker, clinked my glass with his, and drank to his health, hiding my dismay at his lank grey hair, the grog blossoms on his cheeks, the moth-eaten beard.

As I ate, Leon told me that he owed his good fortune in finding the boathouse to his friend Friedensreich Hundertwasser. Alison had studied fine arts at Auckland University and written a paper on the evolution of Hundertwasser's ecological activism, tracing it from the 1960s in Austria when he developed his abstract, colourful paintings with their labyrinthine forms and biomorphic shapes, through his travels in North Africa and the Far East, to his sojourn in New Zealand, where he purchased land to reforest and on which to live a self-sufficient life, using solar panels, a water wheel and a biological water-purification plant. 'No straight lines,' Leon said, echoing Hundertwasser's philosophy of art. 'There's no straight lines in nature. Why should we think of our lives as linear? Thinking cause and effect. Living in boxes.'

'So you came to Northland to meet Hundertwasser?' I asked Alison.

'Yes. I was helping him with his screen printing for a while.'

'Until she met me,' Leon said.

'And then?'

'Then everything spiralled out of control.'

Alison laughed and said she preferred to think of an unfurling fern frond.

Leon took a small tobacco tin from the breast pocket of his shirt and placed it on the table between us. Without a word, I accepted the invitation to share a joint.

I had learned long ago that telling tall stories was Leon's way of turning the tables on the tragic, so it wasn't long before he was regaling me with one of his stories from the period when he was selling pot and hash oil in Auckland.

'I had six kilos of leaf,' Leon said, 'chopped and baled. Usually I made the trip on my own, but Ally insisted on coming along for the ride. So, we get to Warkworth and she's hungry. Wants to stop and buy a pie. I had the bales of grass under some hay bales in the back of my pickup, but nothing disguises that strong smell of hemp, and the last thing I wanted to do was stop in the main street of a town. But Ally was about to throw a tantrum, and I was rattled.'

'That's not true!' Alison protested. 'You were the one who wanted the pie. You were the one who decided to stop.'

'So,' Leon went on, 'we park in the street, and Ally and I go into the pie shop, thinking we'll be on the road again in five minutes max. But in my panic, I left the keys in the ignition. So here I am, racing around behind shops and rummaging in waste paper baskets, looking for a strip of binding tape or some wire to trip the door lock. Even when I get lucky and find something, I'm half expecting a tap on the shoulder and a cop sniffing the air and asking me what kind of hay bales I've got in the back.

'In any event, we get to Auckland, I drop Alison off at her auntie's place in Freeman's Bay and deliver the stash in Ponsonby. The house is one of those old villas, and the buyer's a young Māori guy who introduces me to his grandfather, who's pottering around in the kitchen. The three of us get talking, and before long the old man asks if I'd like to see what he does for a living. I've finished my business, am in no hurry, so why not? I go into one of the side rooms and it's filled with Goldie paintings of Māori chiefs in traditional dress with moko on their faces. I don't know whether the paintings are stolen, or what to make of them. They're all signed C.F. Goldie. And they're beautifully painted. If they're forgeries, they're every bit as good as the originals.

'The old man won't answer my questions. He wants to know what I think of the paintings. I tell him I envy the skills of the person who did them. It's his grandson who puts me straight. His grandfather has been faking Goldies all his life. He even changed his name by deed poll to C.F. Goldie. Then he says, "Why shouldn't he? Goldie wasn't Māori. What right did he have to paint portraits of old-time Māori and profit from them? My grandfather has every right to do this. What's more, Goldie's paintings are the fakes. My grandfather's are the originals."'

I wanted to ask Leon if he was still painting. Perhaps he had gone into the business of art forgery. But what did it matter? We fake so much in life for the sake of getting along, or in order to live with our pasts. Telling stories. Coming to believe our own publicity.

I drifted asleep that night on an old leather sofa, aware of Leon and Alison talking softly in the curtained-off area on the other side of the room, the abrupt sound of embers settling in the stove, then Leon snoring and coughing in his sleep. I woke once and went outside to piss. The wind was lashing the trees. Clouds scudded across the moon. I inhaled the briny, seaweed-saturated odour of the inlet, and felt so much at peace that when I made my way back to my sofa and pulled the army blankets up over me, I could not sleep. I now knew that the landscapes and seascapes of my natal land were as necessary to my spiritual life as curvaceous walls, uneven floors, sod roofs and trees were to Hundertwasser's. For the first time since visiting Leon in Greece, I envied him, though when I pondered this in the light of day I began to wonder whether it was not his relationship with Alison that was the real source of my envy.

After breakfast Alison accompanied me down to the inlet. The wind had fallen. Spring sunlight glinted on the water, and Alison wanted to know what kind of anthropology I did. I told her about my years in Africa, mentioning the psychological cost of pursuing one passion at the expense of another.

'You mean your poetry?' Alison asked.

'Everything that poetry symbolises,' I said. 'The world of the senses rather than the life of the mind. And, paradoxically, everything that cannot be put into words.'

'You and Hundertwasser have a lot in common.'

'The thought occurred to me,' I said, 'when you were describing him last night.'

Alison led me to a jetty with weathered planks. Several yachts and launches stirred at their moorings.

We sat side by side at the end of the jetty, our legs dangling over the water, shading our eyes against the sun.

'Do you mind if I ask you about Leon?' I said.

'Why not ask him yourself?'

'It's just that last time I saw him his health was – '

'It's worse,' Alison said quickly. 'It's always getting worse. If he laid off the weed, whiskey and wine, he might come right, but he won't do that. Or if he ate something that doesn't come out of a tin.'

'What about all the fresh fish you must catch up here?'

'You won't catch Leon fishing. He prefers to sit on his chuff, killing time.'

'It must be hard for you.'

'You mean because I'm thirty years younger than he is?'

'That's not what I meant.'

'It's okay, sooner or later everyone gets around to asking me this. But age isn't an issue for me. Dad was forty years older than Mum. And I've learnt a lot from Leon. Things I wouldn't have been able to learn from someone my own age. And I love it up here, far from the madding crowd.'

We were silent for a while.

'But it's a big deal for Leon,' Alison continued. 'Being so much older. He's always waiting for me to go off with someone else. Someone younger. He even preempts it by pushing me away. I think it's because of what happened to him when he was a child. His parents ditching him the way they did. He won't commit to a relationship, and when he finds himself being drawn into one, he resists becoming attached and pulls up anchor before his boat can be berthed.'

'Pun intended?' I asked.

Alison laughed. 'Appeals to the poet in you, does it?'

'Practically everything here appeals to the poet in me,' I said. 'But whether I could get used to the remoteness is another thing. I'm a bit like Leon, I guess, trying to have it both ways. He wants relationships but cannot commit to them. I want to focus on my creative writing, but can't give up my intellectual life or settle to spending the rest of my life as a university teacher.'

As we strolled back to the boathouse with the sun on our backs, I asked Alison if Leon ever painted these days.

'Hundertwasser tried to encourage him, but Leon claims he's lost the will and lost the knack. He says he doesn't want to make a fool of himself in front of a master.'

'Have you ever met Leon's sister?'

'I met her once. I liked her. She and Leon are very close. It's the one relationship he does trust. If she encouraged him to paint, he probably would. But she's not that kind of person.'

Driving south that afternoon, I pondered my friendship with Leon and why it had endured. 'We go a long way back,' Leon had said, when Alison asked how we met. But was it simply habit that bound us together? Or a similar loneliness, born of a shared love for the same landscapes but a common estrangement from the settler culture that had imposed itself on the land and never come to terms with it? There had been moments the previous night when the past had flooded back with such vividness that I had been moved to tears. Leon's old LPs of Renata Tebaldi singing 'La Vergine degli angeli' from *La forza del destino*, and Bob Dylan's *Blood on the Tracks*. The salt-licked darkness outside, gulls cawing over the inlet as if grieving something that had slipped from their clawed feet and been lost forever. Now, as the bush gave way to denuded hills, skeletal pylons and bone-white bungalows, I remembered the Māori proverb about people passing away and the land enduring. So little of the past remained, neither the great lowland forests nor our youthful promise and vitality, and I was panicked by the possibility that even Emma and Aisha, so constant in my mind's eye, might, even at that moment, be no longer there to welcome my return.

Côte d'Azur

We rented an apartment in the Garavan Palace Hotel. Our living room window overlooked an olive grove and the open sea. Every morning, after seeing Aisha aboard her bus to the Lycée André Maurois, I walked to the writing room. Along the Avenue Blasco Ibanez, cypresses threw pencils of shadow across the stucco gateway to the Fontana Rosa, the decaying mansion of the Spanish author of *The Four Horsemen of the Apocalypse* who lived there in exile in the late 1920s. Tile portraits of Balzac, Cervantes and Dickens were set in the stucco, and a ceramic frieze declared El Jardin de los Novelistas. I turned left into rue Webb Ellis, named for the Rugby schoolboy who, according to legend, picked up a football and ran with it. Forty-nine years later he died in Menton of tuberculosis. Passing the umbrella pines behind the Garavan station, I trudged up avenue Katherine Mansfield and along chemin Fleuri. The writing room was the gardener's shed of the Villa Isola Bella, once described by Katherine Mansfield as 'the first real home of my own I've ever loved'. Here she wrote some of her most celebrated stories. She was thirty-one when she came to Menton in September 1920, suffering from tuberculosis and other ailments. When she left for Switzerland in May 1921, she had only nineteen months to live.

I liked to imagine that Menton had not changed in the sixty years since her sojourn there. On the steep hillsides, terraces were planted with citrus trees. Villas were shaded by chestnuts, figs, olives, oaks, aloes and eucalypts. You inhaled the odour of rotten figs, dry grass, pines, juniper and cypresses. Wisteria tumbled over limestone walls, and African date palms were ubiquitous, though their fruit was inedible. I inhaled the bitter scent of crushed laurel leaves, the rust of railway lines, a Gauloise cigarette, the fresh smell of asphalt when waiters hosed the pavement outside their cafés, my senses alive to everything around me. But there were days when Emma feared that the cancer she suffered nine years ago had returned, and neither of us could settle to our writing. At such times, the violet blossoms and gigantic leaves of the wigandia became sinister signs that our days in Paradise were coming to an end.

If Emma's *Back of Beyond,* now in its final draft, covered her life before and after Hodgkin's disease, the novel on which I was working bore traces of my own struggle to develop a non-didactic form of philosophical fiction. I found myself awash with memories and dreams, sounding depths where everything was amorphous and only vaguely familiar. By day I caught whiffs of Africa in the cloying sea air, the decaying foliage, the acrid smell of burning leaves, the stale odour of urine around the bole of a tree. The musty smell of the room in which I wrote reminded me of the old colonial barracks at Fourah Bay College in Freetown, where Emma and I lodged the week before Aisha was born. Night after night, my dreams returned me to Sierra Leone. Kuranko friends appeared, asking why I had deserted them. In one dream, a calamity of some kind had forced the people of Barawa to flee their homeland. In another, my friend Noah was venturing into politics. I dogged his heels, but he refused to speak to me. What had I done to deserve his censure?

Every afternoon I went for long walks in the Menton hinterland, ascending one of the old mule tracks that led from the coast to Baousset. When I paused to catch my breath, Menton was far below – the cubist roofs of the old town clustered around Saint-Michel, the sea ploughed by a stiff wind racing away to Italy, and the promontories of Cap Martin, Monaco and Cabbé clearer than I had ever seen them. If only my writing could do justice to what was so freely given!

Bypassing Castellar, I took a track through broom, brambles, stunted pines and untended olives, hoping to reach Granges St-Paul and thence one of the old smugglers' paths along the border with Italy. The air was fragrant with juniper and lantana. Above me, against a cobalt sky, the crags of Berceau. After clambering up the scree below the col, I plunged into knee-deep snow and silent pinewoods, marvelling at how instantaneously it was possible to pass, in effect, from one season to another, my mind following suit with fresh sensations and images. Five miles farther on I reached Sospel. Another five and I would be in Moulinet, where Vladimir Nabokov lived in 1938 in 'proud émigré destitution' and on the steep slopes above the village came close to fulfilling his lifelong dream of capturing a new species of butterfly. I sometimes imagined that I was struggling to create a hybrid form of writing that balanced explanation and description, saying and showing, essay and story – a writing that was without pretension, that did not seek authenticity or authority but only fidelity to life as it unfolded, and echoed the ways in which consciousness oscillated between solipsism and sociability, or shuttled between what is past, and passing, and to come.

By mid-afternoon I was back in Menton, listening to Emma's account of her day's work and planning our evening meal. But as winter set in, Emma became increasingly anxious about her health. After consulting a local doctor, we found ourselves repeating our hurried departure from Firawa four years earlier, this time flying to England.

The prognosis was grim. Emma needed to undergo a hysterectomy and begin another gruelling course of chemotherapy. Years of Zen study had prepared her for this moment, and she rejected the oncologist's advice.

We walked away from the hospital in a state of shock. When I prevailed on Emma to reconsider her decision, she became angry and demanded my support. She knew what she was doing. She alone was responsible for her situation. And I remembered what she had once told me about her 'diabolical strength'.

But Emma's resolve was now tempered by resignation, and she cited Mary Baker Eddy's belief that if one attains inner grace, illness cannot take hold of one's body. Emma was convinced that if someone achieves this state of grace, the difference between living and dying becomes irrelevant.

For several weeks we tried alternative therapies, faithfully following the Bristol diet of fresh fruit and vegetables augmented by various vitamin supplements, from ginseng to selenium, vitamin C to echinacea, amygdalin to beta-carotene. There were days when Emma succumbed to bouts of panic and ill-directed anger. Impotent and fearful, I withdrew. As for Aisha, she made friends in the neighbourhood and seemed immune to the darkness that was descending on our house.

Every morning Emma and I went walking on the Downs. We did not speak of her illness or of the future. But as the days passed and her condition worsened, our local doctor delivered his dire prognosis and we decided to return to New Zealand.

Emma was already too weak to walk. She had to enter and exit the airplane in a wheelchair. Back home, the uterine bleeding was impossible to staunch. Shocked at seeing me carrying her mother from the bathroom to the bedroom, then sluicing the blood-stained bath, Aisha wanted to know if her mother was going to die. It was the first time the word had been spoken. It was too abstract. I could not accept it. I told Aisha that Emma loved us and that we must be there for her.

The following day, I sent Aisha to stay with friends and drove Emma to the emergency department at Wellington Hospital. She was placed on a gurney and wheeled into a curtained cubicle. Weakly, she stretched out her hand, and I took it. She was given a blood transfusion, but the doctor drew me aside and told me there was nothing he could do. I was shivering from cold, though the day was warm. Outside the hospital, life went on. The murmur of traffic. Clouds moving over the hills.

A sudden commotion. Nurses running, pushing me aside. Emma had suffered a severe haemorrhage. That afternoon an ambulance transferred her to a hospice. I phoned my friends, asking them to bring Aisha.

When I told Aisha that her mother was going to die, she screamed in pain and protest. When she grew quiet, I took her to Emma's room. 'Be happy,' Emma said. 'You are perfect.'

As evening fell, Aisha left and I sat beside Emma's bed, holding her hand, my guts aching and heart pounding. She dozed in a morphine-induced sleep. Nurses changed her bedding, coming and going during the night as I too lapsed into and snapped out of sleep, checking to see if Emma was still alive, still with me. Aisha returned with the new day, in tears but more composed. She gave her mother a drink of water, refilled the glass. The doctor took me aside to inform me that

Emma would die of renal failure. My mind was distraught and adrift. Organising a funeral, Aisha's future, France, my whole world morphing into memory. I moistened a towel and placed it on Emma's forehead. I kissed her gently. I held her hand. I kept vigil. Lines from a poem by Rex Fairburn came to mind:

> What is there left to be said?
> There is nothing we can say,
> nothing at all to be done
> to undo the time of day;
> no words to make the sun
> roll east, or raise the dead.
>
> I loved you as I love life:
> the hand I stretched out to you
> returning like Noah's dove
> brought a new earth to view.

Aisha left. Hours passed. The daylight faded. Emma surfaced momentarily from sleep. 'I had a bad dream about being buried alive. You won't let that happen, will you?'

'No, my love. I am here. I am not going anywhere.'

Night fell, and a nurse bent over her.

Emma whispered, 'I'm in terrible pain.'

More morphine.

Alone with her again, I took her hand. She cried out weakly, her head moving from side to side. Her neck arched slightly, and her teeth were bared in the ugly imitation of a smile. She gasped for breath, once, twice, three times, four times, and it was over. Utter stillness, her eyelids settling, her mouth agape.

Knowing that she was dead and could not be perturbed by anything I did or said, the most dreadful cries of lamentation burst from my throat, cries of agony that would reverberate for years, despite the poetry wrung from my soul like blood from a stone.

Seven Mysteries

Now write down
the seven mysteries:
why you so young and beautiful should die;
why consciousness prevents
escape into the chestnut branches
where foliage goes soft
with God's vermilion;
why what is said is seldom what was meant;
why men and women work, come home,
cook meals, argue and renew
their vows of silence or revenge;
why we were different;
why there are seven of everything;
why I go on
broken-winded like that horse we saw
on the ridge above Waipatiki
by a bent tree
watching the waves roll in.

Survivors

A few weeks after Emma's death I phoned Molly and asked if Leon was still living in his boathouse at Paihia. 'He left Paihia a year ago,' Molly said. 'He is not well. He's living with me now.'

I drove to Coromandel not knowing what I might find, or even caring. Apart from Aisha, who was with her grandparents, I felt I had little to live for. Perhaps Leon would understand.

Molly had used hessian to plaster over the breeze-block walls of her basement garage and whitewashed the rough surfaces. The window casings had been painted ultramarine to further suggest a Mediterranean villa, and the floor was covered with rush matting. A small sink and fridge were installed in one corner, the double doors of the garage had been replaced with ranch sliders, and Leon's armchair occupied the centre of the room, his signature whiskey and cigarettes on the armrests. My first impression was of a castaway on a white sand beach beside an azure ocean. But then I noticed his pee-stained trousers and food-encrusted jersey and recoiled from his foul breath.

The whiskey he poured for me helped soften the blow of seeing his decrepitude, and I was relieved when he suggested we go outside and get some fresh air.

Native bush overshadowed the house and encroached on the gravel drive. We sat opposite each other in Adirondack chairs, with a wooden table on which Molly had placed an arrangement of flax flowers. Nearby, two tūī alighted on a kōwhai tree.

'How did things work out in France?' Leon asked.

'Didn't you know,' I said, 'that Emma died?'

'I heard. I'm sorry. I remember her fondly, riding to hounds, her Counties accent, her fetching hauteur.'

I hadn't the faintest idea who or what he was talking about.

'I'm thinking of selling the house and moving to Australia,' I said. 'Aisha's having difficulties at school. She speaks fluent French, which embarrasses her French teacher, and her classmates bully her for having airs. To tell you the truth, I've lost my way. My life is a series of chores, helping Aisha with her schoolwork, negotiating with Emma's bank for permission to access her account, giving emotional support to Emma's grieving parents, writing to Emma's friends, preparing *Back of Beyond* for publication. I don't know why I do it but can't do otherwise.'

'Your labour of love,' Leon said.

'And you? Molly told me that you'd been ill.'

'I do not know whether illness is a euphemism for old age or old age is a euphemism for illness. Perhaps they amount to the same thing.'

'I don't see you as old,' I lied.

'I don't see myself as old,' Leon said. 'But everyone else does.'

'It's other people that are my old age,' I said, remembering Sartre's argument against the accusation of being old.

We fell silent, as if neither of us wanted to talk of aging but could not think of anything else to say.

'What happened to Alison?' I asked at last.

'That's water under the bridge,' Leon said.

I wanted to ask what bridge, but I turned my face to the sun, closed my eyes and listened to the tūī chiming and wheezing in the kōwhai. Even as I longed for Emma, I fantasised a new beginning with someone else. Yet in the same instant that it occurred to me to ask Leon if he knew where Alison was, I struck the thought from my mind.

'Life offers us two possibilities,' Leon said.

'And what are they?' I asked without interest. I had wanted to talk about my own possibilities. I had wanted to talk about myself. Why couldn't he listen to me for once? Why did he have to bring everything back to himself?

'We can dream it or we can achieve it,' Leon said.

In the wake of Emma's death I had heard enough platitudes to last a lifetime, and when Leon asked me to go indoors and get his whiskey, I was on the verge of saying no and taking my leave, but it would have been like leaving the house with the gas turned on or a fire unguarded. I went into the garage, found his Johnny Walker and set it on the table in front of him.

He filled his glass and mine.

I had a flashback to the hospice in Wellington. Appalled by Emma's utter stillness and finally able to bring my sobbing under control, I had gone in search of a nurse. After checking for Emma's pulse and drawing a sheet over her bruised hand (where thankfully no more needles would probe for a vein), the nurse hugged me and asked if I would like a brandy. I said no, not wanting to cloud my consciousness. Besides, I needed to call my daughter. I needed … I needed … I needed to descend into the underworld and find my Eurydice again, or join her in the darkness forever …

I was aware of Leon, asking me if I remembered what I had said to him when he was my age.

'What was that?'

'You told me that my life wasn't over, and that I would live to regret it if I did not change my ways. Now I'm giving you back your own advice. Life will look after you. You're not going to end up like me.'

I have no way of knowing what effect Leon's comment had on me, but I suspect that the reason I had once enjoined him not to give up on life was that I had been loved as a child, and that the impulse in me to live was stronger in me than the impulse to die.

Indeed, when Aisha and I moved to Australia a few months later, I felt reborn. Despite my unassuageable grief, I felt that I had been returned to the time when I first met Emma, and I was filled with a sense of boundless possibility. As I began to find fulfilment in new friendships and new landscapes, it was as if her spirit permeated the world in which I now moved, and I was in touch with her at every turn.

> When this bruised medallion, the moon,
> rose tonight
> I thought how solitude
> allows what humankind cannot –
> openness to this hill whose eucalypts
> are my hands,
> the sky that has seen me drown.
>
> I float up
> through these leaves, my skin,
> breathing this blue again;
> the moon
> hangs around my neck,
> under me men move to harvest
> or lie against a golden stook
> eating black bread
> drinking red wine.
>
> The moon is the pupil of my eye
> I go as far as the blue hill goes
> I flow like a river in the dark.

Chiasm

Though Emma was a constant presence, little else of my previous incarnation survived. Apart from Aisha's dressing table and the few books we could not bring ourselves to part with, we had disencumbered ourselves of all that we had owned or called our own. It was only when the half-time temporary position I had secured at the Australian National University came to an end and I found myself unemployed, with time weighing heavy on my hands, that I began to pick up the threads of the life I had all but left behind.

The letter I sent Leon came back to me undelivered. I wondered if Leon was miffed that I'd broken my promise to stay in touch and was punishing me. But when he didn't reply to any of the postcards I sent over the next few months, I wrote to Molly, asking if he had changed his address. Molly wrote back to say she did not know where Leon was. Frantic with worry, she was by turns mystified by his disappearance and angered by his silence. 'It's not like him,' she said. 'I'm thinking of going to the police. He might have had an accident.'

I had given Molly my telephone number in case of an emergency, so when she phoned one evening and I heard her voice, nervously asking, 'Is that you, Mike?', I feared the worst.

Leon had finally contacted her. Several months ago he had suffered a minor stroke, been hospitalised, and was now living in Nelson and making 'a rapid recovery'. Molly gave me his address and urged me to write to him.

In response to the card I posted the following day, Leon sent a lengthy letter, written in longhand on perforated computer paper. 'Still among the living,' he wrote,

> despite my brush with death, though I am haunted by memories of my childhood that for all their vividness may not be memories at all, but hallucinations. My parents appear like strangers, floating out of the mist, looking at me, then floating away. Never speaking. Never touching me. Never really recognising me. But their faces are filled with such unhappiness that I want to reach out to them, only

I can't, because they seem to be in thrall to some power neither they nor I can overcome. The worst thing about these spectres is that they return, over and over again, keeping their appointed round, looking at me, suffering in some mist-swathed wilderness, and I am powerless to do anything but bear witness to them. What it means I have no idea. Sometimes I don't know what day it is. I forget what I am supposed to do or had planned to do. I get frustrated and angry at myself, but when this happens the spectres return, and I am thrown back into this appalling and unresolvable relationship with them, lost for words, stuck in time, going round and round in circles.

'You did well to leave,' Leon concluded, as if I might have become trapped in a similar purgatory had I remained in New Zealand.

I was not so sure. I recalled what a retired judge had once told me about the impossibility of ever knowing whether his decision would change a miscreant's life for the better or for the worse. According to him, the same uncertainty attends the choices we make in our own lives. You might decide to change horses in midstream, but you cannot predict whether your lot will be improved or impoverished by this decision. On his retirement from the bench, the judge and his wife bought a beautiful house near Kimbolton in the Manawatu. Less than a year after moving in and spending a large amount on renovations, he answered a late-night knock at the door. The caller was the previous owner of the house who explained that he had sold the house after the death of his wife, thinking it would liberate him to begin a new phase of his life elsewhere. But his efforts to start over had been undermined by an irrepressible nostalgia for the house he had shared with his wife for thirty years and in which their children had come of age, and he now proposed buying it back from the judge at whatever price he named. The judge and his wife dismissed the offer, but within a week, having thought it over, they decided to accept and buy another house on the Kapiti Coast, which until then would have been beyond their means.

Though unemployment and penury were wearing me down, I was determined not to risk Aisha's newfound happiness by moving again, and despite my longing for the landscapes of my homeland I could not face returning to a place of ghosts.

Leon liked to cite Heraclitus: Everything is in flux (*panta rhei*). One cannot step into the same river twice, for neither self nor river stay constant over time.

I had never known Leon to express regret for the way his life had panned out. Allied to neither Epimetheus nor Prometheus, he seemed to have escaped the extremes of both looking back and looking forward. Whereas his self-description of 'going round and round in circles' suggested a transcendence of time and an indifference to place, my ruling metaphor would have to be one of always changing places, or of forever shuttling to and fro between past and future. I was often besieged by the idea that Emma had sacrificed her life so that I might have mine, as if I was a burden she had chosen to carry even at the risk of breaking her own back. I was also haunted by the idea that Leon and I had changed places through a bizarre twist of fate. When we first met, I was the one who was struggling. The odds seemed stacked against me. By contrast, Leon had everything going for him. He was my intellectual superior, girls flocked to him, the world appeared to be his for the taking. Now everything had been reversed.

Perhaps the one original discovery I had made in my anthropological career was that myths and folktales are constructed chiastically. Each narrative is made up of two halves that are turned against each other, inverted and reversed like playing cards. Consider the story of Cinderella, which pivots on a contradiction between social position and moral disposition. A virtuous and beautiful girl (known variously as Cinderella, Rashin Coatie, Aschenputtel, Finetta, Zezolla, and Yeh-hsien) is initially living in degraded circumstances while her spiteful and ugly stepsisters enjoy the privileges of the well-born. The story involves a crossing over (*chiasm,* from the Greek letter *chi,* which is X-shaped), in which moral beauty is transferred to the high-status position (Cinderella marries a prince) and ugliness is transferred to the low-status position (the stepsisters fall from grace). Thus the tale contrives, through literary legerdemain, an ideal congruence of moral virtue and social status.

In construing my own life chiastically, I became convinced that my destiny lay in completing Emma's and Leon's unfinished lives. Embracing the Kuranko belief that our lives are but extensions of the lives of our predecessors, to whom we are perpetually beholden, I realised that the dead are not shades but significant others. Like the books that change our lives, the ideas we encounter through our reading, the countries in which we sojourn, and the places we are raised, they come to inhabit us as much as we inhabit them. We are all of a piece.

ON THE WATERFRONT

After several years in Australia living on the dole I moved to the United States, where I remarried. In the meantime, Aisha had graduated from art school in Canberra only to find herself adrift and needing my guidance and support. The death of my wife's mother in New Zealand proved equally unsettling, and we moved to Sydney to be close to Aisha and to strengthen the bond between her and our own two children. After a stint of teaching at Sydney University, and a fellowship year at Victoria University of Wellington, I was offered a temporary position in Denmark. When this position ended, we moved back to the US.

During these nomadic years of untenured university positions and family upheavals, I returned annually to New Zealand, wondering whether it would be possible to truly come home again.

That revisiting a semi-derelict hotel should precipitate so many memories proved less surprising than my reluctance to visit Leon, now wasting away in a rest home less than a mile from my motel. In an email, Molly described Leon in terms that made him seem so lost to the world that I told myself it would be pointless to look him up. Just as Leon had once shunned Emma, fearing that her cancer might be contagious, I now cast about for excuses not to see him.

Despite my inhibitions, I knew a meeting was unavoidable. It had nothing to do with loyalty or friendship. It wasn't even a question of seeing in Leon's face what I had seen in the façade of the Albemarle – hard evidence that everything falls apart and passes into nothingness. 'He has emphysema,' Molly had written. 'He has to have his oxygen bottles within reach at all times. Last year he suffered another stroke. He can hardly recognise me, he can't remember recent events, and he can't talk much. This January, he had to be hospitalised. He's now in a rest home in Wellington. If you visit him, he may not know who you are. But if you want to see him, I could go with you. Just let me know.'

The rest home was a stone's throw from the hospice where Emma had passed away. Molly met me in the lobby. We hugged and bantered about the weather and my recently published *Selected Poems* before starting down a long corridor where I glimpsed elderly men shakily sitting on their beds and staring into space. A few were in the corridor, in shabby dressing gowns, struggling to advance a few steps with the aid of walking frames. We found Leon slumped in an easy chair in the recreation room, his oxygen bottles beside him.

Molly repeated her warning that he couldn't speak and might not remember me. But at the sound of my voice, Leon jerked awake, and there seemed to be a glimmer of recognition, though perhaps I imagined this. His skin was blotched and brittle like old newsprint. His hair was thin, and every breath he drew was a pained gasp. I didn't know what to say. I kept repeating my name and gingerly touching his shoulder, his arm, his hand.

The television was on. *Days of Our Lives*. I wondered what he was hearing and seeing. Was it simply a flicker of light, a babble of sound?

Molly walked over to a tea trolley and poured a cup from the urn. I assumed it was for me and was about to call out and say I did not want any tea. But it was for Leon, not for me.

To my surprise, Leon's grip on the handle of the cup was firm, and he had no trouble raising the cup to his lips, sipping some tea, and replacing the cup on the low table Molly had positioned in front of him.

Leon showed no sign of hearing, let alone understanding, anything I said, but I said it anyway. The launch of my poems. The names of mutual acquaintances I had run into. A description of the Albemarle and the old Communist Party headquarters in Marion Street. He sipped his tea, wheezed, and gazed in the general direction of the television.

Suddenly, he appeared to doze off. I said nothing and waited for Molly to suggest we go. But she had settled in for a long vigil, and I curbed my impatience.

After a very long time, sitting in silence and guiltily watching the TV, I asked Molly if we could leave.

I squeezed Leon's arm, and he opened his eyes. 'I'm going,' I said. His eyes seemed to fill with tears. He looked up at me, not with a sign that he now remembered me but as if he had a question he did not know how to ask. I bent over him and held him in my arms.

Molly and I repaired to a café where she described Leon in heroic terms, speaking of his battle against illness and his lust for life. When I demurred, recalling the talent he had squandered, the loves he had let slip away, she protested.

'That's simply not true. If that's what you think, it shows how little you know Leon. Sure, he may not have made much of his life, but he wasn't ambitious. He didn't want wealth or fame. He lived life in his own way, on his own terms. That was his secret. He never wore his philosophy on his sleeve.'

I muttered my apology and said that Leon's friendship had meant the world to me. 'In a way,' I said, 'I owe him my life.'

It was now Molly's turn to apologise. 'I was always over-protective of him. Ever since we were kids. Sometimes I go too far. I know you were close. He spoke of you often, and he read all your books.'

I doubted this. As far as I could recall, Leon had never showed any interest in my work, even though he once said he would give his right arm to be able to sit down every day, as I did, and write.

I asked Molly if she had ever married. She said Mr Right had never come along. Then she confided that she had never really forgiven her parents for abandoning her and Leon. 'I never trusted anyone, I suppose. I never knew for sure whether I would turn out like them. But I've got Lucky, and my garden, and Leon.'

'Lucky?'

'My golden retriever.'

'It's strange how seldom our paths crossed,' I said. 'When Leon came back from Greece, I was gone; when I left New Zealand, he returned. And now I've been in Denmark and the US for so long I've become persona non grata here.'

'You wrote, though,' Molly said. 'You two were always great letter writers.'

I was moved by Molly's efforts to counter my regrets, to mollify me.

I wanted to say something affirmative in return – something that did not offend her idea of her brother. A line of Raymond Carver's came to me. 'Everything depends on whether or not we have been loved and feel ourselves beloved.'

After kissing Molly goodbye I drifted down to the waterfront where I used to work, manhandling cargo in ships' holds or storage sheds, the year before *Truth*, the Albemarle, and Leon. Nothing was as I remembered it. The renovated sheds now housed upmarket restaurants, wine bars and boutiques. One had become a maritime museum. The quay was thronged by young people, all with cell phones in the palms of their hands, eyes fixed not on their surroundings but on their screens as if they were communing with ghosts. I passed a group of teenagers at a table on the quay, thumbing through Facebook posts as if, like Leon after his stroke, they had lost something vital to their wellbeing. Many of the young women carried paper shopping bags bearing the icons of fashion houses. Their possessions and prepossessions seemed superfluous to me, making me feel like a relic from a bygone age. My first impression of Leon had been that he was both there and not there. I now realised this was also true of the city in which I was wandering about like a revenant.

That night I went to Courtenay Place in search of somewhere to eat. I passed gloomy pubs where tattooed men were bawling out their girlfriends. Fluorescent-lit fast food joints stank of rancid fat. In the doorways of shuttered shops, homeless men were hunkering down for the night in grimy sleeping bags – evidence, I thought, of how far we had come in dismantling an egalitarian society that had once been the envy of the world. I had read of entire families unable to even rent a house, of poverty, drug abuse and despair wreaking havoc in the wastes of suburbia. I attempted a count of the bodies, huddled with their shabby belongings, empty wine bottles and mangy dogs, but quickly gave up. Years ago I had feared that this was what would become of me. Even now, this scene mirrored my own degraded sense of myself and my fear of failure – a fear I had undoubtedly projected onto Leon, just as he had once seen himself in Takis Harissiadis.

PARALIPOMENA

The Greek word *paralipomena* designates things we leave behind, shelve or dismiss from mind, yet accumulate as a kind of supplement to the stories we tell. Despite being unfinished and fragmentary, such deleted scenes, outtakes and afterthoughts offer alternative understandings of the events and figures to which the storyteller gives centre stage. They are also evidence of the storyteller's care not to get sidetracked by events unfolding on the periphery of his characters' lives or by the clamouring of his minor characters for attention. To flesh out every individual to the same degree would destroy a story's dramatic tension and undermine its mystery. Yet fiction writers become preoccupied with their characters, just as scholars become obsessed by their theories, and sometimes feel compelled to provide backstories or genealogies for their alter egos.

During his reclusive years in New Hampshire, when no one really knew what, if anything, J.D. Salinger was writing, he was, among other things, compiling meticulous histories of his fictional Caulfield and

Glass families. Buddy Glass, who recounts the life and tragic death of his brother Seymour, is Salinger in disguise.

Paul Auster observes that 'it is possible for stories to go on writing themselves without an author'. This claim reflects Auster's view that every person comprises several selves and that fiction writers flesh out some of these inner personae in their work, as well as events that might have come to pass had they taken a different road in life. The same is true of an ethnographer whose work is peopled by figures that are, in part, projections of his or her own unconscious.

In life as in fiction, we nevertheless cling to the idea of a self that transcends all others. This 'innermost centre within the circle, of sanctuary within the citadel', as William James calls it, this 'nuclear part of the Self', is what abides.

But who is this self that remains constant in the darkness? Can I disentangle the self I was with Emma, or with Leon, or with my present wife? Am I a different person when writing fiction than when writing fact, in the field or out of it, at home or abroad?

In a postscript to *Moravagine*, Blaise Cendrars provides an account of how he happened to write the novel. After describing the insidious way in which the figure of Moravagine entered his life and took possession of him, Cendrars explains that an author can write only one book, *or the same book again and again*, and that all these books are autobiographical.

If it is true that we process the same preoccupations over and over, in everything we write, then perhaps what motivated my memoir of Emma and Leon – and made me feel compelled, when it was done, to go back to the beginning and reimagine it – was the same force that compelled Doris Lessing, having written a novella based on the lives of her parents, to throw the dice a second time and write an account of how her parents' lives actually turned out.

3.

CONSTANT IN THE DARKNESS

....

SAM AND HARRIET

Sam Stillman was a reporter on the *Star*, and the story that came to obsess him was not his story, but one he chanced upon while searching the paper's archives for material on a quite unrelated subject. Unearthing this story, he would later tell Harriet, was almost as fateful as meeting her.

In July 1987 a Taranaki woman helped her husband fake his death by digging up a corpse from a cemetery, then staging a fiery car accident in which the body was burned beyond recognition. It was not, however, the apparent immolation of Andrew Jason Cropper and his reduction to a heap of ashes on the driver's seat of his gutted Toyota Corolla that captured Sam Stillman's attention. It was what happened three weeks after.

Cropper's wife introduced her four-year-old son to Jake Morningstar, her new boyfriend, though he was of course Cropper himself, disguised with a beard and dyed hair.

Sam wanted to know what happened to this bewildered boy when his mother and father were found guilty of insurance fraud and sent to prison. Was he adopted? And how did he survive this traumatic sequence of ambiguities and betrayals?

When Sam's attempts to trace the boy came up against impassable bureaucratic barriers, he began to conceive of a work of fiction in which the bare bones of the newspaper story would be fleshed out. But he felt out of his depth. Although he had published a couple of short stories in an undergraduate magazine and nursed an ambition to write a novel, he knew that this particular story required psychological insights he did not have.

His daily commute to work took him past the School of Psychology at Auckland University. One morning, on the spur of the moment, he went in and asked a flummoxed receptionist if he might talk to someone on the staff about an article he was researching. The receptionist suggested that one of the postgraduate students might help him; all the regular staff members were away for the summer. But no sooner had she provided a name – Rachel Eisenstark – than she remembered that Rachel had phoned to say she wouldn't be coming in that morning. 'I'll ask if her friend Harriet will see you,' the receptionist said, 'though she might not be there either.'

He followed the receptionist's directions to the back of the building and found the door with a plastic nameplate reading 'Lab Manager(s)'. Taped to the doorjamb was a card that bore the names of the occupants. After knocking tentatively, he was summoned to enter by a woman roughly his own age, dressed in a white lab coat, swivelling in her office chair to meet him with undisguised disdain.

Uncertain whether to sit or stand, he identified himself as a journalist, apologised for imposing on her time, and summarised his story, as if haste might lessen the embarrassment he felt in her presence.

He had hardly begun when she interrupted him.

'Why don't you sit down?'

He looked around. The only chair he could see was the one at the second desk in the room.

'You were saying?' she said.

He was captivated by her upper lip, which titled upward slightly like a miniature ship's prow. Arrested by this small detail, he struggled to collect his thoughts, scarcely aware of what he was saying. 'Faking your own death takes a lot of planning. It's a lot harder than murdering someone, because you've got to have a body that will be examined forensically and declared to be you. And then, if you pull this off, you've got to invent a new identity for yourself. And even if you get a fake birth certificate, how are you going to pass yourself off as someone else without a complete makeover? Where are you going to get the money for that? Still, the Croppers are undaunted. They decide on a car wreck and a fire. It seems the mother has found out how you can burn a body in a way that renders it unrecognisable without destroying it completely. But the cops suspect foul play. There are no skid marks on the road, no sign that the driver braked or spun out of control on the corner, and traces of charcoal lighter fluid are found near the driver's seat, suggesting it had been used as an accelerant.'

She was now gazing at him as if looking for a way out of this uninvited interview without provoking a scene.

'I'm not sure I'm the person you should be talking to. I am not a psychoanalyst.'

'I realise that,' he said. 'And I've probably given you entirely the wrong impression about what I'm on about. It's what happened after this fire that fascinates me. I'm thinking of writing a novel about what happened to this little boy when his father returns from the dead, pretending to be someone else, and his parents are jailed. I'm trying to understand the impact this event might have on a four-year-old child.'

It occurred to Harriet that he had once been this child, and that by attributing this story to an archival source he was protecting himself from the grief he still carried within him.

'I think you probably know everything you need to know,' she said. 'At least if you're thinking of writing a novel.' To appease him, she threw out some psychological clichés about separation trauma, though she cautioned him that every case was different, and one could never predict how a traumatic event might affect a person's later life. 'Since you're a writer, why not give free rein to your imagination and trust your instincts? Surely there's something in your own past that might account for your fascination with what happened to this little boy? Why not get in touch with that, whatever it is, and go from there?'

He didn't like being fobbed off. It offended him professionally and personally. Talking to this condescending creature, armoured in a lab coat, was like trying to persuade a doctor to engage in a jargon-free conversation.

'You're probably right,' he said. 'Reading psychology doesn't help one write fiction, and reading fiction probably doesn't help one study psychology. I'll leave you to your trade and get on with mine.'

'I don't think that's the case at all,' she said defensively.

'What's not?'

'What you said about fiction and psychology. As a matter of fact, it was Dostoevsky's *Crime and Punishment* that inspired my interest in psychology.'

'No kidding.'

'Dostoevsky and others.'

'So you think the Croppers might have wanted to get caught?'

'The Croppers?'

'The couple in my story.'

'Oh, them. Yes. Perhaps they did. Or they weren't very bright.'

'So what kind of psychology do you do?'

'It's called attachment behaviour. Attachment and affect regulation.'

'How did you get interested in that, whatever it is?'

She wasn't obliged to explain anything. Certainly not to him. But unaccountably she tried.

'You might be surprised that I don't set much store by the jargon of my profession, and I rather envy you being able to write about something from life without explaining it. Anyway, wouldn't you agree that the way we frame things is less important than how we respond to what's inside the frame?'

He had been about to leave – to save face or escape the curse (or was it the spell?) she was placing on him. But she had lowered her guard, even appealed to him for recognition, and he felt moved to respond.

She was equally mystified that she was so drawn to him. She had better things to do than waste her morning with a reporter who didn't know the difference between tragedy and melodrama. And his retro clothes! He seemed bent on imitating an American writer from the fifties: Oxford shirt, woollen tie, tweed jacket with leather elbow patches, blue jeans and moustache.

They sat in silence for what seemed to them both a long time.

'Well,' he said, springing to his feet. 'I guess that's that. It was nice talking to you. Thanks for your time.'

'Not at all,' she said, and swivelled in her chair to face the open window and the dappled bark and greenery of a plane tree that, for a moment, she felt she had never really seen before.

After leaving her office he walked through Albert Park in a daze, and for the remainder of the afternoon, despite a deadline he had to meet, he could not focus on his work without being suddenly distracted by the thought of her and the way they had been at loggerheads one minute and finding common ground the next.

As for Harriet, she could not put Sam out of her mind. Though moved by his identification with this unknown little boy, she had formed the impression of someone who had yet to find his path in life, someone with a proclivity for dependency, an emotional liability. Yet she felt she owed him something. Not an apology for her initial brusqueness, but something of herself. And so, before the day was out, she mailed a book on trauma to him care of the *Auckland Star*, with a scribbled note expressing her hope that even if it did not prove useful to him, it might serve as an apology for her offhand manner.

Two days later he phoned her, having carefully rehearsed what he would say.

'Thanks for the book. I found it a bit daunting. Perhaps we could meet, so I can return it to you in person.'

She had invited this, but now she wanted to back away. Should she tell him to keep the bloody book, or mail it back to her? She surprised herself by doing neither, unceremoniously blurting out that she went swimming most mornings at the Tepid Baths. 'There's a coffee bar on

Quay Street near the Western Viaduct. You probably know it. The Ca d'Oro. What about coffee around 8:30, if that's not too early for you?'

She was wearing a summer frock – brick-red with white polka dots. A greenstone pendant hung like an exclamation mark around her neck, and her hair, falling damp and loose about her shoulders, gave off a faint odour of chlorine.

All his confident preparations crumbled. He could hardly bring himself to look at her. Glimpses of her bra strap, her knees, her up-tilted lip mesmerised him. As they queued for coffee he was forced to stand closer to her than he could bear. This wasn't the nervousness of a first date, hearts pounding, knees weak, faces flushed as two people make their nervous first moves toward physical intimacy; it was as if his whole life now hung in the balance, and an absolute and irreversible transformation of his entire being was about to occur. Oblivious to everyone but her, he knew that he was drowning and that even if a lifeline was thrown to him, he would be powerless to seize it.

Would it have made any difference had he known that she was experiencing something similar – a desire to touch his shoulder, to run her fingers through his hair and to be touched by him; a yearning to be somewhere else, away from the crowded coffee bar, the harsh light, the two of them alone, cocooned, enfolded in one another, flesh melting into flesh?

The baristas worked rapidly and efficiently, and as the queue inched forward, Harriet felt as if she was on an alien planet, weighed down by excessive gravity. Unless she found something to say, however innocuous, she would face annihilation. And so she asked him what he was working on, only to hurriedly answer her own question: 'I suppose the Commonwealth Games is taking up all your time at the moment.'

'Actually, I've been able to wangle my way out of it. I'm off to South Africa in a couple of weeks. There's a rumour that Mandela is about to be released.'

He had not meant to be so blunt, but her arm had brushed against his and he was burning up.

'I went on a march against the Springbok tour,' she said, 'when I was in high school.'

Not knowing what to say to this, he edged his way toward the counter where their coffees would be served.

At the very instant one of the baristas called Sam's name, she said: 'I envy you.'

'Why is that?'

'I'll tell you later,' she said. 'Shall we find a table outside?'

They found seats at a wonky table on the sidewalk. Coffee spilled into saucers as they squeezed into metal chairs. Despite Sam's attempts to stuff paper napkins under one of the table legs, it remained unstable.

Pressing his foot down on the base of the table, Sam handed Harriet her book.

'To be honest,' he said,' I don't think you believed me when I said I wanted help in understanding childhood trauma, even though you were kind enough to lend me a book on the subject.'

'It's not that I didn't believe you. I was a bit taken aback, that's all.'

'You suspected some ulterior motive.'

'I suppose I did.'

'Like what?'

'Like you were once that little boy.'

'Okay. Well what about this, then? What if I concocted the whole story as a pretext for getting to know you?'

'But you'd never met me. Before you walked through my door last Friday you didn't know my name or anything about me.'

'What if I'd seen you before? And found out who you were and where you worked.'

For a split second she found herself reverting to her first impression of him as a nutcase.

'You're making this up,' she said, determined to mask her susceptibility to his suggestion.

'Then will you believe me if I tell you that within minutes of leaving your office the other day, I wanted to see you again, and that if you hadn't sent me that book I would have found some other pretext to ask you out?'

When they met again, two days later, ostensibly for lunch, they chose a table on level ground.

'What are you going to get?' she asked.

'To tell you the truth, I'm not very hungry.'

'Me neither.'

'I hope you're not going to be like the last girl I took to lunch.'

'Oh?'

'She was obsessed with her weight.'

Harriet laughed. 'Well, that's hardly me. My friend Rachel accuses me of being a fitness fanatic, which I probably am.'

'I used to run. Now I walk fast. I sometimes think I live backwards and it's only a matter of time before I'm crawling again. My mother says the past is more important to me than the present.'

'If you're interested, I can tell you about my last date.'

'Are we on a date?'

'The last time I had lunch with a guy, then.'

'You ordered food?'

'Not exactly. *He* ordered the food. Kept ordering one thing after another but not eating anything himself. He didn't even ask me what I *wanted* to order; he seemed to assume that this was his role – something he had to do *for* me, even if it meant plying me with everything on the bloody menu in order to find something I liked. I couldn't bring myself to eat anything, but when he asked for the bill, he made it clear that he expected me to pay for my half of what *he* had ordered. And then, to add insult to injury, he invited me to choose which of the leftovers I wanted to take home.'

'Did you see him again?'

'What do you think?'

'So perhaps we'd better not order anything.'

There was a screech of brakes from across the road. They turned together in time to see a panel van sitting at an angle in the middle of the road and the cars behind already trying to negotiate their way around it.

'What happened?' somebody asked.

'The panel van hit someone.'

Shoving back his chair, Sam raced across the road to where a weather-beaten man in a greasy, unbuttoned coat was lying on his back, feebly trying to shield his eyes from the sun. Dark red blood was pooling under his head amid fragments of glass from the bottle of vodka he had been carrying. As Sam bent down to him, asking if he was all right, he was aware that no one else was moving. He alone had come to the man's assistance. As he cradled the man's head he was mindful of the blood on his jacket and hands, and of his helplessness, as if he and the drifter had become one, and the crowd indifferent to them both. Removing his jacket, Sam made a cushion of it to push under the drifter's head, dishevelled hair matted with blood, grit and glass. Telling the victim that he would be back, Sam ran into the first shop he came to – a souvenir boutique filled with Japanese tourists off a cruise ship – and ordered a stunned woman to call an ambulance. He then returned to the now comatose man, still lying in the road, as people walked slowly past, staring but not stopping. He wondered vaguely where Harriet was and why she was not there to help him. Later he learned that it was Harriet who had phoned for an ambulance. The woman in the souvenir shop had been freaked out at the sight of him and taken refuge in the back of her shop.

Within minutes, paramedics and police were at the scene. The drifter was gently lifted onto a gurney and rolled into the ambulance. When Sam asked the paramedics if he could accompany them to the hospital, he was told he was not needed, unless of course the man was someone he knew.

It was only then that the driver of the panel van approached him. 'It wasn't my fuckin' fault,' he said. 'The bastard came out of nowhere. I told the cops. I didn't fuckin' see him. I didn't hit him; he ran into me.'

Sam felt the driver was asking for absolution. He thought again of Harriet. He looked across the street to where they had been sitting. She was not there. 'Shit happens,' he said to the driver. 'No one's to blame.'

And then she came to him out of the dispersing crowd, asking if he was all right.

'I'm fine,' he said. 'I'm not sure about my jacket, though.'

'I'll buy you a new one,' she said. Then she took him by the arm and led him away. 'My flat's in Freeman's Bay. You need to get cleaned up.'

'I'm fine,' he insisted. 'I'm not the casualty here. That poor bugger is the one in need of help.'

'Don't argue, Sam. Just do as I say.'

He was now in shock – grateful for her company, but not wanting to talk. But she needed to talk to him, and as they made their way across Victoria Park she asked if she could say something that might offend him.

'Offend me?'

'Did you go to that man's aid just to impress me?'

'What? Unconsciously?'

'I'm sorry, Sam. I don't know why I asked such a thing.'

'I wasn't thinking,' he said. 'I did it without thinking. You were not on my mind at that moment. No one was. Nothing was. Haven't you ever done something spontaneously, without knowing the why or wherefore of it?'

'Yes,' she said. 'Ten minutes ago, when I suggested we go to my place.'

Her lithe loveliness took his breath away. The summer dress discarded, her hair loosed upon the pillow, a dark wreath around her face into which he gazed with astonishment. She moved her hands across his face, through his tousled hair, still wet from the shower, then over his chest, his abdomen, along his thighs, bringing him to readiness, easing him into her, lifting her pelvis to position him, drawing her pleasure from his presence with great gasps and gulps as if she had not drunk from this spring for a long time. His confident and measured responsiveness both excited and soothed her. She lost herself in him, in the surf and sea swell they rode together, the surging tide, the final wave collapsing and spreading up the shelving beach with a soft hiss. When they spoke. it was to share the same thoughts, almost the same words, the total unexpectedness of what had happened, their total unpreparedness, their bewilderment now, cast upon a foreign shore not knowing where to go or what to do.

'I was not looking for this,' she said. 'Another relationship. Not now.'

'Me neither,' he said.

'I was focused on my research. This summer was going to be research. Nothing else.'

'I was looking forward to South Africa,' he said.

'It's when you're content with your own life, when you're not looking for someone or something to fill a void or make good some lack in you – '

'That miracles happen?'

'Yes,' she said.

People sometimes fall in love without the preamble of courtship, though something akin to courtship comes in love's wake, almost as an afterthought. Yet some kind of ritual exchange – of intimacies and information – is always necessary, to wipe clean the slate of the past, to create the illusion of a tabula rasa on which the future can be inscribed. The overture consists of sweet nothings, mirrored admiration, amazement that such familiarity and affinity could exist and wonderment at the chain of events that determined the twain should meet. Then there are the confessed preferences and prejudices, the checklists of favourite foods, colours, pieces of music, ambitions, hangups, and inevitable doubts. Finally (though there is no necessary order to these confidences) there are the family histories that must be recounted, the stories of previous lovers to be touched on and brushed aside.

Harriet was sitting on her bed, a sheet pulled across her body, hugging her knees. Sam was lying on his side, gazing at her.

'I grew up in a series of small country towns in North Canterbury. Dad was a shearer and bushman, a recluse; mum was a termagant. Nothing I did was good enough for her. And she treated Dad like she treated me. I spent more time with animals than with people. In my last year at high school I read a book on attachment behaviour. I became fascinated by how we become attached to abstract ideas, ideologies, and not just people.'

'And animals.'

'Especially animals. Because we *are* animals.'

Sam sat up. 'But can animals love us like we love them?'

'Of course they can! Some of the oldest stories in the world are about animals risking their lives to save people.'

Man's best friend, he thought. Androcles and the lion.

'You said you had a horse when you were a girl.'

'Yes, Rosie.'

'And a dog.'

'My golden labrador, Laika.'

'Wasn't Laika the first dog in space?'

'Yes, I read about her at school. I worried myself sick, thinking about how she suffered, though the Soviets said she gave her life for science.'

'And your Laika, is she still alive?'

'She died years ago. She had to be put down.'

'I'm sorry.'

'You don't have to be sorry. I survived.'

'I read somewhere that people who move around a lot when they are children have poor memories of their early years.'

'My problem was trust, not poor memory.'

Their conversation petered out, and weariness overwhelmed them. As she dozed off, she remembered the Anglican church her mother insisted she attend (though neither parent was a believer), the maudlin Protestant hymns she had to sing. She thought of her boarding school in

Christchurch, the greenery of Hagley Park. In the distance, a small neo-Gothic spire rising above the massed foliage. Lost worlds, sparkling and splendid, tapestries interwoven with swords of mist. Pageantry. Then the foul smell of orange peel, egg sandwiches, apple cores, banana skins, wafting in and out of the corridors as doors opened and closed. She did not belong here. What friends she had made were also outsiders, albeit by choice, not chance. Yet how she wished she did belong, hearing the choir for the first time, those lovely voices swelling like the sea, a stirring Amazonian chorus that made her feel like a visitor among aliens, those arch-patriotic songs swearing eternal devotion, making every sacrifice, extolling the very virtues of peace and gentleness most lacking in that place.

> And there's another country I've heard of long ago,
> Most dear to them that love her, most great to them that know

Their sleep is broken not by the passage of day into night or night into day, but by an unconscious desire to reassure themselves that they are not dreaming, and to physically confirm their new reality by making love. When finally woken by birds singing and sunlight filling the room, Harriet feels an urge to reclaim her immediate past. As Sam sleeps, she casts her eyes around the room as if repossessing it.

When Sam opens his eyes it takes him several seconds to realise where he is.

'How did you sleep?' he asks, and tries to draw her toward him. She slips away.

'Breakfast first!' she declares. Sheathing herself in a white bathrobe. she pads barefoot into the kitchen.

He goes to the bathroom for a pee, then dashes cold water over his face. He inspects the makeup, hairbrush and hair dryer strewn over the faux marble counter top and feels as if he has been given access to a shrine.

The dining room table is littered with books and papers. Crowded House is playing on the radio: 'Now We're Getting Somewhere'. There is a kauri bowl filled with oranges, the aroma of freshly ground coffee. He sits at the table in his boxers and T-shirt, wondering if greater happiness is possible. C'est tellement simple, l'amour.

'What are you thinking?' she asks.

'Just then I was thinking of *Les enfants du paradis*. Something Garance said to Baptiste.'

'The mime?'

'Yes, but I forget what he said to her in return.'

Harriet sets down a pan of scrambled eggs, some slices of toast and a plunger of coffee in a space clumsily cleared among her papers.

'What about you?' he asks.

'I was thinking that you haven't told me anything about your parents.'

'There's not a lot to say. My father's a stranger to me. And my mother's an alcoholic. Has been for as a long as I can remember.'

'How awful for you.'

'It was worse for my father. He walked out on us when I was ten.'

'And then?'

And then I took care of her.'

'How could you have looked after her if you were only a child?'

'No idea. But I did. Got help when she collapsed. Watched over her. She'd go on benders for days at a time, sometimes weeks on end. Then she'd be sober for a while, and loving, and caring, and remorseful, and guilty, and – '

'What drove her to drink?'

'I don't know that either. Though I've often thought of asking her, for all the good it would do.'

'I think I can understand why you were so moved by that story about the – who were they?'

'The Croppers.'

'Didn't you have anyone, any relatives, you could depend on, who could take care of you?'

'My grandfather. Mum's father. He was my mainstay. He still is.'

As Sam was drinking beer with other journos in the Queen's Ferry Hotel that afternoon, Harriet was confiding to Rachel Eisenstark details of the past few days. 'I am drawn to the solitariness in him. I feel utterly myself with him, as if we had known each other in another life.'

Rachel envied her. 'Saint Augustine had a name for what you've experienced. He called it *falsae memoriae*. The Pythagoreans took it as evidence of the transmigration of souls.'

Harriet sometimes felt intimidated by her friend's erudition, but for once she had the edge. She was in love. And all Rachel could do was recite lines from Dante Gabriel Rosetti:

> You have been mine before, –
> How long ago I may not know:
> But just when at that swallow's soar
> Your neck turned so,
> Some veil did fall, – I knew it all of yore.
> Has this been thus before?

Harriet too had authors she could quote. Indeed, an epigram from Borges became symptomatic of the misgivings that now troubled her: 'To fall in love is to create a religion that has a fallible God.'

Sam was also floundering in a sea of emotions, a rip tide against which he could not swim. And though the lovers never breathed a word to each other about their confusions, both secretly looked forward to Sam's departure for South Africa, time to take stock and hopefully regain their equilibrium in the world they had known before they met.

SAM AND ZOE

They first came to the valley a few weeks after Harriet accepted a lectureship in psychology at Massey University. Neither wanted to live in town, and though there were no houses listed for sale in the surrounding countryside, they spent two weeks driving up and down random roads in the hope of finding one. It was an Indian summer, serried poplars sheathed in gold leaf, dark stands of macrocarpas in sun-parched paddocks. Eastward lay the blue-tongued Ruahine Range and a river hole to which they returned every other day to be cleansed in the bush-steeped water. Harriet later described those days as halcyon. It was more by dint of her efforts than his that they found a house that needed only minimal repairs and repainting, only a twenty-five minute drive from the campus.

Within a month of their moving in Sam began work on his novel, and when Harriet fell pregnant Sam irked Harriet by comparing pregnancy with carrying the germ of a novel around in your head but not knowing when or if you'll ever deliver on its promise. But when Zoe was born, Sam suspended work on his book and devoted himself to his daughter: feeding her breast milk that Harriet expressed before leaving for work, keeping house and cooking meals. Indeed, domesticity appeared to give him such satisfaction that Harriet wondered whether it was obliquely connected to his frustrations in caring for his mother. She also found it difficult to focus on her work. Why pursue the academic study of attachment when you can simply yield to living it? She found herself staring out the window at the distant peaks of Ruapehu and Tongariro, or watching the westerly wind playing havoc with the eucalypts. She remembered the night Zoe was born, when rain drowned out her cries of pain and afterward the outside world all but ceased to exist for her as she lay, exhausted but elated, gazing into the steel-grey eyes of her firstborn.

Zoe would become a child of the valley, learning its landscapes by heart – the soughing and creaking of pines, the ominous river hole, the summer shearing sheds and the weather that changed without warning from scudding cloud to driving rain or uncannily sunlit periods of calm. Her first memory might have been of an autumn day when she was carried on her father's hip as he followed sheep tracks around a hill, while her mother skidded and zigzagged down wet slopes, filling baskets with mushrooms whose dark-brown gills and pale skins were covered with a tracery of grass.

With local creeks choked with watercress and their garden overgrown with pūhā, Sam and Harriet took pleasure in the simplicity and economy of their lives. At night, the only sounds were a cattle beast bellowing in the distance or a dog barking. By day, the silence was broken only by the bleating of a lost lamb, or an occasional car or truck passing along the road, spitting stones and churning up dust. Then silence descended again, and Sam turned to his writing or attended to Zoe until, around mid-afternoon, he gave thought to Harriet returning home and what he would prepare for dinner.

For all their happiness, there were differences that might have surfaced, under other circumstances, as disagreement or dissent. For though Sam was utterly fulfilled in Harriet, he was cold toward her friends and would withdraw and sulk when she arrived home late after spending a couple of hours with colleagues in the pub or went off for a weekend skiing on Ruapehu. Nor did they have much more than a token regard for each other's work. When he endeavoured to explain to her the technical difficulties of working out a timeline, developing a character, or finding the right location for each piece of the mosaic he was assembling, she would question his preoccupation with plot, arguing that life is more random and accidental than fiction allows.

She found it difficult to suspend disbelief. When they went to a movie she would complain about the implausibility of events, the sexist or racist stereotypes, and the contrived synchronicities on which the story depended. Exasperated, he would implore her to yield to the story and not sit in judgement on it. In her defence, Harriet would declare that she was a psychologist, not a fantasist. 'Where would we be if we threw reality out the window and lived as if life were a circus?' He grew exasperated by her narrow empiricism. 'I refuse to see life as an experiment,' he argued, 'whose main purpose is to test a hypothesis, so that we are finally able to say unequivocally, this is right and this is wrong.' He cited Tim O'Brien's comments in *The Things They Carried* on the contrast between 'happening truth' and 'story truth'. Fiction opens a door to a world that we haven't actually lived in or a life we haven't actually led; its aim is to capture the emotional truth of existence. Harriet insisted that these so-called emotional truths were all too often delusions, or rationalisations of human ignorance. They would quarrel, not because the issue could not be resolved but because it was a stumbling block between them – something that even their love could not entirely push aside.

Recalling these differences after Harriet's death, he could not find one word to describe what place she now occupied in his life, but he knew that the things that had come between them were no more significant now than the things that had drawn them together, all annulled like a ship's wake through the sea. Overriding every other consideration was the fact was he could not imagine life without her, and that he had become a stranger to himself, his very identity dissolved with her death. She had sustained him, mirrored him, simply by being there, and now that she was gone he could find no book or piece of music, nor conjure any image, to heal his broken heart. Worse, he was forgetting her voice and unable to recall her face. When he thought he was remembering her, he would become aware that it was a photograph of her that he was remembering and that she, whom he had so passionately desired, was no longer physically present to touch him, to arouse him, despite his longing to see her and be with her again.

After the funeral he yielded to Harriet's parents' wishes that he and Zoe come and stay with them in Hanmer Springs. The idea was that they would give one another mutual support. Since Zoe would be starting university in six months' time, she could, if she wished, complete her last few weeks of high school at Hanmer.

From Picton they headed south along the Kaikoura coast. It would be a pilgrimage through places where they had stopped so often in the past – Dead Man's Creek, Blind River, Flaxbourne, Iron Gate Stream – where bleached and amputated driftwood, rusty tins, plastic bags, and decaying entanglements of wrack and kelp had been coughed up by the sea. Zoe was in tears. He put his arm around his daughter's shoulder and looked out to sea. It blurred as he too succumbed. He remembered the telephone call from the hospital, informing him that his wife had been found near death on the Apiti road, apparently a victim of a hit-and-run driver. He remembered Zoe's screams of pain and disbelief, and his own benumbed state of mind as he repeated his mantra of denial, *This cannot be, this cannot be, this cannot be.* He remembered Harriet on life support, her face bruised and misshapen, and the doctor saying that she was clinically brain dead. Zoe could not bear to be in the same room as her mother. 'It is not her. It is not Mummy.' How would he tell his daughter that they had to consider the possibility of letting her go? There was no evidence of brain activity. What would Harriet have concluded? That there was no life, no chance of some miraculous reversal or repair? How could he possibly decide? How could he know whether she was dead or asleep? What if she woke up one day, like Snow White, or that young woman in Pedro Almadovar's *Talk to Her* – a movie Harriet declared implausible? He sat with her. He talked to her. He could not persuade himself that he was doing anything other than talking to himself, arguing for and against what he would do, and how he would live with what he did. Harriet's parents arrived. They told him the decision was his. They would respect whatever he decided. As the reality and finality of the situation sank in, he desired nothing but the same oblivion that had claimed her.

The night after Harriet was taken off life support, he gave Zoe some Valium and sat at her bedside until she fell asleep. He was fearful that if he closed his eyes, some terrible peril would befall Harriet and she would cease to exist. Yet he craved sleep. He wanted to go down into the darkness with her. He wanted to expunge that image of her under a white coverlet, impinged upon by dangling tubes, respirators and monitors, her broken body and battered face a frightful parody of the person he loved.

At last he did sleep, only to jerk awake from a dream in which she came to him across a slope of snowdrifts, in blinding light. He was in a mountain chalet. Through large windows he watched as she came nearer, wearing a white jersey, vivacious and beautiful. But as she approached the glass-panelled door of the chalet he saw that her face was troubled, and when she reached the door she rattled it desperately. Though he could not hear her voice, he could read her lips. *Let me in, let me in!* He crossed the room to the door. Harriet's fingers were fumbling at the letter slit, her nails long and varnished. He touched her fingers. Then he threw open the door, and she hurled herself into his arms, clinging to him, her legs embracing his, her body melting into his, warm and sensual …

At Hanmer he tried to keep his grief to himself for Zoe's sake, though whenever he got away from the house, walking alone on a back road, he would fall prey to uncontrollable sobbing. He and Harriet had walked these roads together – blue borage, thistle and cow parsley along the roadsides, paddocks dry and dun under a cloudless sky, foothills soft and tawny in the evening light. They had held hands, stopped and embraced, made love in long grass, lain side by side, looking up into the blue vault of the sky.

When he returned to Harriet's parents' house, he splashed cold water on his swollen, haggard face before repairing to his room to write in his journal or summon the strength to be sociable.

One evening he came home to an empty house. Zoe's grandparents had taken her to visit old friends and left a note: 'Back at dinnertime.'

He went out onto the veranda and looked toward the mountains, asking himself if they would be the source of his healing. His life seemed so insignificant in comparison, his grief no more than a passing squall. If only he could extinguish his yearning for renewal and become at one with the mountains, he could go on.

The following morning he ran along a deserted road as a soft rain was falling. Pinions of pines and macrocarpas, willows weeping. The sky merged with the land. He felt as if a sudden gust of rain could sweep him out of existence, just as Harriet had been swept away. He thought, I am free for as long as I can think this way – that nothing matters in the long run, or will make any difference to anything, that I am nothing now to anyone, that I am going nowhere.

He drove to the place where Harriet had spent some of the happiest days of her childhood. She once told him that when the house burned down her childhood came to an end, though she was always talking about her childhood having ended before it had run its natural course. He found the site of the house, unchanged from when he had visited it with her: slabs of concrete in the long grass, wild roses. Looking north, he saw the same scene she used to see from her bedroom window, the scree slopes and rocky flanks of Te Rako, the cloud formations – hog's backs, mare's tails – that presaged storms. When Harriet's family moved to Waiongona, her father, Ted, found work driving a grader and digging ditches for the county council. Before this move, Ted had spent his summers away shearing, which, in Harriet's view, made his marriage to Maisie bearable. But in Waiongona, oppressed by his wife's endless carping and depressed by his loss of independence, Ted became restive. He bought fifty acres of mānuka scrub in the back of beyond and one day walked out on his wife and daughter to live in a shack he'd built on the land he intended to break in. Harriet was desperate to join him. She identified with his sorrow and loneliness and yearned to take care of him. And he had always been her ally in her altercations with her mother. Without him she felt vulnerable and gutted. Reading became her refuge. Her horse, Rosie, became her love, and patience her virtue, as she waited for three years to pass before she could go to Christchurch Girls' High School as a boarder.

Now, with Zoe settled in Hanmer, Sam returned to the North Island, crossing Cook Strait in benign weather then driving all night and all day, with brief stops for sleep, to Northland, where he arrived at first light and asked an old man hobbling past the church at Matauri Bay if he knew where Leviathan Reed lived. After receiving confusing directions that nonetheless confirmed what he dimly remembered, he was about to get back in his car when the old man said, 'Tell you what, I'll give him a ring, tell him to come and meet you at the turnoff.'

'It's okay, I'll find him.'

'You sure?' the old man said. 'Make sure you keep left, otherwise you'll end up in the sea. You'll surprise him. He's my nephew.'

The house was familiar. The gravelly crowing of a rooster, clucking hens, duck shit along the path. He parked the car and walked up the flagstone path to the back door. Leviathan greeted him without a word. They hongied. He hongied Lev's brother Jim and their father, Petera. The women enfolded him in their arms. Before eating or drinking they assembled in the front room, where Jim told him that this was his home, adding that it was good that he had come back, to show that the relationship went on, even though Harriet was no longer with them. Lev's mother, Mere, gently upbraided him for coming without Zoe, her mokopuna. School was no excuse. Then Mere and her daughters sang a waiata tangi that alluded to the kiwi's egg – a metaphor for solitude and abandonment. The kiwi lays its egg at the foot of a tree, then leaves it. The egg often rolls into leaves or gets hidden or trapped in a skein of tree roots. For this reason, many kiwi eggs never hatch.

He was treated like a prodigal son. Though he had known Lev since they were undergraduates together, and Harriet and Sam had spent several summers with the family, assisting with the shearing and attending hui around the district, he had not realised until now how much he depended on the unconditional acceptance of this whānau.

On New Year's Eve he accompanied Lev, Jim and Petera to a grove of cabbage trees high above the sea. Lev shinnied up tree after tree, carefully extracting the hearts. Overnight, the kōuta would be marinated in beef fat, then served on New Year's day with pūhā and pork to betoken the power of Life to produce new life from barren or devastated ground.

He slept under an army blanket, listening to the ticking of a clock in the darkness and the timbers of the old house creaking. He looked forward to the new day when they would go fishing for kahawai at the river mouth. He knew the ropes: never to point at the schools or discuss their intentions lest the kahawai move away, how to stand naked in the sea as the fish rubbed against your legs, and how, when you threw one up onto the beach and later gutted, scaled and cleaned it, you ensured that the fish's brethren were ignorant of what was happening. With these observances and beliefs, he felt at home. As sleep overcame him, he remembered what people kept telling him at Harriet's funeral: that time healed all wounds, that he was young and would find someone else. That it was a blessing that he had Zoe to take care of him. He brushed these remarks aside as well-intentioned, though none of them showed any understanding of the inconsolable condition of loss. One remark, from a man he counted as his closest friend, still grieved him when he thought of it. 'Do you think we have the moral right to terminate another person's life?' He had not spoken to Charles since.

But in that moment of utter desolation, when the agony of his decision lacerated his soul, Lev said something that contradicted everything he had been told. 'You will never get over this.' It was the confirmation he needed that he and Harriet would be together for as long as he lived.

He woke at first light and joined Petera, who was sitting outside the back door, cutting some stringy beef from a bone. When the bone fell to the ground, Utu, the family's fox terrier, seized it and trotted off to gnaw it beneath an orange tree. Petera was a man of few words, but he had told Sam that he'd broken his ankle the previous year and it had been slow to heal. Lev had given up his teaching job in Auckland to come home and do the work around the house and on the farm that his father could no longer manage. 'Whatungarongaro te tangata,' Petera said. And Sam completed the proverb with him. 'Toitū te whenua.'

The family saw him off later that morning. 'Don't be a stranger,' Lev said.

Sam embraced Mere and turned to shake hands with Jim. Jim took his hand and pressed into his palm a bone fishhook he had been carving over the last few days.

'For when you go fishing again,' Jim said.

Back in Hanmer Sam told Zoe that he had decided to put their house on the market. Without Harriet's income, he did not know how he could possibly keep up the mortgage repayments.

'That's a terrible idea!' Zoe said. 'What would Mummy think?'

'I know what she would have thought. She would have wanted you to do well at varsity, to follow in her footsteps. She would not have wanted us to sink back into the past.'

'Keeping our house is not sinking back into the past!'

'Perhaps not,' he said, checking himself from saying anything more about money.

He recalled Zoe speaking at the funeral, mastering her emotions and speaking of her mother with such undying love, then standing beside him, holding his hand as if he was the one who was falling apart.

'When you're young', he said, 'the future is everything. But when you're old, there is no future. You look back. You remember. You try to find a pattern in the past.'

She was blinded by tears, and by her anger against him.

'But you're not old, Dad. Forty-three is *not* old. And I'm not so young that I don't have a past. Do you think I have forgotten Mummy? That I will ever forget her? I think of her every day. I go to sleep thinking about her.'

He tried to explain, as if this would mollify her. 'It's not that I don't love the house or know how much it means to you. It's a matter of whether we can afford – '

'What about mum's superannuation, and that insurance settlement you told me about?'

The legal phrases were burned into his brain. Wrongful death suit. Punitive damages. Lost-wage compensation. He could not bear the thought of her life and death being subject to some kind of calculation, 'a lifetime's loss of earnings,' a 'compensatory package,' or her loss mitigated by her drunken killer being given a ten-year sentence ...

'Do you realise how ghoulish you sound?'

'And you do realise how pitiful you sound? You sit around for hours on end playing solitaire and listening to sad music on YouTube, like you did at Hanmer.'

'It's not sad. It's *saudade.*'

'Dad, it's *sad*. And selling the house will make you even sadder.'

There were times when he could persuade himself that Harriet was in another room or had gone out for a bike ride and would soon return. He would set out two mugs on the counter and brew tea for two. He would walk through every room in the house as though he might feel her presence, hear her voice. In their bedroom he buried his face in her clothes, inhaling her. Each night, as silence wrapped the house in its dark vice, he lay in bed conjuring her, imagining them walking together in the dusk, the green of the river flats buoyant, palpable, permeating their consciousness. The air scented by rain-drenched fennel and lupine and the damp gravel of the road. At nightfall the moon-blanched landscape opened itself up to them as they walked arm in arm toward the river. A row of poplars writhed and rippled in the wind, an embankment of them, swelling, lifting, pulsing like dark water, and the hills bathed in a pale green undersea light. The moon sailed out from behind scuds of cloud, the shadow of the poplars laid out on the grass like shrouded bodies. He and his beloved were one again, stones among stones.

He once read about a prisoner of war who, during several months in solitary confinement, recovered his earliest memories and journeyed from the distant past to the immediate present, postponing for as long as possible the moment when he would have to face the future.

Sam proposes to do the same, only in reverse. He will work his way back through the labyrinth of their twenty years together, back to the very beginning, and find her again, as Orpheus found Eurydice.

It does not work out as he planned. He gets distracted. New experiences delay and interrupt his idyll.

He happens to watch a rare film on YouTube – Pablo Casals playing Bach's Suite No. 1 for Cello. The film was shot in the Benedictine Abbey of Saint-Michel-de-Cuxa in southwest France in 1954. Casals was a refugee from Franco's Spain, and this was one of his first public performances after several years of silence.

Listening to Bach, Sam is moved to tears. He draws an analogy between his own sense of exile and the exile of the 77-year-old Casals, seemingly alone in this roofless French abbey, playing for no visible audience.

The video reminds him of something he had read and photocopied when he worked for the *Star*. He finds it in his filing cabinet, under 'Ideas for Stories'. The story had appealed to him because it hinged on the kind of synchronicities that are the magical glue holding a narrative together, as well as the mysterious force that brings two people into one another's orbit at exactly the right time.

Almost thirteen years after the film was shot, and only a few months before Casals' 90th birthday, the American writer Norman Cousins travelled to Puerto Rico where the cellist and his wife, Maria, were then living. Although Casals' favourite composer was Bach – he owned several original Bach manuscripts – he confided to Cousins that his favourite composition was not by Bach but by Brahms, and offered to show his visitor the original manuscript of Brahms's B-flat Quartet – one of the most valuable music manuscripts still in private hands. After taking it down from the wall, where it hung framed behind glass, Casals told Cousins how the manuscript came into his possession.

'Many years ago,' Casals said,

I knew a man who was head of the Friends of Music in Vienna. His name was Wilhelm Kuchs. One night in Vienna – this was before the war – he invited several of his friends for dinner, myself included. He had what I believe was one of the finest private collections of original music manuscripts in the world. He also owned an impressive collection of fine musical instruments – among them violins by Stradivarius and Guarneri. He was wealthy, but he was a simple man and a very accessible one.

Then the war came. Kuchs had no intention of spending the rest of his old age under Nazism. He moved to Switzerland. He was then more than ninety. I was eager to pay my respects. Just seeing him again, this wonderful old friend who had done so much for music,

*was to me a very moving experience. I think we both wept on each
other's shoulder. Then I told him how concerned I had been over
his collection of manuscripts. I had been terribly apprehensive that
he might not have been able to keep his collection from falling into
Nazi hands.*

*My friend told me there was nothing to worry about; he had
managed to save the entire collection. Then he went and got some
items from the collection – some chamber music by Schubert and
Mozart to begin with. Then he placed on the table before me the
original manuscript of the Brahms B-flat Quartet. I could hardly
believe my eyes. I stood transfixed. I suppose every musician feels
that there is one piece that speaks to him alone, one which he feels
seems to involve every molecule of his being. This was the way I
had felt about the B-flat Quartet ever since I played it for the first
time. And I always felt it was mine.*

*Mr Kuchs could see that when I held the B-flat Quartet
manuscript in my hands it was a special and powerful emotional
experience.*

*'It is your quartet in every way,' Mr Kuchs told me. 'It would make
me very happy if you would let me give it to you.' And he did.*

*I couldn't thank him adequately then, but I did write him a long
letter telling him of the great pride and joy his gift had brought to
my life. When Mr Kuch replied, he told me many things about the
history of the B-flat Quartet I had not known before. One fact in
particular stood out. Brahms began to write the quartet just nine
months before I was born. It took him nine months to complete it.
We both came into the world on exactly the same day, the same
month, the same year.*

Sam remembers Harriet's reaction to this story. She cast doubt
on the coincidences. She demanded to know about the element of
contingency. 'Would you use the word *fate* if Brahms had begun his
quartet eight months before Casals was born, or eight years after?
What of all the coincidences we don't remark or remember, because
they did not pander to our need for our lives to express some hidden

design? I don't mind fiction, Sam, but I draw the line when we lose sight of the difference between what is real and what we imagine to be real.'

He knows she was right. The idea that Harriet was fated to be riding her bicycle on the Apiti road at precisely the same time that a drunken farm labourer sped south to meet his mates in an Ashhurst pub is so outrageous that he cannot forgive himself for entertaining it.

He wakes at six. Knowing Zoe will not be awake for another two hours, he prepares a breakfast of muesli with fruit, fresh orange juice, toast and black coffee. He does not turn on the radio, or check emails or listen to music. After washing up, he puts on his boots and parka and heads down the gravel drive to the road. There is no traffic. The sun is still below the range. The air is cold. Dank paddocks are swathed in mist. He takes the track to the river, where he undresses and plunges into the water. It knocks the breath out of him. Gasping, he turns onto his back. He is thinking of Harriet, planning his day's writing, so that when he returns to the house with the rising sun at his back he will know what he is going to write. He is ghost-writing her biography, entering into her earliest experiences and converting them into a narrative, a stream of consciousness, becoming her.

Within days he realises that he possesses only fragments and will never be able to compose a meaningful mosaic with them. He agonises over whether he knew her at all, and whether loving someone, living with them from day to day, is a matter not of knowing but of something beyond our conceptual grasp – like the genius of Django Reinhardt with his two paralysed fingers, Bach's counterpoint, or simply the inertial force of habit. Even revisiting in his imagination the places and people he met through Harriet fails to bring her back to life. The backcountry she knew as a child, Cloudy Range, the inland Kaikouras, Emu Plains. Landmarks that helped her get her bearings: Te Rako, Pyramid Valley, the homestead at Greenboro. At Hanmer she used to point out to him mavericks and misfits who never seemed to age or die: the miserly recluse who lived in a poky windowless room behind an abandoned shop, surrounded by a midden of newspapers, greasy paper bags, bottles and cardboard boxes. The town drunk who lurched red-faced homeward at 6:15 every evening, his self-mortification dating from the day his wife died of cancer. The irascible and overweight 19-year-old mother, her legs already shapeless and varicosed, shepherding her preschool kids in and out of the local milk bar. And then old Frank McLaren, the panty snatcher, chipping weeds and grinning inanely at Harriet as if he still had a pair of her knickers tucked away in his bottom drawer. Harriet spoke of Frank with affection. But for her school friends she felt only pity, dreading becoming one of them – married to a farmer, darning socks, getting the roast on, gossiping tirelessly about domestic intrigues, road accidents and who'd been done for speeding.

He turns to compiling a list of the things he misses most about her. The smell of her body and her hair. Her indecipherable handwriting. Her teeth, which were almost perfect. Her irrepressible laugh. Her shoes, now his fetishes. Her political commitment, marching for every cause and getting baton bashed while he cowered on the sidelines, finding excuses for not taking part. Her kindness, visiting distressed neighbours, going out of her way to help an exchange student, caring for stray animals. Her garden. The human names she gave to her favourite animals, and the animal names she gave to her least favourite colleagues. Her ability to cook Asian food. Her hand-knitted scarves and jerseys. Her insistence on celebrating birthdays and anniversaries (which he forgot). Her patience, reading Zoe bedtime stories until mother and daughter fell asleep together. Her homemade bread. Photos of her as a child, before he knew her. Photos of her as a young woman, after he had met her. Her love of the mountains. Her intolerance of pretension. He is smiling as he remembers the American couple Harriet invited to the house for Sunday brunch. The husband introduced himself as a biochemist. His wife was in Mensa. He was tall and gangly, like John Kenneth Galbraith. She was short and dumpy, with close-cropped peroxide hair and two plastic earrings that matched the bracelets on her chubby forearms.

'The thing about Mensa,' she explains to Harriet, 'is that we can travel anywhere in the world and always find someone of our own intellectual calibre to talk to.'

'That must be nice for you,' Harriet says.

'Oh yes, we'd find it very hard otherwise. Bob's always being invited to international conferences so we travel a lot. Without Mensa we'd be quite lost.'

'What kind of IQ do you have to have to get into Mensa?' Harriet asks, and Sam can already tell that she is not going to suffer this fool gladly.

'Oh,' croons the woman, with hushed seriousness, 'there's only a small percentage of any population who can qualify.'

'I see,' Harriet says. 'You must feel very privileged.'

'Not privileged. I'd say we feel *responsible*. We have a duty to the less gifted members of society. Bob's work, now. I mean his epidemiological research will someday alleviate so much unnecessary suffering in the world.'

'About suffering they were never wrong,' Harriet says.

'You know, it's really great talking to you, Harriet. Travelling around as much as we do, you run into an awful lot of folks that don't know what you're talking about if you use polysyllabic words.'

'Pray tell,' Harriet says, 'what does polysyllabic mean?'

He belatedly writes letters to friends who sent condolences. He arranges for Harriet's bank balance to be transferred to his account (because there was no will, he has been obliged to show evidence both that he and Harriet were married and that she is now deceased). He pays Zoe's university fees and finalises arrangements with her hall of residence. Then Zoe begins to complain of splitting headaches and does not want to eat. He takes her to the doctor, who prescribes medication, though there is no cure for this pain, this desolation. Yet Zoe continues to astonish him. She buys the texts she will need for university and begins studying them. Days pass in which he sees no evidence of her grief, though she sees the anguish in his face and places her hand on his or smiles at him. He feels that his heart is literally broken. There is an aching, fractured sensation in his chest, a wound that will not heal.

He drives Zoe to Auckland and settles her into O'Rorke Hall. Zoe says this is the beginning of her own life. She tells him she is happy, and she wants him to be happy for her.

For two days he is glad to have the house to himself. On the third day he takes the sugar bowl from the kitchen counter and runs hot water over the hardened sugar, cleaning the bowl with the back of his forefinger. He does not take sugar in his coffee. Zoe does. Did. He places the upturned bowl on the drying rack, and as he does so he suddenly realises that Zoe has gone. He stumbles through the house moaning and whimpering like a wounded animal. He enters Zoe's bedroom. Clothes discarded on the floor. Empty beer bottles. He is doubly bereaved. He has lost them both.

Some days he cannot write and has no desire to walk. He takes the car and drives blindly into the landscape, abandoning all thought of where he might end up. One winter afternoon, north of Turakina, he takes a turnoff toward the sea. A sandy track leads to the mouth of the Whangaehu River. Blackbirds screech in the boxthorn hedges. A sea mist hangs over the valley. He leaves the car near a fisherman's whare and walks into the wind, sand grains stinging his face. He picks his way around heaps of grotesque driftwood, the sea wind plastering his hair, caking his skin with salt. Then the sea is before him. Breakers tilt and butt against the outflowing river, heaving logs into the air like beheaded dinosaurs or the prows of Viking longships. Above the maelstrom, gulls wheel and shriek. He squats out of the wind, his back to the detritus and drift. He picks up a piece of dirty pumice. Nearby is the bloated carcass of a cow. A gloom descends. The darkness seeps into him. Wasn't this the river that, fed by a deluge of volcanic mud, swept away the railway bridge at Tangiwai, causing the night train to plunge headlong into the void? He sees the wrecked trees, bark stripped away, a decaying animal, a filthy pumice stone, and weeps.

Rereading Sartre's *Nausea*, Sam is arrested by Roquentin's distinction between the commonplace and the adventure. 'Two years ago it was wonderful. I had only to close my eyes and immediately my head would be buzzing like a beehive. I would conjure up faces, trees, houses, a Japanese girl in Kamaishi bathing naked in a barrel, a dead Russian with a great gaping wound, his blood pooling beside him. I could recapture the taste of couscous, the smell of olive oil that fills the streets of Burgos at noon, the smell of fennel that floats through the streets of Tetuan, the piping of Greek shepherds. I was moved … But this joy has worn away … I can't see anything anymore. However much I search the past, I can only retrieve scraps of images and I am not sure what they represent, or whether they are remembered or invented … Nothing is left but words.'

He opens Malcolm Lowry's *Under the Volcano*, once his favourite book. If Roquentin's life is bereft of meaning, the consul's life is inundated with it. The consul drinks to quell this overwhelming tide of meaning. Everything around him conspires to form patterns, suggest hidden histories, reveal hermetic correspondences. Nothing is devoid of sense unless it is his own life. A sign in a garden, the repetition of the number seven, a black dog – all portend some awful and inescapable ending, willed upon him who cannot will. He cannot break free of the wheel of fate and begin anew. He is trapped by the past. And the present is preeminently a narrative – an artificial world of plotted connections that he takes to be real. His madness lies in the way he confuses living with recounting, assuming the artifice of the latter to be the essence of the former. But life is gratuitously, insufferably arbitrary. And Sam remembers Harriet's injunction: If you never lie, you never have to remember anything. You are liberated to live in the here and now.

As winter grudgingly gave ground to spring, he received an email from one of Harriet's colleagues who did not want to intrude on his privacy but hoped he wouldn't object to a meeting to discuss the data and unpublished material stored on the hard drive of Harriet's laptop. 'When we helped you clear out her office, we did not deem it appropriate to ask if we might access and examine this material, but we are hopeful you will agree to us doing so now.'

He had become so inured to isolation, so estranged from old friends, that it came as a shock to realise that he had been living for many months as though time had come to a standstill and the world itself had come to an end. The landscape had replaced people in his affections. Emotions once centred on Harriet now found expression in the exhilaration of wading a flooded stream, clambering up a steep track, thrusting his way through leatherwood and arriving breathless on the summit of the range, tussock underfoot, mist swirling about him, then breaking into a run and plunging headlong into a bank of cloud. Battered by wind or walking blindly into the rain, he was in his element. These were his spiritual compass points – the black bog through which he waded, the drifts of snow, the cloudburst, the swollen river, the sodden paddocks, a stand of kahikatea, a pine plantation, the amputated macrocarpas, the sun porch where her ski pants were still hanging on a rusty nail, the garage where her crumpled bicycle collected dust, the laptop he had not touched, her books that he could not bring himself to sell, the nesting pāua shells they had gathered with Zoe on a beach near Akitio, a wind-abraded stone. The only people he saw were Hans and Kirsten, a Danish couple who owned ten acres across the valley, not far from the two-roomed school that Zoe had gone to. They never intruded on his grief. Perhaps they did not know what to say, or what to ask. But in their company he experienced an oasis of calm.

Virginia Kinsey introduced herself and immediately apologised for butting in. Even when he ushered her into the kitchen and made an espresso for her, she continued to ask if this was a good time. He knew she was struggling with what to say, deciding whether to commiserate or get straight down to business, but he could not find it in himself to help her. He set the coffee down on the dining table and let her founder. He did not even ask if he could take her coat, though a puddle of rainwater was forming on the floor beneath her chair. Did he resent her presence – the first woman who had crossed his threshold since Harriet's death? Did he resent her accessing Harriet's files, or suspect her of stealing Harriet's research? After sipping her espresso and declaring it to be superior to any available in town, she explained what she wanted. Harriet had been engaged in cutting-edge research. Much of it had been collaborative. There was data on the hard drive of her laptop that was vitally important to the research Virginia and others were now preparing to publish. He said he understood and had the laptop ready for her. She could take it with her and return it when she was done.

'We miss her dreadfully. But for you, it must be – '

'Yes,' he said. 'It is all that and more.'

'I went through a divorce three years ago. But bereavement must be so much harder.'

'I would have thought the opposite,' Sam said. 'When you are bereaved, you are still in love with the person you have lost.'

'I will never forget her,' Virginia said.

'It is strange,' he said, surprised that he would confess this to a stranger, 'but I am forgetting her, and this is the most painful part of it all, not even being able to hold on to her memory.'

'Memory is not as constant as we are,' Virginia said.

'I know. Harriet often said the same thing.'

'Mourning involves a lot of changes in the way we recall the past.'

'What do you mean?' he asked. Was she presuming to counsel him now?

'There is a tendency in us all to idealise those we have lost, in the same way that we demonise those we do not really know.'

He allowed her words to settle like dust, and the silence to remain unbroken.

'Well, I really must be going. I've taken up quite enough of your time. You have been most understanding, and we are all in your debt.'

He saw her to the door. On the veranda she turned. 'You are lucky to be a writer,' she said. 'You can work through your grief with words.'

When she had gone, Sam got out the journal he had kept during his first two years with Harriet, before they moved to the Manawatu. He located the notes he'd scribbled about the day they first made love. 'The day that passed into another day without a night.' He had been convinced that going to the rescue of the drifter on Quay Street and falling in love with Harriet were the catalysts that made him shed the persona of being a writer and begin the hard work of writing. 'Harriet has made me real,' he had written. 'With her there can be no more pretending.' What he did not write of at the time, though now recalled, was Harriet's later refusal to have him idealise her, her rejection of the role he wanted to cast her in. 'It was the *Star* folding that made the difference,' she had told him. 'It was only when you found yourself out of a job that you finally focused seriously on your writing.'

A month later he received another email from Virginia Kinsey, inviting him to a barbecue at her house near Himaatangi. Harriet's old colleagues would all be there. They would be delighted if he could join them.

The house is in the lee of a sand dune covered with bracken fern. Cobwebs in the gorse. Sky-blue hydrangeas. Flax pods like fire-blackened beaks and bills. A slick of dew on the grass. When Virginia Kinsey greets him, he blurts out an apology for not taking her coat when she called on him, obliging her to sit in a pool of water. 'It has weighed on my mind,' he says. She smiles and takes his arm, leading him over to the other guests, most of whom had known Harriet and been at her funeral. They shake his hand. They touch his arm. One woman gives him a bear hug. How long, he asks himself, will I be seen as an amputee, disabled by tragedy?

Virginia clearly wants to take him under her wing. She tells him that she shared Harriet's passion for the mountains, that she has a glider pilot's licence, teaches guitar and scuba dives. Is he bored, or simply indifferent to all this worldliness? The cheap red wine in a plastic cup, the charred sausages on a paper plate, the garlic bread and coleslaw? He is aware of his surliness, his unwillingness to make small talk, and wanders away to where a Māori guy is tinkering with his guitar. He glances back, meeting Virginia's gaze. For a moment he is aroused at the sight of her freckled skin and buxom body. Startled by the flicker of life he feels in his loins, he appraises her at a distance – not lustfully, yet surprised by this stirring in a body that has lain dormant and benumbed for almost a year.

That night he wakes in the small hours from a dream in which he is fishing with his grandfather on the Tongariro River. He has failed to catch anything. Again he baits his hook and casts his line into the snow-fed stream. There is a tug on the line, but when he reels it in there is nothing. He walks across a ridge of greywacke stones to a turf shelf where his grandfather has left chunks of fish bait. As he makes his way back to the river, Harriet appears and tells him not to use so much bait. He argues that the piece he has taken is not that big, and he wasn't overdoing it. Her upper body is naked. He presses his face into her flesh, between breast and armpit, and is overcome by a sense of sensual tenderness and love.

Was he too desperate to 'catch' another woman? When Jim Reed gave him the carved fish hook at Matauri Bay 'for when he next went fishing', did Jim mean what Sam now thought he meant?

A few nights later he has another fishing dream. This time he is on a jetty in Amazonia, lowering into the water a basket of bait that resembles red pine mushrooms rather than fish. The basket becomes heavy, and when he attempts to haul it up he loses his footing and has to dig his heels into the jetty to keep his balance. When he finally brings the basket to the surface the bait has gone, and there are only a few small fish to repay his efforts. Then Harriet appears, telling him she is going to embrace religion. He tries to dissuade her, assuring her that she has all the love she needs. In tears, he takes her in his arms, assuring her that she is loved, that she need look nowhere else for love …

Zoe phones him every few days, excitedly telling him about a lecture she has heard on Shakespeare's London or Dickens' *Great Expectations*, as if no one else, himself included, knows of these marvels. He envies her, for whom everything is new, because as his days drag by, he is beginning to think that there is nothing new for him under the sun, and he will not live to see another spring. Perhaps his daughter detects this morbidity in his voice. She urges him to drive up to Auckland, pay her a visit, meet her friends. One of her lecturers knows his work and would like to meet him. He asks her to come back to the valley for a while and be with him. 'I'm simply too busy,' she says, 'and during winter break I'll be away tramping in the Waitakeres. You come here. It'll be fun. And when you come, can you bring Mum's Shakespeare? It used to be in the bookcase in the hall.'

He takes the dark red Morocco leather-bound volume from the shelf. There is an envelope between the pages, and the book falls open in his hands at page 216. It is the fourth act of *A Midsummer Night's Dream*, and there is a pencilled cross beside the speech by Demetrius in which he confides that his infatuation with Hermia has 'melted as the snow' and 'seems to me now as the remembrance of an idle gaud which in my childhood I did dote upon'. Demetrius then confesses, 'all the faith, the virtue of my heart, the object and the pleasure of mine eye, is only Helena'.

Sam's face is on fire as he opens the unsealed envelope and unfolds the letter inside. It is a love letter. Tears scald his eyes, blurring the handwriting. Charles' crabbed hand, Harriet the object of his desire. It is clear to Sam, reading between the lines, that this desire was requited. Allusions to a ski lodge at Ruapehu, to skiing as a sensuous prelude to making love, now confirm what he suspected eighteen years ago when he returned from an assignment in Samoa and Harriet asked for space, for quiet, to finish an article she was working on …

He reads the letter again and again, from the romantic banalities with which it begins to the lines from Anaïs Nin with which it ends. 'Faithfulness in love is unnatural. Morality is man-made ideology. Self-denial the most selfish thing of all.'

Sam had flirted with infidelity. Who, he asks himself, has not? But she had actually *been* unfaithful, and with someone he had once considered a close friend. Yet what grieved him most was that she had kept the affair hidden from him, a guilty secret lying in ambush in the pages of *A Midsummer's Night's Dream*, awaiting the inevitable day when he would fall foul of it. Then what? Would they have talked things through? Would he have forgiven her? Or would he have taken his revenge? Anger, hurt, confusion contend within him as he turns back to the play, wondering what Shakespeare might have to say about the shadow side of the imagination.

> More strange than true …
> Lovers and madmen have such seething brains,
> Such shaping fantasies, that apprehend
> More than cool reason ever comprehends.
> The lunatic, the lover, and the poet
> Are of imagination all compact.

But who was he, and what was he to do?

SAM AND MAXIM

After half an hour with Zoe it was obvious to Sam that much as she wanted to see him, she wanted to be with her friends even more. As their conversation faltered and the coffee cooled in their cups they agreed to meet next morning for breakfast, though each was aware that an irreversible transformation had occurred and would have occurred even if Harriet were alive.

Sam sauntered into Albert Park. He sat on a bench, mesmerised by the desultory fountain and three scruffy sparrows waiting for crumbs. To his right was a band rotunda. On a long-ago night he and Harriet had made love there.

He stood up. Should he go downhill into the city, or walk toward the rotunda?

He did neither. Leaving the path, he made a beeline for the Auckland Art Gallery, where he sought out Colin McCahon's images of stark and solemn hills slashed by what could be waterfalls or roads.

These paintings had illuminated the darkness of his pre-Harriet years. He pondered them now, repining for the valley, his house, his refuge.

He wandered on through some of the smaller rooms of the gallery that he had not visited in the past. In one of these rooms he came upon a painting by Maxim Suvorin. Using house paint on hardboard, the painter had rendered his vision of a West Coast landscape in broad brushstrokes, suggesting burnt umber road cuttings, black iron sand beaches, the turbulence of surf and blinding summer light.

Hadn't there been some kind of connection between Harriet and Maxim Suvorin?

The question nagged at him as he continued through the gallery. He vaguely remembered a friend of Harriet's, though he could not recall her name. Harriet used to complain about her friend's indifference to the white rats whose cages they cleaned and whose water bottles they filled. While Harriet pitied the shell-shocked animals, padlocked in their metal cages, unable to see or interact with one another, her friend appeared to regard them as inferior and dispensable life forms whose sole existential value was to help students write academic essays about self-evident aspects of learning and perception.

Then he recalled the connection. Around the time he met Harriet, her friend was in a relationship with Maxim Suvorin, who was at least twenty years older. Though baffled by this dalliance, Sam had not questioned it on moral grounds. Besides, his obsession with Harriet had blinded him to the affairs of others. Even when Max Suvorin resigned his teaching position to focus on his art (it was rumoured that he'd been dismissed for impropriety), and Rachel (that was her name!) went to the UK, neither event left more than a momentary blip on Sam's radar.

But he now wondered what had become of them, and again recalled the psych lab, the white rats, the water bottles rammed into mesh cages, the smell of urine-soaked straw, and this couple walking away, arm in arm, under the sodium lights and great plane trees along Symonds Street, as he and Harriet went in the other direction. He knew that Max Suvorin was a painter back then but did not perceive him as anything but Rachel Eisenstark's (there, at last!) rumoured lover. Yet he had just seen a work by this artist that had brought tears to his eyes, and though its creator had probably passed away, this abstract landscape had suddenly brought Sam back to life.

When he asked if the gallery owned any other Suvorins, he was told no, the artist was no longer active.

He felt disappointed, as if for a moment he had allowed himself to believe that this figure from the past possessed a magical key that would reconnect him with Harriet. Though he could not remember exchanging a single word with Max all those years ago when he and Rachel were an item, Sam now wanted to know everything there was to know about him.

Once again, he tried the patience of the woman at the front desk by asking if she or anyone else on the staff might know how he could contact the painter. 'It's very important,' he said, though hesitated to say it was a matter of life and death.

Ten minutes later a young man informed him that Maxim Suvorin lived at Makara Beach, near Wellington. The gallery had no mailing or email address and no telephone number. 'As far as we are concerned,' the curator said, 'he's effectively dead.'

Sam drove south, playing a CD of indie rock that Zoe had burned for him. *It's never as it seems. Losing my religion. Life's too short to even care at all. When there's nowhere else to run. The dog days are over. Nantes. Home is wherever I'm with you.* He played the twenty tracks over and over, wondering whether they were intended as cryptic messages – Zoe insinuating what she could not bring herself to say to his face. Whatever the intent, his spirits lifted, and he changed his mind about taking a detour to Ruapehu and stalking the ghosts of Harriet and Charles in a landscape of black volcanic ash. He slept that night in the valley and went on to Makara the next day.

The sky was overcast, and the beach café was appropriately called the Bitter End. When he asked if anyone knew of Max Suvorin he was quickly told where he could find him. 'You can't miss it, mate. Just look for the sign.'

Live life to the Max.

The faded, handwritten sign was nailed to a lamppost, and a driveway of crushed shell led to a Fibrolite bach that had seen better days.

Sam steeled himself for another disappointment. He was not only nervous about intruding on the privacy of a near stranger. He was also wary of what he might encounter.

Max had aged, of course, though his eyes were startlingly blue. Only his gaunt features, deeply lined face and liver-spotted hands testified to the work of time. And despite the impression Sam had been given of a hapless neurotic who had turned his back on the world, he quickly discovered that a fire still burned in Max Suvorin's soul, stoked by bitter memories, visionary experiences and voracious reading.

'*Two Sides of the Same Coin*!' Max proclaimed, astonishing Sam that the painter knew of his first novel.

'*West Coast Landscape*!' Sam said, though to little effect.

'They say you should never judge a book by its author,' Max said.

'I'm sure,' Sam replied, 'that I'm not the first writer to hope that his work will prove more interesting than he is.'

Max rarely had visitors, and was baffled by Sam Stillman's motive for calling on him. Rather than invite him into the house, Max suggested they take a stroll down to the beach.

And so it was that Sam found himself dogging the steps of this old man of the sea, climbing a steep track through gorse and matagouri and descending to a rocky foreshore where, southward across Cook Strait, the snow-capped Kaikouras were clearly visible. The going was not easy. Sam noticed how warily Max picked his way along the track, and how unsure of himself he seemed on the foreshore, dropping into a crouch and feeling his way around boulders until he found one on which to sit.

Sam's eyes now turned toward the distant range. Harriet had spent her childhood beyond that region of cloud and scree. And as Sam remembered the summers he had spent there and the life they had shared, he was filled with rage at the drunk who had taken her life, and the false friend who had clandestinely loved her for almost as long as he had, only to hold him accountable for taking her off life support.

'You okay?' Max asked.

Drawing his forefinger across one eye and down his cheek, smearing the tears, Sam endeavoured to compose his face.

'My wife died a year ago,' he said. 'It doesn't take much to set me off.'

'You sure you want to go on? We can go back if – '

Determined not to be an object of sympathy, Sam recounted how the staff at the Auckland Art Gallery had given him the impression that Max was a recluse who no longer painted.

'One supercilious young curator in a pinstripe suit and red bow tie was convinced you were dead.'

'Dead to his world, maybe, but not this one,' Max said, and gestured toward the sun glint on the sea, the weed-strewn rocks, the wind-flattened banks of matagouri.

'You may remember my wife, Harriet,' Sam said. 'She was a close friend of someone you were dating in Auckland around the time Harriet and I met.'

'Rachel Eisenstark.'

'Yes. What became of her?'

'She ran off with an English academic who had a fellowship at the University of Auckland. I think they went back to the UK and got married. At least that's what I heard. You're not alone in wondering what became of her.'

'You never kept in touch?'

'Why would I do that?'

'Sometimes love affairs metamorphose into friendships.'

'Yes, and sometimes they don't.'

The two men were now sitting on the same sea-smoothed boulder and watching two interisland ferries, heading in opposite directions, pass in the strait. Sam inhaled the brine-filled air. Offshore, a ragged patch of dirty foam rode the heaving sea. The bulldozer blade of a wave formed then broke with a hollow roar, flattening and falling back before gathering itself again for another onslaught.

'Did you and Harriet have children?' Max asked.

'We have a daughter. Zoe.'

'Life!'

'Yes, she's well named. I visited her a couple of days ago. She's a fresher at Auckland University.'

'I was also an only child. Perhaps I am only a child. I don't think I was ever capable of being a parent.'

The two men sat in silence, until Max suddenly asked if Sam had known Rachel.

'I knew that Harriet and Rachel were friends, but I don't think I ever met her. Not face to face, that is. Not as far as I can remember.'

'You might have had a lot in common.'

'How so?'

'Just a hunch. You never know.'

'Was there any truth in the rumour that you were sacked because you were having an affair with a student?' Sam asked.

'Is that what they were saying?

'I seem to remember something along those lines.'

Walking back along the foreshore, Sam observed a gull plunge sheer into the sea then surface with a fish in its beak, while another, flying low over the water, scooped up its prey and, with a wet slapping of its wings, made off into the splintering sun. When Sam drew Max's attention to what he had seen, Max's eyes remained fixed on the stony path. He dismissed the image of seagulls, as if it was an everyday occurrence and hardly worth remarking.

Though initially mystified by Sam's visit, and half inclined to turn him away, Max now knew what Sam was searching for, and no sooner had Sam driven off than Max regretted not offering him consolation in his loss. His regret, however, almost immediately gave way to a spate of memories, leaving him devastated by the power of the past to wound him.

That night he went through it all again, in thrall to a story that had no end.

He had always told himself that their first mistake was living together rather than keeping their own apartments. It visited an unwanted codependency upon them. Both felt stifled by the domestic adjustments they had had to make, deciding whose turn it was to shop or when they would eat dinner, or their trivial quarrels over clothes left lying on the floor or dishes left unwashed in the sink. Max needed long hours alone, not only to paint but to await the inspiration to paint, while Rachel needed time with her friends, to be free to come and go as she pleased. Within weeks of moving in with Max she was leaving notes on the kitchen table, saying she was working late in the lab or meeting some friends for drinks. If they made love, Max felt it was an act of pity or duty on Rachel's part, and he felt ashamed every time he imposed himself on her. When she muttered goodnight, he was reminded of the way one puts a slip of paper between the pages of a novel before laying it down on the night table and going to sleep.

He knew she was destined to leave him for a younger man, but when it happened, he felt cast away, like a piece of garbage or a broken toy. He could not paint. He could not sleep. If he lay down a dead weight settled on him, squeezing the life out of him. So deep was his hurt that he could easily understand why, in some countries, murder is treated as a crime of passion. He remembered a story someone had told him, of an abandoned wife who lured her husband's mistress to her house on the pretence of having a heart-to-heart talk, only to pull a knife on her, bind her wrists with rope, cut her clothes from her body and send the terrified woman into the street stark naked. He could not bear to think that Rachel was alive in a world that was now dead to him. He imagined her with the man who had displaced him. The thought of them clawing at each other, mouthing their romantic crap, filled him with renewed rage. He pictured himself plunging a knife into her without a qualm. It was like the drive to suicide, this drive to kill. A way of annulling the pain, even though he would be extinguished with it.

When Sam returned to the valley, he was aware that something had changed in him during his week away. He put it down to Zoe's joyful independence, his meeting with Max at Makara, his sense of liberation from his cloistered life. Playing the tape that Zoe had made for him reinforced this sense of new growth appearing on barren ground, and he hoped that a second visit to Makara hard on the heels of the first would not be pressing his luck.

To his surprise, Max seemed relieved to see him and this time ushered Sam inside, asking if he would like a cup of tea.

'I trust I'm not intruding,' Sam said, aware that he had become like a renunciant whose awkwardness with the spoken word reflected his difficulty with sociality itself. Even Max's friendly overtures could not dispel Sam's belief that he had no right to be alive.

'You're not intruding,' Max said. 'In fact, I'm happy you've come back. I felt bad about showing so little sympathy last time you were here.'

Sam followed Max inside, observing his torn tartan shirt and dungarees fastened around the waist with binder twine.

'If you're in the middle of something – '

'You're going to have to learn to stop apologising for yourself,' Max said. 'That's my job. Sit wherever you can. I realise the place is in a mess. I can't even find my own way around it.'

As Sam watched Max rinsing cups and clumsily prising open the lid of a Chinese tea caddy, he wondered how someone so maladroit could handle a paintbrush.

The explanation for Max's apparent uncertainty over where to place his hands or feet, or how to locate a cup, a doorknob or a light switch, or even where to focus his eyes when Sam moved about the room, was not long in coming.

The living room led into a studio roofed with transparent polycarbonate sheets. On a paint-spattered easel in the middle of the studio was a large painting. Its impasto surface was like a bed of anthracite or the surface of some planet of perpetual night – small hillocks, gulches and mesas of pitch-black paint squeezed straight from a tube. A heap of empty, thumbprinted and flattened paint tubes lay on the floor beneath the easel.

'Welcome to the world of dark matter,' Max said.

Sam placed his cup on the floor and bent to inspect the painting. As the light caught it from different angles, new features of the Stygian landscape appeared.

'This must be what it is like,' Sam said, 'to look back for the last time on one's life from the threshold of oblivion.'

'I can see why you're a writer,' Max said. 'And you're not wrong. My inspiration is Lao Tzu. Colour blinds us. Blackness allows us to see the truth.'

'Why blackness?'

'The blackness of dark matter, which can't be seen.'

Sam did not get what Max was telling him. He was too absorbed in a second painting that was leaning against the wall. Done in Indian ink with broad brushstrokes, the painting brought to mind kelp beds stirring in an underwater current, pumice stones, waving fronds of wrack, and a light source far above the surface of the sea.

'It's not what you see that matters,' Max said, 'it's what you feel.'

'I feel as though I am swimming through this painting,' Sam said. 'I can feel the currents. It's remarkable what you have achieved here.'

'Art is easy,' Max said. 'It's life that's hard. Years ago, when Rachel left me, I tried to lose myself in painting. I couldn't do it. I lost all will to work or live. I began drinking. Drowning my sorrows in a quart of whiskey a day. When you said you became an anchorite after your wife's death, I knew exactly what you meant. That urge to withdraw. Only for me it lasted more years than I care to remember.'

'And yet you found that will again,' Sam said. 'You did get back to painting.'

'Sure, but at a price.'

'Your work wasn't selling?'

'I sold enough. A couple of exhibitions. Some memorable reviews. Steady sales to private collectors. Nothing that led to fame or fortune. I lived on the smell of an oily rag, and still do, as you can see.'

'But you did turn things around – '

'Things turned around, yes. Whether I was the one who did the turning is another matter. I went to Hanmer Springs to dry out. But rehab wasn't what made the difference. It was something that happened after I returned to Auckland. I'd moved from Grafton Road to a flat in Mt Eden. Another alcoholic had the flat across the landing. Gin in his case, whiskey in mine. We knew each other's first names and exchanged small talk about the weather if we passed each other on the stairs, but we never really talked. Brothers of the bottle, you might say, though I saw him as the lost soul, not me. I went off to my studio every day. All he did was watch TV.

'Well, to cut a long story short, the poor bugger up and died. I hardly noticed the absence of gin bottles on the landing. And because our paths so seldom crossed, it never occurred to me that he was no longer in the land of the living. Ten days passed before he was found. The landlord was upset about the junk mail spilling out of his mailbox in the lobby, and the unpaid rent. I got home one evening to find police cars in the street, gaping neighbours, and an awful stench coming from his open door. His body had been taken away by the time I arrived on the scene, but I learned that he'd been found watching TV One. And someone mentioned that the entire front room of his flat was a beautifully sculptured and painted landscape with an electric train running through it. I remember asking if the train, like the television, had been running when he was found, but no one knew the answer, or they thought my question a bit weird. But I couldn't help wondering why he'd want to play with a toy train, and I could not get the image out of my head of this engine and its empty wagons going round and round in circles, getting nowhere.

'Anyway, I was deeply and inexplicably unsettled by this bloke's death. Maybe because he was my age. Maybe because I felt guilty about never asking him over for a drink or getting to know his name, which I later discovered was Jay. A couple of days after his body was found, a notice appeared in the foyer announcing the funeral at St Alban the Martyr Church. Everyone was welcome, and there'd be a reception afterward in the church hall. The notice was signed, Auckland Steam and Model Railway Club. Though I had misgivings about gatecrashing a private gathering, I went anyway. There was quite a crowd at the wake, as well as at the reception. And everyone was friendly and thanked me for coming. I thought they must be Jay's family, but they were all from his club. In fact, Jay had severed all connections with his family thirty-five years ago. I also found out that Jay had worked as an electrical engineer for the Shaw Savill shipping line during its last decade of operations and sailed to every corner of the world. When he left the sea, he worked as an electrician for Farmer's department store. He was the artist that built the miniature railway on the third floor. And I learned that in his youth Jay had been madly in love, and when this woman broke up with him, he was desolated and never entered into another relationship with a woman. He was likeable, I was told, but pig-headed.'

As Max went on with his story, Sam was wondering why some people fall apart in a crisis, while others seem to discover some inner strength. He remembered the night Harriet was killed, when a nurse had offered him a brandy to 'keep up his spirits'. He had refused, with words to the effect that he did not want to dull his senses, to run away from what had happened. Perhaps unconsciously he knew at that moment that he was in danger of becoming like his mother. Maxim Suvorin had accepted the brandy and come to depend on it, trying to hide, yet hounded by what he could not escape.

'Do you think pig-headedness can explain why one person survives a tragedy, but another person doesn't?' Sam asked.

'To go back to Jay's funeral,' Max said, 'a few days after it I got a letter from someone who'd been a mate of his during his years on the Shaw Savill boats. He hadn't spoken to me at the funeral, but he'd noticed me and thought from my face that I had lost a close friend. He wanted me to know that Jay hadn't always been the person who cut himself off from the world. "Jay and I were dealt very different cards in life, and our lives went in very different directions. But I always respected Jay, and felt great affection for him, even though he was too stubborn to listen to anyone else's advice and ended up drinking himself to death." Jay's friend enclosed a photo of Jay in his salad days, a slim and handsome young man, smiling bashfully in front of an immense K locomotive.

'It was like seeing myself as I had once been,' Max said. 'Or like seeing myself from afar, in another incarnation. It was like a conversion experience. As if I was suddenly liberated from my sick self and saw this other healthy self and wondered how I could leave my sick body and pass over into that other body. At the same time I was saying to myself, if you do not do this you will remain as you are for as long as you live, which probably won't be for long, and if you do it, even though it takes more resolution that you think you have, then you may still have a life. You won't have given your life away to someone like Rachel Eisenstark.'

'I sometimes ask myself,' Sam said, 'how far one needs to fall before one can begin to get back on one's feet. And how much one can accomplish alone.'

'You can do fuck all on your own,' Max said.

Again, Sam thought of his mother, wondering if he had given up on her too soon, shutting her out of his life as his father had shut him out of his.

'There was a doctor at Hanmer called Jameson,' Max continued. 'One of those people who isn't taken in by your bullshit. He got me to think back to when I was a child, to when I wasn't a piss-head. He told me, "You were different then. You've *become* like you are now. *You* changed, so *you* can change back."'

'Nothing happened overnight,' Max said. 'In fact, I checked out of the hospital and went up into the Wairarapa and found a hotel on the coast where I could hole up and drink. That first evening I went downstairs to the bar, intending to get blind drunk. But something stopped me in my tracks, and I walked straight through the bar and out onto the beach. It's all sand dunes there. Sand dunes for miles, peppered with fragments of moa eggshell and siliconised mangroves from a time when the climate was subtropical. The hills beyond the beach were getting dark as the sun went down. God knows how far I walked. But I began to feel the power of the landscape entering me. I felt small and insignificant, but I also felt a part of the land.

'That's when I knew my day of reckoning had come. For a long time I had had this monstrous black dog that went everywhere I went. How can I describe it? It was a dog but not a dog. I don't know whether I loved it or hated it. But I was so used to its presence that I couldn't imagine it not being there. Anyway, in the middle of the dunes, out of sound of the sea and with the darkness falling, I let it off the leash and screamed at it to scram. It didn't want to be abandoned, and kept coming back, licking my hand. I threw a stick at it, then a handful of sand. It turned away, and I turned away from it. And then it was gone.

'I felt free, but completely alone, mourning it, I suppose. But when I got back to Porangahau, my head was lifting off like the lid of a packing case, a ripping jangling sound like static. I thought I was going round the twist. But I was determined to stick it out, even if I did go mad. It took three days. And then the noises went away, and I went back to Hanmer and saw Jameson again and told him what had happened. And then, when I retold my story in a group session at the hospital, a Māori guy told me that Porangahau is based on the idea of a night, or te pō, and of rangahau, which means tracking something down. I knew then that I had been given another lease of life.'

Had Sam not doubted his own sanity many times in the aftermath of Harriet's death, he might well have ended his incipient friendship with Max Suvorin after his second visit to Makara. Instead, he continued to visit Max every weekend over the next few months, and even suggested they collaborate on a book in which a selection of Sam's recent prose poems would be interleaved with small abstract seascapes by Max. It could be published, if necessary, at Sam's expense.

Exasperated by Sam's ignorance of his condition, Max was obliged to spell out what should have been obvious to Sam all along: that he was suffering from advanced macular degeneration and could hardly see.

Sam's abject apologies fell on deaf ears. And when Sam reappeared at Max's door five days later, Max cynically asked if Makara had become his new place of penance. 'You may feel that you owe your late wife a debt you cannot repay,' Max said, 'but you owe me nothing.'

Despite Max's pleas to be left to his own devices, Sam found an advertisement in the Bitter End offering domestic help. It had been posted by a local woman, who agreed to buy provisions, do Max's laundry and clean the bach once a week. When Max protested, Sam explained that Max would be doing *him* a favour by accepting his help. An insurance settlement had been reached based on what Harriet would have earned had she lived. For Sam, the money was tainted by its association with Harriet's death, and though most of it would go into a trust fund for Zoe, it would bring him peace of mind to have some of his ill-gotten gains used to make Max's life sustainable and to build him a small pottery studio and kiln. In addition, Sam insisted on working with the City Art Gallery in Wellington to schedule a retrospective of Max's work. He even proposed collaborating with Max on a biographical essay for the exhibition catalogue. 'This isn't penance for anything,' he said. 'I'm doing us both a favour.'

RACHEL AND MAXIM

On the day Harriet Hempton was hit by a speeding car on a New Zealand country road, her old friend Rachel Murchison (née Eisenstark) signed her divorce papers in Cambridge, England – a coincidence that Sam would undoubtedly have found intriguing had he known of it. After all, it was Sam who once wrote that 'any story taken from life involves such curious concatenations that one would be hard pressed to say exactly where one person's story ended and another's began. Everyone's story contains others, like Chinese boxes.' Nor could Sam have been aware that had it not been for Rachel's divorce, she would never have taken seriously the invitation from the Wellington City Art Gallery to contribute to a catalogue for Maxim Suvorin's 2012 retrospective. And she might never have asked her college for compassionate leave and flown to New Zealand had not a Russian friend, in a common-room conversation, so poignantly raised the question of belonging. 'I feel as if my Russian self and my English self are like two weather fronts colliding inside me,' her friend said, 'passing right across my soul. It was easy to leave Russia behind for a new unknown world, but it has proved more difficult to leave behind the person with whom I shared my life there. How can one reconcile this passion to live one's own true life with one's sense of obligation to one's homeland?'

Rachel had no answer to Masha's dilemma, because it was also her own. What is this thing about Russia, she asked herself, that it should have inspired my research on memory, mediated my closest friendship at Cambridge, and figured in my adolescent affair with Max Suvorin? (She was thinking of A.R. Luria's 'little book about a vast memory', *The Mind of a Mnemonist.*) And why should I now waste my time on *him*, of all people, scraping together my recollections of him? I owe him nothing. As for his paintings, what could I say except that they were background to the life we shared for four years? I know these exhibitions. They are like rehearsals for the artist's death, when one can finally forget the real person and begin the work of creating his posthumous persona. I want no part of such an insidious rehabilitation, Maxim transmuted into an icon, his trespasses forgiven, his debts written off, his failings forgotten. I refuse the rebranding, the reincarnation of a flawed and tormented man as an uncompromising genius. Art critics may come up with smart and saleable labels for his work. It may no longer be written off as unclassifiable and crazy; but I will be no part of the makeover.

The last thing she did before locking her house in Owlstone Road was to sit at the piano. After straightening the sheet music, she placed the palm of her hand on the polished surface of the lid. Then she lifted the lid and gently laid her splayed fingers on the keyboard. It had been many months since she had played. But she found the notes as if guided by a ghost, unsure of herself at first, then, with growing confidence as she played the Chopin étude she had once taught her daughter to play. But her daughter was gone. And her husband had pillaged and burned the landscape of her life, leaving only ash.

She had become accustomed to look away. To glimpse herself in a bathroom mirror or plate-glass window was enough to bring home to her how shamefully dependent on him she had become. In love, as in loathing, one falls under a spell that can only be lifted by being alone. If she was to have a life, she would have to rediscover the person she had been before she met him.

Plagued by nightmares of her apartment filling with water, she felt like Alice, drowning in a pool of her own tears. She thought that if she swam underwater toward the front door she'd be able to surface there, take a deep breath, dive again and get out of the building. Then she realised that water had already filled the space between floor and ceiling, leaving her no air to breathe and no way out. Some nights she would try to avoid falling asleep for fear of yet another such nightmare. She would stand at the window and look down. The bamboo was black against the eastern sky. She was overcome with vertigo. There were no walls around her. Nothing secured or contained her. She fell back against the washbasin, grabbing the cold tap. I will not let myself be like this, she muttered. I will not exist in his shadow, as the one in the wrong, the abandoned one, carrying the burden of shame. What he could not give, I will not ask of anyone else.

Shattering though her divorce had been for her, its greatest impact had been on her daughter, who began neglecting her homework, staying out until the small hours of the morning, coming home drunk, vomiting in the toilet and refusing to get out of bed in the morning or go to school. Curfews were imposed and broken. Before Rachel fully comprehended what was happening, her daughter was drinking heavily every day and confronting her mother with an inane smile on her face as Rachel by turns berated her and begged her to consider the harm she was inflicting on herself. Lucy's volatile relationship with her boyfriend only exacerbated matters, and when he dumped her she fell apart completely. No one understood her. She hated her life. She hated Cambridge. At night, Rachel would hear her coughing and sobbing in her room. She would go to her, but her long, patient talks ended in Lucy's histrionic outbursts against her uncaring, stupid mother. 'I hate you. You've never been there for me. You don't understand a thing about me.' In desperation Rachel arranged for her to see a counsellor, but Lucy refused. She tried grounding Lucy and tested her urine every morning for traces of drugs. 'Do you realise how stupid you are!' Lucy railed. 'How farcical this is?' Despite the shouting, Rachel knew it was better that Lucy vent and rage against her mother than resort to dope or worse.

Then the unexpected happened. Rachel even ventured to call it a minor miracle. One Sunday Lucy went to church with a friend and was transformed. Saved, she said. The pastor had told the congregation that God wanted everyone to live their own lives and not be tempted or persuaded by what someone else thought they should do. It sounded corny, but Lucy had taken back her life and now wanted to determine her own path. Not succumb to peer pressure. Refuse the bong when it was passed around. Ignore the derision when she would not smoke or drink. She would focus on her work, collect money for the Red Cross or help raise public awareness of the dangers of climate change. But Lucy's salvation had come at a price. After months of being out of her mind with worry, Rachel had fallen into the habit of blaming her ex-husband for Lucy's unhappiness, imagining all the sins of omission, the lapses, the negligence that had culminated in his affair and their divorce. With Peter no longer around to vilify or blame, Rachel felt stifled by her own fury.

At the beginning of Lucy's college year Rachel drove her to Oxford, thinking she should help Lucy get settled. But no sooner had she parked her car than Lucy made it clear that she did not wish to be seen with her mother and that she wanted the moment of separation over and done with. Rachel found herself lugging her daughter's suitcases up a flight of stairs and trying to give her some last-minute advice, only to be rebuffed by a crowd of excited first-year students bearing Lucy away as though they were already best friends.

On the drive back to Cambridge Rachel experienced flashbacks – Lucy as a baby, Lucy starting preschool, Lucy arguing to have a butterfly tattooed on her ankle, Lucy with a tear-streaked, swollen face remonstrating with her and saying she wanted to die. Eighteen years had passed in the space of a day, and Rachel had been washed up on a windswept shore with nothing to look forward to and no way back. For several days, sick to her stomach, she could not eat. She would walk into Lucy's room with hot tears welling up, her chest and throat choked with emotion. The empty nest syndrome, they called it. It was worse than the divorce. And she struggled to remind herself that this was the beginning of her daughter's life, not the end of hers.

Her field was autobiographical memory – the mysteries of why we remember almost nothing before our third or fourth year of life, why time seems to gather speed as we grow older, why our childhood haunts seem so reduced in size and scale when we revisit them, why we remember life's humiliations more sharply than its joys, and why we believe that at the moment of death our whole life will flash before our eyes. In writing about these experiences, Rachel had used words like *fidelity* and *betrayal*, as if one's relationship to the past resembled one's relationship with a lover, a friend, or a spouse – ideally constant despite the vagaries and vicissitudes of life. 'Our closest relationships seem to undergo the same sea changes as our memories,' she had written. 'After decades together, we can no longer remember what we once saw in each other, or why we fell in love. Something akin to dementia obliterates the details of our shared life. Passion dies as memory dims. And there are times when we feel that we are aboard a bullet train, surrounded by pitch darkness, desperately searching for some still sanctuary of light in the black hills, where another existence awaits us.'

On the first leg of her flight to the Antipodes, lulled by the drone of the airplane and the long night, Rachel yielded to memories of the tawny stubble and dark pines of the Wairarapa. Though born and raised in Wellington, she had come to feel at home in the old homestead near Martinborough where she stayed every summer during her late teens with her close friend Holly. She remembered the day she walked past the Bee House for the first time on her way to the river for a swim, and a gangly individual dressed in a paint-blotched boiler suit had appeared out of nowhere with paintbrushes in his hand and playfully asked where she was going. Holly had already warned her away from him – the old soak whom Holly's father allowed to live in the Bee House in return for producing a painting of the homestead (a painting that never materialised). When Rachel asked Holly if she had actually seen any of his work, Holly shuddered, either at the thought of his paintings or the thought of him. 'What could someone like that create? Apart from ugliness.'

'But isn't that what Bohemians do?' Rachel retorted. 'Live on bread and dripping, and create things of great beauty?'

He asked how old she was and stood there, grinning at her.

'What's it to you?'

'It's an innocent question.'

'Eighteen,' she lied.

'You going to uni?'

'I'm starting next year.'

'To study what?'

'Psychology,' she said.

'Why psychology?

'I'm interested in people.'

'That makes you an interesting person,' he said.

Max's father was Russian, his mother a dyed-in-the-wool Kiwi (the phrase was his), and there were times when he was convinced that everything that had befallen him in life had been foreshadowed by his father's exile from Russia and his parents' disastrous marriage. Max's father had been conscripted into the White Army when he was twenty, or so he said, and fought the Reds in the Far East for three years before escaping Russia and joining the White émigré community in Hong Kong. In the late thirties he moved to Paris, where he met Max's mother. He approached her in a café and confessed that he'd been unable to take his eyes off her from the moment she had sat down. He begged her to appreciate his dilemma. He knew that nothing could be more unsettling for a beautiful young woman than the unwanted attentions of a stranger twenty-five years older than she was. But she was partly responsible; she had made him forget himself.

Alone in Paris, this young New Zealander was as captivated by this suave and handsome foreigner as she was afraid of what might happen if she responded to his overtures. But she was vain enough to want to know if his flattery was genuine, and made the fatal mistake of allowing him to buy her a drink. She was not inexperienced in the ways of the world, and she'd come to Paris half hoping for a love affair. But in this soi-disant Russian prince she met her match. And so did he, for with her refusal to give herself to him unless he married her, Nicolai Suvorin broke his vow never to settle down.

They lived for a while in Nice where he had 'contacts' – a conspiratorial assemblage of émigrés who slept by day and haunted each other's apartments by night, smoking Russian cigarettes, playing cards and plotting counter-revolution. Following the fall of France in 1941, and desperately homesick, Max's mother persuaded her shiftless husband to move with her to Wellington, where Max was born the next year. His earliest memories were of a windswept hillside covered with yellow gorse, of a moving ceiling of cloud that threatened to carry him away, and of a night when his father came into his room not to recount one of his stories from the steppes of Central Asia but to say he'd been called away and didn't know when he would be back. Max remembered throwing his arms around his father and pleading with him not to go. But Nicolai Suvorin's voice was theatrically grim as he exhorted his son to be brave. 'I must go,' he said. 'The matter is out of my hands.'

Max could hear his mother in the next room, weeping so uncontrollably that he struggled to hold back his own tears in the belief that this would alleviate her grief.

Max's father came back to New Zealand from time to time, but just as unpredictably he would disappear again, and when Max asked his mother where he'd gone, and for how long, he was told that his father had gone away because his life was in jeopardy. This word bothered him. He would go over the phonemes and their associations in his head as he walked to school – leopards, pardons, parties, leapt – conjuring exotic and improbable images of his father escaping his Red enemies. In *Alice in Wonderland* he found confirmation of the heroic battle between white and red that his father had alluded to, and he fantasised about falling down a rabbit hole into a fabulous and exotic world where his father was enthroned or fighting the Bolsheviks.

Max's mother told him to forget. Many of Nicolai's family had been assassinated before the war, and if the Reds discovered his whereabouts, who knew what might happen to him, or to them? Max was sworn to silence. To mention a word about his father at school or to his friends might jeopardise his safety. It never occurred to Max that his mother was struggling to hide her shame, her lacerating remorse at having ruined her life. Nicolai wrote from Java, from Bali, from San Francisco, sending his wife money orders, telling her to buy herself something nice. She gave the stamps to Max and gave the money to charity. She wanted nothing from him. She wanted everything from him. She vowed never to marry again.

Rachel's initial reaction to Max's account was that he was proposing they replay his parents' story as if, through some kind of magical abreaction, *their* unfortunate history might be rewritten and *his* life might be redeemed. Though Max's mother had allowed herself to be conned by Nicolai Suvorin, Rachel was determined not to be seduced by his son. Yet within days she was falling for this man, old enough to be her father. By the time she moved to Auckland to attend university they were lovers, and within a year Max followed her north and found a part-time teaching job at the art school.

As the aircraft droned through the night, and the women on either side of her slept bolt upright with blankets drawn over their heads, Rachel stared at the blank screen in front of her, recalling the names of the paintings Max had finished that first year of their affair: *Blind Corner. Fiery Furnace. Pillar of Salt. Lakes Entrance.* Each name dissolved into an image: making love on the shingle beach at Lakes Entrance, his sunburned face and neck, the scrawny body that never saw the sun. In the water, then, their legs and arms entangled, bodies wedded beneath the surface, her lips sealed with his and in her nostrils the sour tang of the water.

She gasped as she realised how long ago these traces had been lost, more scar tissue than memory.

She pulled Orhun Pamuk's *The Museum of Innocence* from the seat pocket and tried to read, but she could not get past his observation that 'the longing for art, like the longing for love, is a malady that blinds us, and makes us forget the things we already know, obscuring reality'. She marked the page with her boarding card and shoved the book back into the seat pocket, now knowing why she had been unable to write anything usable for the exhibition catalogue. 'We want the focus to be on Max's art,' Anne Merriweather, the curator, had written. 'There will be biographies, of course. But for the moment we want to foreground the paintings. I know you do not write on art, but as someone who knew him intimately during a critical phase of his career, I am sure you will have important insights into his oeuvre.'

But Rachel could see neither Max nor his work dispassionately. Both dwelled in her, not apart from her, as indefinable and fleeting as an aftertaste, or the odour that clings to discarded clothing.

Convinced that Anne Merriweather was less interested in what she might have to say about Maxim Suvorin than in her Cambridge affiliation, Rachel resolved to avoid any encounter or conversation with the curator. She wanted to see the retrospective. She wanted to visit her mother's grave. Beyond that, she thought vaguely of hiring a car, driving around the country, and seeing where the road might take her.

Her steps echoed in the gallery's white spaces. She could have been at the Hermitage or the Tate. But within seconds of standing in front of the first work – *Road Sign* – she was home, in a landscape she knew by heart, more deeply ingrained in her psyche and senses than anywhere else in the world, despite her twenty years away. Most of all, she was with Max again, remembering him joking about the Bee House ('Not B House. *Bee* House, as in honey bee') and explaining that the owners of the homestead had used the old worker's cottage to store frames and process the honey from their hives, the wax forming an impasto on the matai floorboards, the honey permeating every room, tinting the windows amber. She remembered racks of unframed canvases, the paint-encrusted floorboards, badger-hair brushes crammed into jam jars, and the sun-baked plain beyond the open French doors, the air redolent with dry grass and pines.

She saw Max's canvases as if through a glass darkly. The life course of their friendship was laid out here, each work a cryptic allusion to a place or event in their shared past. She read into every canvas, every painted board, every collection of found objects, some experience they had undergone together. She was reminded of things she had forgotten: his passionate identification with Cézanne, the pilgrimage he made to Aix-en-Provence (the only time, as far as she knew, that he had left New Zealand), the depth of his feeling for the Wairarapa, his startling vision – the world reduced to a fragment of pine bark, a single pine needle, the surface of a river stone, an indecipherable letter on a yellow ground. And yet the work refused any specific reading. Veiled messages could be projected onto the paintings, but they defied interpretation. The landscapes were bereft of anything personal, any sign of life. No portraits, no suggestion that anyone inhabited these places, or haunted them. No evidence that anyone had handled these stones, fenced these paddocks, walked under these pines, painted these signs. The beauty of his canvases lay in their emptiness.

She had to sit down to deal with her emotions, to take stock. She returned to the first gallery where a black upholstered bench was placed in the middle of the room, positioned to offer a view of the great triptych *Wairarapa*, with its hints of stippled sunlight on a vast lake beneath a cloudless sky.

When she heard her name, she thought she was deceived – or that Anne Merriweather had found her.

'Rachel, is that you?'

She half turned, then stood.

'Holly?'

'My God, it *is* you! What in heaven's name are you doing here?'

'I could well ask you the same question.'

'I thought you were in England.'

'I am. I was. I came to see Max's show.'

'Were you at the opening?'

'I couldn't stand the thought of it. All that chardonnay and cheese. Not being able to see the paintings for the people. I snuck in this morning, thinking I'd be alone.'

'Same here. I came in yesterday for a while. It was rather overwhelming. So I thought I'd take a second look today. Then who do I meet but you!'

'Me and Max both. In the same room.'

'In the same room. I can't believe it. How *are* you?'

'I'm fine, considering. You?'

'Oh, you know me. Boxing on.'

Holly was wearing a black suit. Her hair was pulled back from her forehead and tied with a red ribbon.

'Black becomes you.'

'It's my job. I have to look professional. No colour.'

'I wasn't being critical. You look fabulous.'

'Why thank you, Rachel. At our age one does not look for compliments, but one hopes for them.' As Holly tentatively placed her hand on Rachel's arm and laughed, Rachel half expected her old friend to tell her that she didn't look a day older. Something flattering, if dishonest. But as if the spot they were standing on had suddenly become a bed of hot ashes, they moved off, peering at the paintings, respecting the taped white line.

'Remember that day at the Pinnacles?' Holly asked, nodding at the work titled *Lot's Wife*.

Rachel did not respond. Holly had detested Max and derided Rachel for falling for him. A dirty old man. A bloody rogue.

'Have you two kept in touch?' Holly asked.

Again, Rachel could not find the words she needed.

'There was a piece about him in the *Dominion* last week,' Holly went on. 'He's practically blind, you know. Lives out at Makara, I think. I saved the article, if you want to read it.'

Rachel moved toward *Wind Gusts*, remembering the road, the air filled with the stitch of cicadas.

'Blind?'

She was in a daze. Though she wanted to know more, she did not trust anything Holly said.

'Until this morning, I had forgotten everything,' Rachel said. 'The paintings have brought it back. And now you materialise, out of thin air, as if my remembering brought you back to life.'

'But in black,' Holly said. 'Back in the day, you were the one who wore black.'

'My daughter wears nothing else,' Rachel said. 'Gothic punk. I sometimes wonder if our children inherit our shadows.'

'You have children?'

'Just one. Lucy. And you?'

'Mark's fifteen. Angela's eleven. I would love for you to meet them.'

'That would be nice.'

Holly suggested they go somewhere for coffee. There was a place across the road. It would give them more privacy than the gallery café.

'As long as it's not Suzy's,' Rachel said.

Holly laughed. 'It's not Suzy's now. It's called Grounds for Happiness.'

As they walked toward Panama Street, Rachel commented on how much the city had changed. Holly said she hadn't noticed. 'Living in the city, seeing it every day, year in and year out, you don't really notice the changes, or remember what things were like before the changes began. But then, change is always going on, isn't it? Like with one's kids. I hardly remember what they were like when they were babies. One lives in the present. When they leave home, maybe then I'll start to look back.'

Rachel hesitated to share. Besides, she was trying to get used to this person she thought she knew.

They waited for a bus to pass then crossed the road to the café. Both ordered lattes before finding a seat near the window.

'You're quite famous,' Holly said, almost as a question.

'Famous? For what?'

'Word gets around. And there's the internet. Our spy network, Bob calls it. I looked up your Cambridge web page. I wouldn't have recognised you from your photo.'

'I cheat. I use a photo taken ten years ago.'

'And I dye my hair.'

'I would never have known.'

'So, do you have photos? Of your Lucy?'

'Of Lucy, no, I didn't think to bring any. But you must show me yours.'

'I can do better than show you photos. I can arrange to have you meet them. How long are you going to be in Wellington?'

'I haven't decided.'

'Then let me decide for you. What is it today? Thursday. No, Wednesday. So how about Saturday? For lunch. We can do something in the afternoon together. Drive up the Kapiti Coast if the weather's okay. I remember you loved it there.'

'That'd be nice.'

'Good. Now let's talk about you.'

'You probably know all you need to know about me from my web page.'

'I mean gossip, Rachel. The stuff we hide. Like why you should come all this way to see Max's work if you didn't want to see him.'

'Did I say I didn't want to see him?'

'No, but you didn't say you did.'

Rachel told Holly how she had been asked to contribute an essay to the exhibition catalogue. How it didn't work out. How it had led her to toy with the idea of writing a memoir about her early life. How this, in turn, had led her to mull over some of the what-ifs and might-have-beens of life. 'It's uncanny running into you,' Rachel said. 'Please forgive me if I say I had not planned to look you up. Or Max. Or anyone. I can't believe I am here. Seems it was only yesterday we were running wild at your parents' homestead and you were pissed off at me for getting involved with Max. It's like I've died and returned to a previous incarnation.'

'It's good to have you back, Rachel. Can you believe it? The way we bumped into each other. Talk about coincidence!'

Rachel was beginning to warm toward Holly, even feel glimmerings of the affection that had bound them together in high school. Without the severe outfit and the swept-back hair, Rachel thought, she could pass for someone in her late thirties, someone in whose soul a fire still burns. Something has been resolved in her. She does not run for cover. That judgmental side of her has gone.

After they finished their coffees Rachel walked Holly to her parking garage on Jervois Quay. Though Holly asked where Rachel was staying, she did not extend an invitation to stay with her. 'So,' she said, 'let's say Saturday, at noon. Come earlier if you like. And if you want a lift from your hotel, just call. Either Bob or I would be happy to drive down and save you the walk.'

'Walking's fine,' Rachel said. 'I need the exercise. Besides, I need to get to know the city again.'

That evening she rang Holly to cancel their weekend meeting, pleading jet lag. But when she asked Holly if she knew Max's exact address, her cover was blown. 'You haven't changed,' Holly said. 'I knew it as soon as I saw you in the gallery this morning. Coming all the way from England to see his paintings. I knew you'd come to see him. I knew you didn't want to see me. When did you ever?'

She could not argue. 'I'm sorry,' she said, and closed her phone.

Next day she hired a car and drove to Makara. We will be strangers to each other, she told herself. There will be nothing to say. I will drive back along this same road this afternoon, having accomplished nothing. But I will have laid a ghost. I will not have to live with the memory of someone who probably never forgave me for leaving him.

She parked on the foreshore and walked a little way along a beach strewn with driftwood. She watched the toiling waves, their eternal curving act, and remembered her battle to get away, to escape his shadow. His jealous rants and abrupt withdrawals. His child-like pleas that he could not live without her. 'Don't you see,' she told him, 'my whole life is you! I have to exist in my own right. I came to you too young. I have grown old before my time.' Why then should she now be risking all that she had gained by tracking down the person who had held her spellbound for so long, to whom she had sacrificed the best years of her youth?

Determined to get it over with, she retraced her steps to the car. As she felt in her jacket pocket for her car keys she suddenly changed her mind. Uttering a small cry of exasperation she set off toward Max's bach, following the directions the woman in the café had earlier given her.

A mailbox bearing the name 'Suvorin' in black handwritten letters had been nailed to a macrocarpa tree. Clumsily painted on the lintel above the plywood door she made out the faded words 'Live Life to the Max'. She was trembling now, trying to work out what she would say, and suddenly aware he might not be able to see her.

When he answered her knock it was as if he saw right through her, as if she were invisible – she the spectre, not he. The nearby sea hissed, withdrawing from the stony beach.

There was shock, too, at his appearance. He had aged terribly, collapsed in on himself. His blue eyes were clear but clearly unseeing, his hair uncombed and beard peppery.

He showed no surprise, only offering a matter-of-fact invitation to come in if she could get past the junk. It occurred to her that he hadn't the faintest idea who she was and that she should tell him. But she could not bring herself to do so, and waited, as he sought and found his armchair and sank into it.

'It's Rachel Eisenstark,' she said.

He did not respond.

'Rachel from Cambridge,' she said.

'Yes,' he said, 'I don't need to be reminded. You're the only Rachel I know.'

'I think you're the only Max I know.'

'So, what brings *you* back, stranger?'

'Your retrospective,' she said.

'A concession to those who have no prospects,' he said.

'It must be awful for you,' she said, casting her eyes over the shelves above the kitchen counter, looking for something she might usefully do, like make a pot of tea.

'Only when people feel sorry for you.'

'I didn't mean that.'

'Compassion, then? When you become an object of people's compassion.'

'Do you mind if I make a cup of tea?'

'Help yourself. There's some teabags on the fridge.'

Waiting for the water to boil, she asked trivial questions, killing time. How long he had been there. When he had moved from Auckland. She told him she'd run into Holly.

His curt answers made her feel as if she was interrogating him, or as if he was waiting for her to get the message and leave.

After placing a mug between his hands, she sat at a small Formica dining table, wondering whether they had already exhausted all possibility of closing the gap.

'So what about you, Rach? Still at Oxford?'

'Cambridge.'

'Still married to that English joker?'

'Divorced.'

He sipped his tea. 'Who dumped who?'

'Does it matter? Though if you must know, I was the injured party.'

'The injured party,' he repeated. 'Is that the legal term for it?'

She had expected anger and resentment and was determined not to take it personally. She was not at fault.

She drew a deep breath, and plunged back in. 'When I said it must be awful, I meant it must be hard fending for yourself, especially out here – '

'It's not all that bad. A local woman comes by every day to clean up and prepare a meal. And I have a few good friends. In fact, you probably know one of them. I call him my Good Samaritan. He helped build my pottery studio and the kiln. I suspect he was the brains behind my retrospective. He was married to Harriet Hempton, that girl you did psychology with in Auckland – '

'Harriet? Is she in Wellington?'

'Not anymore. She was victim of a hit-and-run accident. You didn't know?'

'You mean she's dead?'

'Yeah, she's dead.'

'Oh, my God – '

Max did not see her cover her face with her hands. He went on as if she was still breathing, still able to speak.

'My pension is more than enough to pay the rent and buy the few things I need at the store. Sam flogs my paintings on the art market, which gives me a windfall from time to time. My main difficulty is getting my hands on the clay I need.'

She was aware that he could not see her grief.

'For sculpture, you mean?' she stammered.

'What?'

'The clay. You need it for sculpture?' she said, forcing the words from her throat.

She looked toward the window. The salt sting of her tears and the unwashed panes gave the impression that mist had drifted in from the sea, cocooning them.

She went to the sink. It was smeared with clay, filled with wizened tea bags, cracked cups, unwashed plates. Does he really have a cleaning woman? She remembered the Bee House and how she could not resist cleaning up his mess. Their first argument had been over her need to rehabilitate him. She rinsed her tannin-stained cup, inverted it on the draining board, and left it at that.

'Do you think we could go for a walk?' she asked, desperate to be elsewhere, even though it would be with him.

He rose from his armchair and felt his way to the door, where he took a torn Drizabone from the hook, slipped it on, and asked Rachel to hand him his cane.

'Shouldn't we lock up?' she asked.

'I've nothing anyone would want,' he said. 'And I trust people here.'

She led the way, Max on her arm, down the overgrown driveway.

'I'm sorry if I say the wrong things,' she said. 'It's been a long time.'

'Look at it my way, Rachel. I see vague shapes. I can tell the difference between night and day. And I hear the sea, day and night. I smell it. I listen to the gulls. And I have my clay, that I pound and thumb and cut and throw. I want for nothing.'

She asked him how it happened.

'Does it matter how? Does understanding something help you live with it?'

She focused on negotiating the path, holding back some sodden fern fronds so he could pass.

'Is it true,' she asked, 'that you develop other senses?'

'Ah, the famous sixth sense.'

'I wondered if the other senses compensated, that's all.' She felt foolish and out of her depth.

'No,' he said. 'Nothing compensates. Least not for me. The answer's in appreciating what you still have, not in bemoaning what you've lost.'

As they pressed on along the coastal track, Rachel asked Max to tell her when he was ready to turn back. He was happy to keep going, he said. He didn't get out as much as he'd like. So they walked on, arm in arm, until Rachel suggested they stop and find somewhere out of the wind.

They sat without speaking, Rachel with closed eyes, her face lifted to the sun. She was listening to the sea's unflagging inhalations and exhalations on the beach and thinking of Harriet, trying to summon her from the mists and explain to herself why they had lost touch.

'Why so quiet?' Max asked.

Rachel took her eyes off the distant Kaikoura Range, the cloud formations on the horizon, the surface of the sea, and asked if it was still possible to dive for pāua.

She was remembering the times they had driven out to Auckland's west coast beaches together. Diving for pāua and kina. Cooking the seafood in a pan over a driftwood fire. Sharing a bottle of beer. Walking for hours, windblown, across iron-sand dunes and hills. But she did not risk confiding her thoughts to him, wounding him with memories.

'Well,' he asked, 'you going in or not?'

'I haven't brought my swimmers, or a towel.'

'Is there anyone here but us?'

'Not as far as I can see.'

'Then I won't look if you don't.'

She would have to get used to the fact that he had not lost his sense of irony, was not a victim.

She stripped to her bra and panties, he to his jeans. He held out his hand. She took it and led him to the sea that slathered around their ankles, much colder than she had anticipated. It was impossible to keep their footing on the stones. The water chilled her to the bone and she had to let go of his hand as she stumbled toward deeper water. Before plunging in, she turned to warn him that the water suddenly deepened in front of him.

He said nothing, groping his way forward. But once in the water he was her equal, and they swam in tandem through beds of dark brown bladder kelp and into the breaking waves.

'I'm diving,' she shouted.

Underwater, no longer buffeted, she allowed her body to be taken by the current. Kelp caressed her, slippery, leathery. Stones and seaweed, anemones and limpets gave her the impression of an enchanted garden, the water tinged with green, like bottle glass. She surfaced, gulped in air, dived again, pulling herself down into a crevice, along the flank of a boulder, looking for pāua.

Again she surfaced. Again she was overwhelmed by this feeling of being in her element, stripped and cleansed.

Several yards away, Max was treading water.

She called his name and said she was going further out.

She pulled herself strongly beyond the breakers, then turned to see the immense hill rising above the beach, studded with flax stalks and giant aloes. Clouds like cotton spilled from seamless bales.

Max had mentioned that the kai moana had been plundered, and he was right. A solitary octopus was all she saw, holding its ground as her hands moved toward it.

She was breathless when she returned to him.

'Poseidon,' she said, laughing. 'You look like Poseidon.'

They supported each other into the shallows, slipping on submergèd stones, clambering back to the beach. She was glad he could not see her. And she averted her eyes from his sagging body and bedraggled hair in a vain attempt to equalise the situation.

Within minutes her drying skin was taut with salt.

'It doesn't seem fair that I can see you and you can't see me,' she said, slipping her dress over her head and thinking of what she looked like now, having borne a child, having weathered so many years.

'I do see you, Rachel. In my mind's eye, and through your voice. Your hand guiding me into the water. Some things don't change.'

'Except the pāua,' she said.

'Who needs pāua?'

'I do. I'm hungry.'

On the way back to the bach he bade her gather small pieces of pumice and shell toggles.

As she made toasted sandwiches with sliced tomatoes and sweet corn, sprinkled with cracked pepper and Italian parsley, he rummaged in a chest of drawers for a bradawl and began boring into a piece of pumice. Then she cleared the table, quietly in case he objected to his papers and spatulas being moved where he would not be able to find them.

'Whenever you're ready,' she said.

On the beach it had been easy to talk. Now she felt inhibited again.

'Where do you do your work with clay?' she asked.

'In the studio Sam built.'

'Do you have a wheel?'

'Go through and have a look.'

She did, half-eaten sandwich in hand. She saw the bulbous ceramic pots, craters and urns and rubbed her hand across unglazed, gritty surfaces. She came back to the dining table and asked how he fired them.

'Like I told you,' he said, 'I've got a kiln.'

The light was fading now, the shadow of the hill engulfing the house.

'I admire the way you cope,' she said.

'Man is a creature that can get used to anything. Isn't that the line? That line from Dostoevsky you were always quoting.'

'Yes, except I said woman!'

'I have had this gift all my life, Rachel. I used to think it was a curse. Not being able to forget. Having perfect recall. Without it I might well have been unable to cope, bereft of my vision. As it is, I retain an exact picture of every square inch of this house and the paths around it, just as I remember you. I can sense you now, the smell of your body, your hair, the sound of your footfall. When you were making the sandwiches, I could see you perfectly. I knew you wanted to clean up, to rearrange things, to bring some order into the house. I could feel you struggling not to, struggling with the memory of how we used to argue over such things. And as I drilled holes in the pumice and braided the flax we bought back from the beach, I was struggling too.'

'Against what?'

'Not against anything. Struggling to believe you are actually here. That I am not hallucinating.'

'Because I turned up out of the blue?'

'The indigo, Rachel. The dark blue. The blue of night.'

'I will have to go soon,' she said. 'But I will come again, if you don't mind.'

He pushed back his chair and went to where he had placed the pumice and shell necklace. He handed it to her. 'It needs finishing,' he said. 'But it will serve as a souvenir if you don't come back.'

She thanked him, then paused. 'Could you tell me something about Harriet?' she said. 'How long ago did she – '

'I only know what Sam's told me, and that's not a lot. I think he's still in mourning. But you could always ask him. He lives up in the Manawatu. I'll give you his address if you're interested.'

She squeezed his hand and left, returning to her car where she sat for a long time, looking out at the darkening sea, a necklace of lights along the Kapiti Coast, the black whale bulk of the hills, the first stars appearing in the sky. She really did want to know about Harriet, but not from some stranger. It was not a narrative of Harriet's life she wanted to hear; it was Harriet she wanted to see. But nothing anyone told her would turn time back on its tracks and make that reunion possible.

Back at her hotel Rachel read emails from another world, including one from Lucy asking what on earth she was doing in New Zealand.

What *was* she doing here? She threw herself down on the bed and stared at the ceiling. She thought of Lucy, awakening to her life as she yearned to be reawakened to hers. She thought of Cambridge in its midwinter grip, and her unfinished monograph on the mysteries of memory. She thought of Harriet, and of the difference between losing touch with someone you assume to be alive and losing forever the possibility of seeing that person again. Did I write Harriet out of my life, along with Max and New Zealand, effectively dying to them? Or did I deep down keep faith with them, knowing that I would one day return and reconnect? Things change. The pāua gets plundered. Places change without heeding us, just as we change without heeding them, and to return to anywhere that was once part and parcel of one's life is to be reminded painfully that the world goes on without us and we are destined for anonymity. She rolled to the side of the bed and thought of showering, of standing in the shower until she was calm, but she could not bring herself to sponge the sand from between her toes, wash the salt from her skin, shampoo the spume from her hair. She did not want to expunge those residues of the coast. She wanted to dwell on them, dream of them, lose herself in them, and not go back.

On her second visit to Max she brought cornflowers, ground coffee, Vogel's bread, fresh salad ingredients and mangoes. Max said she shouldn't have bothered. 'Please don't bring *things*,' he said as she placed the flowers in a jam jar and prepared fresh coffee. 'I don't want you buying stuff I don't need.'

'What if it gives me pleasure?' she said.

'You sound like Sam.'

'Do I? And who do you sound like, Max?'

'Do what you like, then. You always did.'

She ignored the remark. She made sandwiches. Then they left the house and retraced their steps of two days before to a stony beach where they sat under a flax bush, out of the wind.

She had not bothered with makeup. She was wearing jeans and a white blouse. She passed him a sandwich before turning her face with closed eyes toward the sea.

Max was the first to break the silence.

'You said your husband left you.'

'He found someone else. A younger someone else.'

'What goes around – '

'Comes around,' she said, completing the cliché. 'I should have known you'd say something like that.'

'I didn't mean to imply that you were to blame.'

'Perhaps no one is at fault in these cases,' Rachel said, 'despite our tendency to apportion blame. I certainly blamed myself. For not being a good enough wife. For not being worthy of love.'

'It was the same for me when you left for England. Yet unlike you, I blamed everyone but myself. Blamed you for letting me down. Though I always knew you'd have to go, that you'd die if you stayed. I'm sorry about your husband. He was unworthy of you. But you're a survivor, Rachel, like me.'

'You think so?'

'Birds of a feather. Washed up on the rocks like a couple of uprooted trees.'

'I'm not sure which metaphor works best. But I get the message.'

She was stunned by the familiarity she felt, despite her years away, with Max and the wind-blown hills that descended to that wild coast, bearing the scars of winter storms, torn seaweed, shattered driftwood, broken shells and carapaces among the sea-worked stones. She could not account for how the place she called home could be suddenly eclipsed, replaced by this aboriginal elsewhere inhabited by people she had written off as dead. How could she have put it all so completely from her mind?

She did not like to look at him for long. It was too much like staring. Max was unable to look back. But she looked at him now with emotions she could not name. Pity? Compassion? Love? This ancient mariner, his matted hair and beard, his dark green Swanndri and shapeless corduroys. Except he had no pressing story to tell, nothing he had to unburden himself of. No albatross.

'Penny for your thoughts?' he said.

'I was thinking,' she said, 'of how one can forget whole swathes of one's life, then remember them again with such overwhelming vividness.'

'Like what?'

'This place. Harriet Hempton, when we were students in Auckland. You.'

'But if you're remembering me, you're not seeing the person I am now.'

'You haven't changed, Max. Despite the fact that you have.'

'Can I touch your face, Rachel? To see if you are still the person I remember.'

'That would be only to touch the surface. I'm not talking about appearances. Not what we look like.'

She edged toward him as he stretched out his open hands. She was aware of the strange similarity between handing him a cup and placing her head between his hands, of being held.

His fingers moved across her face as her fingers had moved across the keyboard of Lucy's piano the day she left Cambridge. He ran his fingers through her hair, dislodging her hairband only to dexterously smooth it back into place. Gently he touched her eyebrows. His forefinger traced the line of her mouth. He caressed her neck. She had the impression she was like one of the stones on the beach or one of his clay urns.

'You'll find plenty of lines,' she said.

'It's what can be read between the lines that matters.'

When they returned to the bach Max asked if she would cut his hair. She demurred. She didn't know how. She would make a mess of it.

'A worse mess than it's in now?'

'Don't you remember how you hated me trying to tidy you up?'

'This is me trying to tidy myself up, Rachel. Please. There's scissors in my studio. Jar on the table to the left as you go in.'

She had him bend over the kitchen sink with a towel around his neck and shoulders while she shampooed him with a cake of laundry soap. After rinsing, he sat at the dining table while she moved around him, sizing him up, combing out knots, figuring how to use comb and scissors together as she'd seen in salons, where to make the first cut.

It proved to be less difficult than she'd imagined. She was pleased with her handiwork.

'You look ten years younger,' she said. 'And now that you look presentable, I have a favour to ask. I would like to see your retrospective again, but with you. If I came back tomorrow, would you – '

'There is no one else I would say yes to. Sure I'll go. You can be my guide.'

'Your seeing-eye dog.'

'My Braille. My white stick.'

She was surprised that they could laugh about such things.

When she picked him up the following day, she hardly recognised him. Not only was his hair shorn, but he had shaved off his beard and was wearing a plaid shirt and pressed trousers. 'My disguise,' he explained. 'If we're going to the gallery I don't want to be recognised. That bloody opening was enough to last me a lifetime.'

Climbing the Makara road in second gear she had a sudden vision of them dodging curators, like a couple of schoolkids sharing a furtive cigarette behind the bike sheds. Yet wasn't this what had drawn them together all those years ago? His irreverence reinforcing her love of mischief, the anarchic cocktails they mixed. On the night of the Four Square grocers' annual ball, they snuck in a back door, located the main switchboard and killed the lights. As pandemonium broke out, they slipped into the street and fled, shrieking with laughter.

She wondered when this part of her had died. When the fun had gone out of her life. Or was it youth that had given way to middle age?

'Did I mention that I came back to Wellington when my mother died?' Rachel said.

'You didn't think to get in touch?'

'I wasn't thinking much at all. I had to organise the funeral, sort through her things and put her house on the market. I toyed with the idea of staying longer, but – '

'Your heart was in England.'

'Perhaps. Even then I suspected that Peter wanted something he could not find in our marriage. For all I know, he was already looking for someone else.'

She could no longer drive and talk. She pulled over to the edge of the narrow road. There was a sagging fence, lank grass, and a steep hill terraced with sheep tracks descending into a valley of shadows.

'The truth is,' she said, 'I don't think I ever really recovered from Mum's death. It probably changed my feelings toward Peter, which changed his feelings toward me. My heart had been broken, Max, and I didn't know how to piece together the broken shards.'

'Give me your hand,' he said.

She offered both hands, trembling, and he took them between his own and held her.

'When I went to England with Peter, all those years ago, it never crossed my mind that I was losing anything. My mother. My motherland. But what about you, Max? Did you ever think you might flourish somewhere else?'

'Never. Everything I needed was here. Right before my eyes.'

'I wish I could say the same,' Rachel said. Then, because nothing was going to be resolved on that narrow windswept road, she pulled away from him and started up the car, as if moving might lift the darkness that had stolen over her.

It seemed to work. By the time they entered the art gallery her thoughts were no longer centred on her own dilemmas, but on Max. Holding his arm she led him around the exhibition, telling him what she was looking at and what it brought to mind. *Pillar of Salt* … Lot's wife, Orpheus and Eurydice. 'You are right,' she said. 'Looking back is dangerous. The past turns you to stone.'

'Like art,' he said. 'You begin with something alive and you petrify it for all eternity. Those limestone pinnacles were once a sea floor, brimming with life. How can we undo the spell that has been cast on us by history? How can we kiss or paint life back into being?'

She did not want to question him too deeply, to pry. Certainly she did not want to comment on the phallic presence of those limestone fingers.

'What are we looking at now?' he asked.

'Your triptych,' she said. '*Wairarapa*.'

'I wanted to call it *The Pursuit of Wairaka*, but the gallery thought it might offend Māori sensibilities, and went for the more neutral *Wairarapa*.'

'Why *The Pursuit of*?'

'She figures in Rangitāne legend. The wife of Haunui-a-nanaia. Ran off with a lover. Hau went after them, travelling along the coast, naming the various rivers as he went. Whanganui for its size, Turakino where he crossed the river by throwing a dead tree across it, on south to the Manawatu where he stepped into the cold water and the breath was knocked out of him. By the time he reached Otaki, he was close to overtaking the runaway lovers and used an incantation to locate them. At Waikanae he found their footprints in the sand, and at Pukerua Bay he caught them. He killed his wife's lover with a blow from his mere, but for Wairaka he'd planned a subtler revenge. Complaining he was footsore after his long journey, he sent her down to the sea to fetch water. When she returned he said the water was dirty and sent her out into deeper water for more. This went on until she waded into water so deep that she lost her footing and drowned. Reciting more incantations, he turned her to stone. The stone's still there at the southern end of Pukerua Bay.'

She felt cold. These allusions to petrification. To betrayal.

'Are you still with me?' he asked.

She took his arm again.

'I used to wonder why my parents called me Rachel,' she said. 'One with purity, like a lamb. I used to feel so impure, as if I was to blame for my parents' misery. I used to rack my brains for what I had done wrong.'

'Your parents were that unhappy?'

'No more than most, I suppose. But they were. And I never knew why.'

'Like mine,' Max said.

'This room is mostly your road signs,' she said.

'Did they hang *Blind Corner*?'

'It's there. Why wouldn't it be?'

'Sensitivity, I suppose, to my blindness. Like Anne Merriweather not wanting to refer to Wairaka. Creating the right impression. Doing the right thing. You spend your life trying to create things that ring true, that are real, and then the vultures descend and carry your work off to their own make-believe world. What can you do?'

'The work does not allow it,' she said. 'The work subverts them. Nothing they could ever do will blemish or eclipse these images, Max. They're stunning. It's like throwing a window open in a darkened room, and suddenly the place is filled with light. Not painted light, Max. The light of day.'

He laid his free hand on hers.

'Shall we go now? Or do you want to see more?'

'No, let's go. I don't want Anne Merriweather finding us here and turning us to stone.'

On the way back to Makara she asked him when he had painted the eucalypts and pines. She had not seen them before – the two series of small canvases in which he focused entirely on the bark, so that one had no sense of the tree itself, only this meticulously painted miniature.

'I sometimes think,' Max said, 'that things mean more to me than people. Perhaps this comes of working with clay. Perhaps it explains my affinity for Paul Cézanne.'

'Cézanne?'

'He also gave more life to things than to people, and that included his wife and son. "The landscape thinks itself in me, and I am its consciousness," he once said. That's why his landscapes are really abstract images, not of rock and pine but of the flesh. Look at his portraits of his wife, Hortense Fiquet, and you'll see that the reverse is also true. This man who could not bear to be touched, and whose passion for landforms was stronger than his desire for human contact, turned his wife to stone. He didn't just treat people as objects; he treated objects as persons. And to achieve this, everything had to be sacrificed or made secondary – home comforts, relationships, even physical health. He distanced himself from everything that could hook him. He even stayed away from his mother's funeral in order not to lose a day's work. At the end of his life he suffered from diabetes, headaches and bronchitis, yet he painted outdoors every day, relying on his son to take care of Hortense as well as the day-to-day chores at home. Eight days before his death he collapsed while painting in the rain. He was brought home in a laundry cart. Even at death's door he got out of bed and went to his studio, determined to work.'

'But you were never like that,' Rachel said. 'That self-mortification, I mean.'

'I came close. When I lived in the Bee House I lived like that, pushing myself to the limit. When you went to England I went back to the same regimen. Punishing myself. Throwing myself into work in order to blind myself to the torment within me. I even swore off women, took a vow of chastity!'

'You, chaste!'

'Rita Angus did it.'

'Yes, but at what age?'

'Thirty-four.'

'*That* surprises me.'

'Decided to devote herself to art. No more marriages. No more attempts to bear children. Lived alone, jealous of her privacy, frugal to a fault, and to hell with promoting her work.'

'And you followed her example?'

'No, I came to my own decision. I only found out about her much later.'

'What changed for you?'

'Cézanne didn't seem bothered by the local kids that followed him every day as he trudged to his studio, throwing stones at him as if at a stray dog. But I balked at being the village idiot, the butt of local jokes. I wanted reality on my side, but not the whole world turned against me. Maybe you can't have it both ways. Perhaps greatness in art requires the sacrifice of one's life. What would I give to have painted that *Mont Sainte-Victoire* that hangs in the Courtauld. It was the first painting that ever moved me to tears. I don't know whether you know it. There's a pine tree on the left, leaning away, with a single bough extending across the top of the painting. You can feel it moving in the wind, actually see the effect of the wind on the pine needles and smell the resin. And then, across this breathtaking plain that reminded me strongly of the Wairarapa, the lilac mountain –'

'I don't think I've ever seen it,' Rachel said. 'But I will visit the Courtauld when I get back to London.'

'When's that?'

'I'm not sure. My students need me. But when I think of my empty house, my old routines, I quake at the thought of returning.'

'Why not stay?'

'My work is there.'

'Couldn't you find work here? My friend Sam tells me that Harriet's old job has been advertised at Massey. Maybe you could apply for it.'

'Teaching psychology? No. But it's not only England. It's a lot of things I can't put my finger on. Half a lifetime there, for a start. Could *you* pull up stakes and settle somewhere else, after all the years you've lived here, painting this country?'

'I'm sixty-six, Rachel. Blind and old. Where would I go?'

'I don't see you as old, or blind. But I know what you're saying. There are points of no return in life. It's not that we choose the path ahead, rather that we become aware that we cannot go back along the path we have already travelled.'

He was recalling the marked paths at Aix, the so-called pictorial routes that led to the Bibemus quarries – Tholonet, Lauves, Bellevue and Montbriand, each marked by a different colour. He did not know which path to take, or if it mattered. All that mattered was that first glimpse of Sainte-Victoire, the breath knocked out of him, the reality of the paintings affirmed by the reality of the mountain itself, its presence as compelling as it had been for Cézanne. He knew then that art completes the world: it makes it noticeable, it lends it significance, it draws our attention to things that would otherwise remain unremarked, rendering them memorable. And this was as true of art as it was of love, for with Rachel the Wairarapa had come alive, and it was this region, infused with his passion for her, that he had painted. Without her he would have looked at the landscape but not seen it.

At Karori Cemetery she was sure she remembered the location of her mother's grave, but after walking up and down the rows of concrete slabs and marble headstones, she felt she was in a labyrinth and sought help.

An irritable sexton was working on a new grave, attacking the clay with his pick, shovelling soil with such furious concentration that Rachel was loath to disturb him.

'I am trying to find my mother's grave,' she said. 'If I gave you the name, would you be able to help me find it?'

'I'm busy right now.'

'I can wait.'

She waited. He resumed his angry digging for long enough to make his point. Then, clambering from the pit, he muttered: 'You'll never get over it, you know.'

With no context, she had no choice but to leave this comment hanging. She followed him to his shed where he consulted his registry and found her mother's plot number. Though she asked him just to point her in the right direction, assuring him that she could find the way, he insisted on leading her to the plot and waiting while she confirmed that it was indeed her mother's.

'Mary Eisenstark?' he said.

'Yes.'

'No, you never get over it,' the sexton muttered. 'I buried my son seven years ago, and every grave I dig is his grave.'

'I'm sorry,' she said. Again, she waited for him to go away, but he remained there, silent.

She was becoming annoyed. She needed this time alone, time to think.

'I'll leave you to it, then,' he said.

'Thank you for your help.'

'Should have known the name,' he muttered. 'I pride myself in knowing most of them, keeping up with the new ones, knowing what's going on.'

After he had wandered off, she pulled a few weeds from the gravel, examined the name and the dates, felt a rain squall coming across the hills. But no vision of her mother came to her, no memory. By the time she returned to her car she felt more alone than she had since Peter had walked out on her. And when she finally switched on the ignition and drove slowly out of the cemetery, she knew that she could not return to the city. Not yet.

Turning left she drove to the summit of the range. After parking the car, she climbed a fence and picked her way over the broken ground. The wind was whining in the metal struts of a telecommunications tower as if frustrated in getting its message out or maddened by the obstruction in its path. At the edge of a small plateau she gazed down at the bony and eroded hills, the dark green belts of macrocarpa and pine, the glint of a farmhouse window, a verdant valley and the South Island beyond. Ten thousand miles away her daughter was studying for an exam. At Makara Max was pressing tabs of clay onto a metal armature, or throwing a kneaded clump onto his wheel, his hands cupping what remained real to him. She suddenly wanted to throw herself headlong down the slope, taking wing as the wind gathered her up, bearing her into the blue never-never of the sky. She knew why she had sought this place. It was her Reinga, the headland from which the dead sailed into the afterlife, the sea's contending currents far below them and the tribulations of their earthly incarnation left behind. Yet oblivion was not for her. The only wings that would bear her anywhere were the wings of an Air New Zealand aircraft flying to London in two days' time. No Reinga awaited her, no respite, no Utopia. Only an empty house, an unfinished manuscript, a hundred emails, a queue of needy students.

That evening she emailed Lucy to say when she would be back. She was surprised how emotionally exhausted she felt. She had come all this way, but to what end? She could discern the shape of what had come to pass, but she did not yet know that the exhausted woman who lay on the hotel bed switching channels in an effort to find distraction or sleep was passing from one life to another.

Rachel and Sam

Dear Sam Stillman,

*I bought your novel several months ago when I was in New
Zealand. I read it on my flight back to the UK and enjoyed it so
much that I thought of writing to you at the time to thank you
for this beautiful and unusual piece of writing. I knew of you,
even before I read your book, through our mutual friend Max
Suvorin. It was Max who told me that you had been married to
Harriet Hempton, who was a close friend of mine when we were
postgraduates at the University of Auckland. In fact, you and I
very possibly met back then, albeit briefly. I was also surprised to
learn that you had a hand in organising Max's retrospective and
have been helping him out in various other ways. These discoveries
moved me, finally, to write to you. Please don't feel under any
obligation to respond, but if you are ever in the UK it would be
nice to meet and talk about these connections from so long ago
that seem to have followed us into the here and now.*

With kind regards,

Rachel Eisenstark

Sam and Rachel

When Sam and Rachel met they had no memory of each other, yet felt
they had met before. Rachel would observe that the passing of time
plays tricks with the mind. Besides, their appearances had undoubtedly
changed dramatically, and since they had never actually spoken to each
other in the past, all they had in common were Harriet and Max. With
Max's death, even that last tenuous connection had been lost.

It rained during the funeral, a relentless drumming on the chapel
roof that drowned out the platitudes and paeans of those bold enough
to speak. Later, as the small crowd huddled under umbrellas or sought
shelter under the macrocarpas at Makara Cemetery, someone said that
the rain was a sign of how even nature grieved Max's passing. For Sam
and Rachel, however, nature had played a very different role in Max's

death. Neither had accepted invitations 'to view the body', which had been washed ashore on the stony beach they had separately walked with him. Neither wished to see the grotesquely repaired sea damage to his face or join the debate over the cause of death – accidental drowning or suicide. But both had needed to be there, to see the unembellished pine casket lowered into the grave on wet ropes and toss their token handfuls of clay onto it, perhaps the same refractory clay from which Max had fashioned his earthenware.

In the months that had passed since Rachel wrote to Sam, a few awkward emails had been exchanged. But tentative fantasies and overtures had been suppressed, so that now, when their eyes met briefly across the rain-blinded paddock, surrounded by higgledy-piggledy fences and bruised hills, they wondered what words they could summon for the occasion, whether of sorrow for Max or small talk about the weather.

There was no formal reception, though many mourners drove back to Makara for sausage rolls and pots of tea at the Bitter End, 'now under new management'.

Rachel struggled free of her raincoat and hung it on a peg near the door. Sam was standing in a pool of rainwater, wondering how to approach her, when she breezed up to him and introduced herself, adding that they probably needed no introduction.

Sam suggested they take the table in the corner before anyone else did. After draping his parka over a chair, he ordered a corn toasted sandwich at the counter. Rachel took one look at the asparagus rolls and cream buns in the glass cabinet and settled for a cup of tea.

'It's bizarre,' Sam said, when they returned to their table. 'I feel I know you, yet we're complete strangers.'

'We know each other through people we loved,' Rachel said. 'We've come to know each other through osmosis.'

Sam laughed.

They talked of their children. Lucy and Zoe had finished their degrees and had both taken gap years to go travelling. Lucy had flown from England with Rachel but immediately headed south to go whale watching with a New Zealand friend she'd made at Oxford. Zoe was in Australia.

'Why Australia?' Rachel asked.

'It's not New Zealand, but not so far away that she can't fly home if the money runs out or she gets into trouble.'

After a long pause, Rachel asked Sam if he was working on a new book.

'Working on one,' Sam said, 'but making very slow progress.'

'Do you mind me asking what it's about?'

'Since you're a psychologist, I could describe it as a book about intergenerational trauma. It's called *Fathers and Sons*.'

They both looked around, taking stock of who had come to see Max off. Both recognised Anne Merriweather from the Wellington gallery, though they made no cynical comments about her. Most of the mourners were unknown to them, though Rachel assumed Sam would know them all.

'I had even less to do with the art crowd than Max did,' Sam said. 'Anyway, since Harriet's death I've become a bit of a hermit. Writing also drives you in on yourself.'

'I think I've done the same,' Rachel said. 'We seal ourselves off from the world, not wanting to be hurt again.'

'Max told me that your husband left you.'

'Yes.'

'What about your life in Cambridge? I would have thought you'd be inundated with sherry parties and students.'

'It's easy to be lonely in a crowd.'

'When do you go home?'

'To England? I don't know. I haven't booked a date. I was thinking vaguely of meeting up with Lucy and travelling around the South Island, seeing if I can reconnect with New Zealand.'

'If you ever come north,' Sam said, 'you'd be welcome to stay with me.'

'That's most kind of you, Sam.'

'It's a very beautiful part of the country. I'm sure your daughter would love it.'

'The Manawatu?'

'No, I sold my house there and bought a place in Northland, near Pakiri Beach.'

'Pakiri! I know it well. In fact, Harriet and I ... this was well before you two got together ... we went up there with our boyfriends and lit a bonfire on the beach and raved and sang folksongs all night and welcomed the new day with the last of our champagne. Harriet was so open to life, so irreverent of everything that got in the way of living openly and passionately. You must miss her very much.'

'But life goes on, doesn't it?'

'Ah, life!' she exclaimed, suddenly remembering the other time she'd gone to Pakiri with Max and their mad friend Cam, in a pink Cadillac convertible, and drunk whiskey sours on the beach. Then, almost in a trance, she was thinking how lives pass away while life itself goes on. Max had gone, but the sea he loved was out there in the rain, beating up on that shingle beach, obeying its own deep rhythms, beholden to no one.

When Sam and Rachel went their separate ways it was with a promise that they would keep in touch. But for Sam, no promise was needed; he wanted to see her again, though he hesitated to confess his feelings lest she take it as presumptuous and intrusive.

Every few days he received an email from her with details of her peregrinations. Walking the Milford and Routeburn tracks with Lucy, becoming fitter than she'd been for years. Staying in forest lodges, swimming in mountain tarns, Lucy obsessively taking selfies for her Facebook page, with mountains, waterfalls and sunsets in the background. Rachel did not, however, mention coming north or taking up Sam's invitation to visit Pakiri, and he began to feel that his reticence had been interpreted as indifference and that he would not see her again.

He emailed his friend Leviathan, saying that he had to kill his desperate fantasy of recovering his life with Harriet, of there being someone else he could love as he had loved her.

Leviathan had his own experiences of loss to contend with. His first marriage had ended disastrously, and to escape the ruins he had taken a teaching job on a Pacific atoll where he had met Rima and persuaded her to come with him to New Zealand. Though his homesickness had been overcome, for Rima it was the beginning of a long period of suppressed mourning, and after the birth of their second child she returned to Aitutaki, taking the children with her. It wasn't a divorce, but for Lev the separation felt like a prelude to something more permanent, and he was oppressed by the thought that Rima might not return to New Zealand and he would lose touch with his children.

When Lev wrote back to Sam he reminded his friend that everyone lives in the shadow of loss. The loss of something or somebody. 'If we're thick-skinned or wise enough,' Lev wrote, 'we can survive it, and not need to fill the void. But sometimes, when we least expect it, something or someone enters that vacant space and fills it for us.'

Some years ago Lev had begun researching the seismic causes and social effects of the 1886 Tarawera eruption, which destroyed ten Māori settlements and covered the central North Island with millions of tonnes of volcanic ash, mud and debris. Sam regarded this project as an expression of his friend's need to come to terms with the devastation of traditional Māori life in the nineteenth century. But Lev's research had been interrupted by false leads, misleading evidence, and his inability to distinguish between the archival facts and photographs he had unearthed and images from a series of unsettling dreams. Unable to control the contamination of his data, Lev took a long break from his project. One night he woke from a nightmare in which he was walking down a country road. A figure emerged from a farmhouse and proceeded to cut the telegraph lines that ran alongside the road. This figure now mounted a bicycle and sped past Lev, who turned and gave chase. The cyclist had a ten-year-old boy with him, and on the cyclist's orders the boy attacked Lev and beat him up. Then Lev found himself poring over a book whose text was laid out in a funnel shape on the page. On waking, he scribbled down on a Kleenex box two sinister lines that had come to him in the dream:

The happy children dance around

the soul goes down the funnel underground.

When Lev recounted this dream to Sam, Sam asked if anything had happened to Lev when he was ten. Lev was stunned. He suddenly knew what the dream was about. Ten years before, his wife had aborted the child she was carrying, neither telling Lev what she had decided to do nor giving him any say in the matter. It spelled the end of their marriage. Lev had never forgiven her, and he had not forgiven himself for allowing the abortion to occur, even though, as Sam pointed out, he could not have known what Angela was doing. The boy in the dream was his ten-year old son punishing his father for allowing him to be murdered before he had had a chance of life.

Sam had never forgotten Lev's dream or the ethical reflections it occasioned, so when he received an email from Rachel asking for directions to his house, he realised that he had been carrying his own burden of guilt from the day he signed Harriet's life away in a Manawatu hospital. Now, by turns, he was distraught and elated at the prospect of seeing Rachel again.

He spent the day preparing the house. After making up the bed in Zoe's room for Lucy, he cleared out his bedroom for Rachel and placed a vase of pōhutukawa flowers on the night table. He would doss down on a futon on the floor of his study. Finally, he set about making the bathroom look and smell as if it had never been used.

They arrived that evening as shadows lengthened across the paddocks and the wind veered toward the sea. He stood on the veranda as they lugged their suitcases up to the house, unable to bring himself to help. Disarmed by Rachel's presence, he fussed over her daughter in an attempt to neutralise his emotions, all the while wishing Zoe were there as a go-between.

Having shown them around the house and urged them to make themselves at home (thankfully Rachel said nothing about displacing him from his bedroom), he suggested they might like to go down to the beach while he prepared dinner.

With the house to himself again he regained his composure, uncorked the wine, and simmered puttanesca sauce for the pasta. He set the table with the plates Harriet had bought when they first moved to the Manawatu. Finally, he lit candles on the table, kindled a fire of mānuka logs and dimmed the lights in the room, so that when Rachel and Lucy walked back with the setting sun on their faces, he would be able to say, in all honesty, that they were glowing.

At dinner the focus was again on Lucy, though she was sensitive enough, or had been prepped by her mother, to excuse herself early and go to her room, leaving Sam and Rachel with the wavering candles, the firelight reflected in their wine glasses, and their unnerving conversation. Rachel suggested they sit by the fire, and as Sam poked at the logs she kicked off her shoes and ensconced herself in the armchair beside him. Sam then hoisted himself onto the couch opposite to begin the conversation for which he felt totally unprepared.

She asked about his progress with *Fathers and Sons*. In response he asked if she was working on anything herself.

'To be honest, Sam, I'm working on reaching you.'

'Am I so hard to reach?'

'Physically, no.'

He took the bottle of wine from the coffee table and attempted to refill Rachel's glass. But she placed one hand over the glass and said no, no more, and with her other hand gently touched his arm.

'Here we are,' she said, 'trying to relax with wine, when all we need to do is relax with each other.'

'I have wanted to be with you from the moment you and Lucy went on your way south,' Sam said. 'It was difficult, getting your emails, answering them, but knowing it wasn't enough to write, that I wanted something that could not be set down on paper or put into words.'

As he replaced the wine bottle on the coffee table, she moved from her armchair to the couch. He looked into her eyes and was about to speak when she touched her fingers to his lips. 'No words,' she said. 'We don't have to say anything.'

Sam passed the night in shallow sleep, coming awake with a soft jolt to find her beside him. To experience the oceanic aftershock of the hours in which they had made love, caressing, bruising each other with kisses, expressing wonderment that they had not met twenty-five years ago.

Toward dawn, he woke to find her gazing at him.

'I don't want to lose you,' she said.

'You won't,' he said. 'And we won't lose each other.'

'Before you woke up,' Rachel said, 'I was thinking of Max. I felt his presence, as if he was giving us his blessing. '

'And it came to pass,' Sam said.

'What do you mean?'

'It's from the Bible. I love the phrase. I love the idea that the most momentous things in life sometimes happen without our will, as if there's some benign and unfathomable conspiracy that brings us together or tears us apart.'

'Yet you gave me the impression that you'd do anything but let things happen in their own good time. Your emails were always so cagey. I felt you were willing yourself not to yield to the stream of things. And when I saw you at Max's funeral I so wanted to give you a hug, but I felt it was prohibited.'

Sam laughed. 'It probably was.'

'And last night?'

'I didn't want to embarrass you with my feelings. Had you not made the first move I would have remained as landlocked as you first found me.'

'I am flattered that you lowered your guard. That you even wanted me. I'm not a young woman anymore.'

'Nor am I a young man. But love annuls time. It renders the past impossible.'

'What a strange thing to say.'

'I feel as though I've gone back to before I met Harriet. Only I'm not the person I was then, but the person I am now. Does that make sense?'

'Yes. It's the same for me.'

By the time Lucy emerged, bleary-eyed, out of Zoe's bedroom, Sam and Rachel were drinking coffee at the kitchen table and making plans for the day. Though a little self-conscious about their overnight transfiguration, they were relieved that Lucy appeared unsurprised by their evident happiness and intimacy. Even when her mother leapt to her feet and took Lucy in her arms, Lucy gave no sign that something life-changing had occurred. That it was a possibility she had known from what her mother had confided one morning on the Routeburn track. But that it had actually happened, transforming her mother from an anxious adult into a slightly ditsy teenager, would take time to accept. It made Lucy feel not abandoned but suddenly rather lonely, and she was grateful for Sam's solicitude, as if he sensed, better than her mother, the repercussions of what had occurred.

'I thought I would take you to see my friends Lev and Rima this afternoon,' Sam said. 'They're keen to meet you both, and their daughter Tara is back home for a while. She's your age, Lucy, and though I know what a pain it is when someone tries to set you up with someone else, I think you two might hit it off.'

As if the fates were for once on Sam's side, Lev phoned him minutes later, and Sam explained that he and Rachel and Lucy were thinking of driving up to Matauri Bay that afternoon. After welcoming the idea, Lev put Tara on the phone. She would be happy to take Lucy riding and could lend her some jodhpurs and riding boots.

'Have you ever ridden before?' Sam asked when Lucy got off the phone.

'It was probably the only useful thing I did learn at Oxford.'

Rachel was interested to know more about Lev and Rima.

'I admire their marriage,' Sam said, 'and I am the beneficiary of their kindness. And I admire the way they have learned to live off the land.' Sam described how Lev had fertilised the sandy soil around their house with compost, and how Rima grew vegetables while Lev supplemented their diet with kai moana. A local barter system enabled Lev to exchange fish and vegetables for wine, and in the winter he worked on nearby farms, chartered his boat to tourists, or sold home-grown marijuana on the Auckland market.

They reached Matauri Bay late in the afternoon and, at Lev's insistence, Lucy and Tara were immediately sent to the tack shed and Rachel and Sam ordered to go swimming. As if he knows what's going on, Sam thought. As if he knows me better than I know myself.

Rachel was the first to dive into the deep cleft. Bioluminescence streamed from her body as she plunged though the translucent water, and when Sam joined her they found themselves encased in an incandescent chrysalid.

'This must be what it's like to be born,' Sam said.

'Or reborn,' Rachel said, diving again into the luminescent water.

When they described their experience later to Lev, he told them how unpredictable the phenomenon was. 'I've seen it at sea a few times, like electric mercury around the boat. When we go fishing tomorrow we may run into it again.'

Rima had woven a panama hat – a gift for Rachel should she be silly enough to go out fishing with Lev and Sam. Rachel instantly warmed to her, and though Sam had mentioned that Rima said very little, preferring gestures to words, she admired Rima's subtle assertions of independence. Sam had been right when he had described Rima as a loving, attentive presence to whom one could confide almost anything and feel, though she gave no advice, more at peace for having shared one's thoughts with her. Sam had also told Rachel that she should not be surprised if Lev regaled her with the story of how he and Rima found their house. 'Apart from the birth of their children,' Sam said, 'nothing has given them more pleasure than finding this house and naming it after Rima's island.'

It happened just as Sam had predicted. After a salad of red lettuce, pūhā and watercress, and servings of baked groper and sweet potatoes washed down by Matakana wine, Lev launched into his story.

'I wanted to be close to my home marae,' Lev said. 'And we wanted to be close to Auckland for when the kids started high school. We spent two years before we found the house we were looking for. It hadn't been advertised for sale. And it seemed a lot more isolated than it does now. The gate was unlocked and I walked up the drive to take a closer look. Rima was spooked and stayed in the car. My heart was racing as I approached the house and saw that it was derelict, the paint faded and peeling on the weatherboards, the veranda rotted through in several places, the corrugated iron roof streaked with rust. Several windows were broken and boarded up and two of the back rooms had been used to store bales of hay. But I was already forming in my mind a plan of action – to buy the house, rehabilitate it and make it the place where we would spend the rest of our lives.

'As soon as I stepped inside I felt I already owned it. As if the previous owners had left it for me. The kitchen table was covered with an oilcloth. One plate was laid out with cutlery beside it. The usual phalanx of salt cellars and pepper shakers, toast rack and ketchup. On the stove were two saucepans, the contents shrivelled and black. A white plastic drying rack held a single Willow Pattern soup bowl. I thought *ghost ship*, and *Goldilocks*, wondering what had befallen those who once lived here, the dining room deserted, food uneaten. The main bedroom only deepened the mystery – twin beds, one made up, the other with the sheet and blanket, as if its occupant had risen only minutes before.

'But the strangest discovery,' Lev said, 'was the living room piled high with broken furniture, stacks of newspapers clumsily tied with baling twine, and all manner of household trash. Festering organic matter had rotted through the floorboards. I imagined a family that had broken up, a sole survivor staying on, filling the rooms with rubbish until the house became uninhabitable, then one morning abandoning ship. On every windowsill I noticed what looked like old loofahs or dead processionary caterpillars. When I picked one up and realised what it really was, I dropped it in disgust. The last occupant of the house must have been a woman, still young enough to bear children, but traumatised enough to arrange her sanitary pads in this poignant testimony to what had befallen her.

'My suspicions were confirmed by the realtor I tracked down a few days later. He had tried without success to get the woman to leave the house, put it on the market, move into an apartment, seek help. But the woman was determined "to go down with the ship".'

'What happened?' Rachel asked.

'The old story. Husband walked out on her. Wife cracked up.'

'And how did the story end?'

'Ended quite well according to the realtor. Husband got tired of the other woman. Went back to his wife, begged her forgiveness. She forgave him, and they walked away from the house and didn't look back. I tried to find them, but they'd succeeded in disappearing without a trace. To start over, I suppose. The house a painful reminder of what had happened. They got back together, but the house had gone to rack and ruin and they wanted no part of it.

'We eventually found the couple living in Kaitaia. At first, they didn't want to talk about the house, let alone discuss selling it. But we persisted until they agreed to let it go for a fraction of its market value and never have to think about it again.'

Rachel, who had been rapt until this moment, interrupted to ask Rima whether she had had forebodings about inheriting this accursed property.

Rima appeared not to understand the question, but Lev answered for her. 'It's amazing how different a thing looks when you put body and soul into rebuilding it. You make it yours. And that's what we did with Aitutaki. We brought it back to life.'

Determined to goad Rima into speaking, Rachel asked if she missed her homeland.

'It's all very well calling a house Aitutaki, but my placenta is buried there, not here.'

'But your children,' Rachel asked, 'were they born here or there?'

Rima got up from the table and went into the kitchen, leaving Rachel to wonder if she had given offence or whether this was simply a sign, as Sam had suggested, of Rima's reluctance to talk about herself.

That night, lying in bed, listening to the sea whose susurrus reminded Rachel of traffic on a distant road, Sam assured Rachel that she had not spoken out of turn.

'Were you thinking of England when you asked Rima about missing her homeland?'

'No, I was thinking of New Zealand.'

'Homesick?'

'I'm not sure,' Rachel said. 'The last two days have muddled things so much that I don't know what I'm thinking from one moment to the next.'

'You need time. To think things through.'

'No, Sam. I don't need time, or space. I just need to know you are there for me. Everything will resolve itself if we are patient.'

'You'll go back to Cambridge, though?'

For a split second she might have been talking to Max.

'Of course. I have to go back. I can't just walk away from my life there even if I want a life here with you.'

'Perhaps you'll become a godwit,' Sam said. 'They fly from the Antipodes to Alaska each year, some returning, some not. Each summer they nest in the sandhills and on the beach, vulnerable to heedless kids and the hooves of horses. Rima spends hours patrolling the beach, marking their nesting sites with small flags or watching over them.'

'I can easily imagine her doing that,' Rachel said.

'You might even become like Rima,' Sam said. 'Lev told me that when Tara finished high school, Rima took her to Aitutaki. On their first night on the atoll they spread woven mats on the concrete grave slab of Rima's parents and slept there. Next day Rima took Tara to the church where, at Tara's age, she had sung in the choir. They visited the grove of coconut palms her uncle had planted for her when she went away. They waded through the warm shallows of the lagoon, and Rima taught Tara to catch rahi, manini and ava by sweeping a seine net through the water. And they sat together on the veranda of the family house, where the women worked red pandanus fibre or the fronds of young coconut palms into fine white threads and wove them into handbags, platters, sandals, fishing nets, baskets, mats and hats. When Tara disdained these things, or was embarrassed, her mother knew that the circle had been broken, that she had become one of the godwits who would not make the journey back.

'She put Tara on the boat, charging a cousin to see that her daughter got back safely to Auckland. Then she turned to making peace with her family, whose advice she had ignored when she went to New Zealand and married Lev.'

'So what are you saying? That I will be faced with a similar choice?'

'No, Rachel. That's not what I'm saying at all.'

At the boat ramp Lev reversed his trailer into the water and quickly launched the boat. He asked Sam to hold the boat against the incoming tide while he drove the trailer back to a parking lot beyond the dunes. Waves thudded against the aluminium hull. The boat strained like a leashed animal. Sam felt out of his element. But then Lev was back, clambering into the boat and urging him to get in. Within seconds Lev had got the outboard going, turned up the throttle and was forcing the boat through breaking waves and blinding spray.

'Where are we heading?' Sam shouted against the noise of the outboard and the banging of the boat against the swell.

'The Cavalli Islands,' Lev said, and nodded toward their blue outline on the horizon. 'We should get there just as the tide turns.'

It was only after Lev had stopped off at a small bay, baited his lines and thrown them into the turquoise depths that Sam asked how long Rima had stayed in Aitutaki after returning there with Tara.

'About a year. I thought she wasn't coming back. I still don't know if she came back to be with me or the kids.'

'It can't have been easy for you.'

'Harder for her, I'd say. She's always felt bad about leaving the islands. She thinks her parents blamed her for abandoning them and died of heartbreak.'

'The guilt of every expatriate!'

'I wouldn't know. But we all leave home, don't we? Leave one life for another. One person for another. Does it have to be seen as a betrayal? Isn't this the way of the world? Moving with the tide, the wind, the weather? Look at me. Those dreams I had of writing a book about history and catastrophe. I don't regret the choices I made. They weren't even choices. Angela aborting our child. Meeting Rima. Having kids. Finding the house here. It's just the way things happened. It's not something to moralise about. I'm happy with my lot. I think Rima is too, despite her misgivings. Look around. Does it ever get any better than this?'

Sam pulled his cap down on his forehead, shading his eyes from the glare, and studied the thin line of white sand between the ocean and the inland hills.

Lev was baiting another line. Sam observed his hands, reddened and hardened by hauling in lines, scraping rust, digging clay. And because he could not imagine himself living such a hand-to-mouth existence, he asked Lev bluntly if he ever gave any thought to the roads he had not taken.

'I leave that to Rima.'

Lev caught several snapper. Some were legally undersize and he threw them back into the sea, where they swam in dazed and listless circles before making a sudden dash for safety. But several six- or seven-pound fish now lay at Sam's feet, pink blurring into silver, the eyes already glazing over.

As Lev gunned the outboard and turned the boat into the wind, a school of dolphins suddenly appeared beneath the bow. As they picked up speed, the dolphins surged through the water ahead of them, nose against nose, effortlessly slipping in and out of reach.

'Duskies,' Lev shouted. 'They often guide me home.'

Sam watched, transfixed. For a moment neither he nor they were moving. It was as if they had been buried alive in the glass coffin of the ocean, while he hovered above it, in thin air. And as the school guided the boat back to the beach, flipping, arching, diving, scampering through the translucent water, Sam tried to remember what the ancient Greeks had said about dolphins and their mythical association with Delphi. Did it have something to do with their ambiguity – being at once fish that live in the sea and mammals that breathe air? Inhabiting two worlds, being in between?

As suddenly as they had appeared they were gone, peeling away through the water, weary of the two men or drawn elsewhere to forage or flaunt, gambol or guide.

On the veranda of Aitutaki Lev had built a sink and countertop. That afternoon Sam watched as he scaled and filleted the snapper, his big hands deft and practised, the bone-handled flensing knife slicing cleanly through the exposed flesh, guts and fins tossed into a plastic pail, the cutting board sluiced clean.

Sam envied him and said so.

'I'd give my right arm to write the way you do,' Lev said.

'Sometimes I think that words are a curse. All the life we leave unlived as we struggle to write about it.'

'You think too much, Sam,' Lev said. 'That's your problem.'

'You know that I am in love with Rachel?'

'Now that's something you didn't need to spell out! Do you know what I think, Sam? I think of fishing. Of waiting. Of that constant vigil we keep, waiting for the fish to bite. We must put time, skill and effort into perfecting the hook, but beyond a certain point we must simply wait for fish and fishhook to come together. Rima says that on Aitutaki people believe that the world is divided into two regions, one above and one below the surface of the sea. The fishhook connects the fisherman with the lower depths, and every fishhook is a lure to bring fish from the deep into our world, the world of light. The fishermen do not say they "catch fish", because most of their hooks are not even baited. The hook itself is the bait, made to look like a fish. There is a spiritual connection between the hook and the fish.'

ACKNOWLEDGEMENTS

I wish to express my sincere thanks to Rachel Scott for her editorial advice and guidance, and to Erika Bűky, whose painstaking copy-editing helped me avoid numerous stylistic blunders.

Thanks are due to the following copyright holders for permission to cite previously published material in this book: Victoria University Press, Wellington, New Zealand, for ten lines from A.R.D. Fairburn's poem 'A Farewell', published in *Selected Poems*, ed. Mac Jackson, n.d.; Auckland University Press, for two excerpts from Derek Challis and Gloria Rawlinson, *The Book of Iris: A life of Robin Hyde*, 2002, pp. 410, 616; Indiana University Press for '"The Two Momoris": An oral tale by Keti Ferenke Koroma', translated and published in Michael Jackson, *Allegories of the Wilderness: Ethics and ambiguity in Kuranko narratives*, 1982, p. 179; Penguin Random House New Zealand for the description of 'Emma' in Michael Jackson, *The Accidental Anthropologist*, first published by Longacre Press, Dunedin, in 2006, p. 120; John McIndoe, Dunedin, for 'Seven Mysteries' and 'Full Moon', from *Duty Free: Selected poems 1965–1988*, pp. 61, 64.

Notes

1. Theme and Variations

Epigraph – J.M. Coetzee and Arabella Kurtz, *The Good Story: Exchanges on truth, fiction and psychotherapy* (New York: Viking, 2015), 137.

Losing the Plot

chaste compactness – Walter Benjamin, 'The Storyteller', in *Illuminations*, ed. Hannah Arendt (New York: Schocken Books, 1968), 91.

Lost Fortunes

A disease is never a mere loss – Oliver Sacks, *The Man Who Mistook His Wife for a Hat* (London: Picador, 1986), 4.

Zazetsky was under no illusions that his scribblings would constitute a coherent narrative – A.R. Luria, *The Man with a Shattered World*, trans. Lynn Solaratoff (Cambridge, Mass.: Harvard University Press, 1987), pp. xx, 86, 84.

Hannah Arendt speaks of this capacity as natality – Hannah Arendt, *The Human Condition* (Chicago: University of Chicago Press, 1958), 246.

In Solitary

What makes me happy is creating a unique work of art – Mu Xin, in *Dreaming against the World: A portrait of Chinese artist Mu Xin*, dir. Francesco Bello and Tim Sternberg (Grasshopper Films, 2014).

His central concern was for 'directly, actually demonstrable concrete facts' – Hannah Arendt, introduction to *Illuminations*, trans. Harry Zohn (New York: Schocken Books, 1969), 11–13.

The past carries a secret index – Walter Benjamin, 'Theses on the Philosophy of History', in *Illuminations: Essays and reflections*, ed. Hannah Arendt, trans. Harry Zohn (translation modified by Thomas Schwartz Wentzer), (New York: Schocken Books, 1968), 254.

Hudson Rejoins the Herd

Although I am in pain, I write partly to convince myself – Claude Houghton, *Hudson Rejoins the Herd* (New York: Macmillan, 1939), 9.

What so startled me in reading this book – Henry Miller, *The Books in My Life* (New York: New Directions, 1959).

Si j'étais

I did not like my work – Quoted in Sven Broman, *Conversations with Greta Garbo* (New York: Viking Press, 1990), 271.

If I were Greta Garbo – Blaise Cendrars, 'Si j'étais', in *Trop c'est trop* (Paris: Denoël, 1957), 215–20.

The most elaborate form of communication between the living and the dead – Piers Vitebsky, *Living Without the Dead: Loss and redemption in a jungle cosmos* (Chicago: University of Chicago Press, 2017), 1.

Thoroughly social in character – Vitebsky, *Living Without the Dead*, 121.

Memories fade (masuna) as their rememberers too change with time – Vitebsky, *Living Without the Dead*, 121.

It'll Come To Me

To be 'drawn from without' – 'It is clear that Homer invokes the gods in order to account for the observation that a central form of human excellence must be drawn from without. A god, in Homer's terminology, is a mood that attunes us to what matters most in a situation, allowing us to respond appropriately without thinking.' Hubert Dreyfus and Sean Dorrance Kelly, *All Things Shining: Reading the Western classics to find meaning in a secular age* (New York: Free Press, 2011), 84.

Penned in, heaped up, like cattle, in poorhouses – Blaise Cendrars, 'The Art of Fiction,' interview with Michel Manoll, trans. William Brandon, *Paris Review* 37 (1966), 118.

I come back tired, alone, and utterly dejected – Blaise Cendrars, 'Easter in New York,' trans. Ron Padgett, in *Blaise Cendrars: Collected poems* (Berkeley: University of California Press, 1992), 11.

En cendres se transmute – Jay Bochner, *Blaise Cendrars: Discovery and re-creation* (Toronto: University of Toronto Press, 1978), 27.

Mary Magdalene, 'the lover of Jesus Christ' – Blaise Cendrars, *L'homme foudroyé* (Paris: Denoël, 1945), 265–66.

The book is sustained on its own axis – Anaïs Nin, preface to Henry Miller, *Tropic of Cancer*, 8.

It is now the fall of my second year in Paris – Miller, *Tropic of Cancer*, 11.

I have no money, no resources – Miller, *Tropic of Cancer*, 11.

The Book of Iris

The New Zealand writer Iris Wilkinson – See Derek Challis and Gloria
Rawlinson, *The Book of Iris: A life of Robin Hyde* (Auckland:
Auckland University Press, 2002).

When she gave birth to a child out of wedlock – An earlier pregnancy had
ended in a stillbirth, and Iris adopted the name she would have given
her son as her own nom de plume, Robin Hyde. Challis and Rawlinson,
The Book of Iris, 173–74.

Our country is right at the tail end of the map – Iris Wilkinson, letter to
her family, 19 May 1938. In a second letter dated the same day, she
reiterates the same view: 'My New Zealand is too good to be a safe,
smug, barricaded little country – it can lose its littleness for ever in the
greatness of reaching out to other peoples, studying their languages and
cultures, respecting their integrity, trying to work with them, not as an
affair of small half-sincere wholly ineffectual clubs or cliques, but as a
national policy.' Quoted in Challis and Rawlinson, *The Book of Iris*,
616–18.

The trip and the story of the trip – Lorrie Moore, *Birds of America* (New
York: Knopf, 1998), 237.

In a similar vein, Martin Amis observes – Martin Amis, *Experience*
(Toronto: Knopf, 2000), 7, 361.

The possibility of being at home in the world – Here lies another uncanny
connection between Wilkinson's work and my own. When I published
At Home in the World in 1995, I had no idea that she had written
an 'autobiographical fragment' published posthumously in 1984 and
titled *At Home in This World*, the theme of which presaged mine. 'I
am looking for … a home in this world … I don't mean four walls and
a roof on top, though even these I have never had … As often as not
… four walls and a roof get in the way, are the very point where one
is fatally side-tracked from ever having a home in this world. I want a
sort of natural order and containment, a centre of equipoise, an idea –
not a cell into which one can retreat, but a place from which one can
advance: a place from which I can stretch out giant shadowy hands, and
make a road between two obscure villages in China, teach the Arab and
the Jew to live together in Palestine, tidy up the shack dwellings and
shack destinies of our own thin Māoris in the north.' Quoted in Challis
and Rawlinson, *The Book of Iris*, 410.

The Expatriates

In his memoir, The Dreaming Land – Martin Edmond, *The Dreaming Land* (Wellington: Bridget Williams, 2015), 103.

Mentioning my book on the figure of the limitrophe – See Michael Jackson, *Harmattan: A philosophical fiction* (New York: Columbia University Press, 2015).

Past, present and future are so mixed – Martin Edmond, *The Expatriates* (Wellington: Bridget Williams Books, 2017), 10.

2. SIGNIFICANT OTHERS

The Albemarle

During the year I lived in the Albemarle – During this period I read extensively on the history of trade unions and workers' struggles, blissfully unaware that the egalitarian spirit of my homeland would be undermined by Rogernomics, the pig-headed divisiveness of the Muldoon years, and the advent of neoliberalism.

So friendly and gentle-spoken that I warmed to him – Mark Twain, *Roughing It* (New York: Oxford University Press, [1872] 1996), 88.

Leon

To move away / From the hissing of the spent lie – Dylan Thomas, 'I Have Longed to Move Away', *The Poems of Dylan Thomas* (New York: New Directions, 2003), 43.

Human kind / Cannot bear very much reality – T.S. Eliot, 'Burnt Norton', *Four Quartets* (London: Faber and Faber, 1940).

The Ordinance of Time

I have never believed in miracles – Michael Jackson, *The Accidental Anthropologist* (Dunedin: Longacre, 2006), 120.

Of the persecution of members of the Left, of the concentration camps on Makronisos and Yaros – See Neni Panourgia, *Dangerous Citizens: The Greek Left and the terror of the state* (New York: Fordham University Press, 2009).

Mikis Theodorakis's Kaïmós – For this reference and other details of the period of the junta, I am indebted to Michael Herzfeld's *Portrait of a Greek Imagination: An ethnographic biography of Andreas Nenedakis* (Chicago: University of Chicago Press, 1997), 225.

Envois

What lips my lips have kissed — Edna St Vincent Millay, *Selected Poems* (New York: Harper Perennial, 1992), 41.

Sierra Leone

My book would take several years to complete – See Michael Jackson, *Barawa, and the Ways Birds Fly in the Sky* (Washington, DC: Smithsonian Institution Press, 1986).

No advantage without limitation – See Michael Jackson, *Minima Ethnographica: Intersubjectivity and the ethnographic project* (Chicago: University of Chicago Press, 1998), 15.

Blue Cold Rough Water

The fault … is not in our stars / But in ourselves – William Shakespeare, *Julius Caesar,* act 1, scene 2.

The Two Momoris

Each of us is several, is many – Fernando Pessoa, *The Book of Disquiet,* trans. Richard Zenith (New York: Penguin, 2003), 327–28.

Menton

Proud émigré destitution – Quoted in Brian Boyd, *Vladimir Nabokov: The Russian years* (Princeton: Princeton University Press, 1990), 486, 488.

Survivors

It's other people that are my old age – Jean-Paul Sartre and Benny Levy, *Hope Now: The 1980 interviews,* trans. Adrian van den Houten (Chicago: University of Chicago Press, 2007), 72.

On the Waterfront

Everything depends on whether or not we have been loved – 'And what did you want? To call myself beloved, to feel myself beloved on the earth.' Raymond Carver, 'Late Fragment', *A New Path to the Waterfall* (New York: Atlantic Monthly Press, 1989), 122. Carver's lines echo William James's comment that 'the most peculiar social self which one is apt to have is in the mind of the person one is in love with'. William James, *Principles of Psychology*, vol. 1 (New York: Dover, 1950), 294.

Paralipomena

It is possible for stories to go on writing themselves – Paul Auster, *The Red Notebook and Other Writings* (London: Faber and Faber, 1995), 37.

Auster's view that every person comprises several selves – See Paul Auster,
    4 3 2 1 (New York: Henry Holt, 2017).
This 'innermost centre within the circle' –James, *Principles of Psychology,*
    vol. 1, 297, 298, 299, 302.
In a postscript to Moravagine – Blaise Cendrars, *Moravagine* (Paris:
    Grasset, 1956), 223.
Doris Lessing, having written a novella – See Doris Lessing, *Alfred and
    Emily* (London: Fourth Estate, 2008).

3 . Constant in the Darkness

Sam and Harriet

You have been mine before – Dante Gabriel Rosetti, 'Sudden Light',
    in *Dante Gabriel Rosetti: Collected poetry and prose,* ed. Jerome
    McGann (New Haven: Yale University Press, 2003), 174.
To fall in love is to create a religion – Jorge Luis Borges, 'The Meeting in
    a Dream', in *Other Inquisitions, 1937–1952,* trans. Ruth L.C. Simms
    (New York: Simon and Schuster, 1964), 99.

Sam and Zoe

The American writer Norman Cousins travelled to Puerto Rico –
    Norman Cousins, *Anatomy of an Illness as Perceived by the Patient:
    Reflections in healing and regeneration* (New York: Norton, 1979),
    79–88.
Faithfulness in love is unnatural – *The Diary of Anaïs Nin, 1934–1939,*
    ed. Gunther Stuhlmann (New York: Harcourt Brace, 1967), 13.
More strange than true – William Shakespeare, *A Midsummer Night's
    Dream,* act 5, scene 1.

Rachel and Max

The longing for art, like the longing for love, is a malady that blinds us
    – Orhun Pamuk, *The Museum of Innocence,* trans. Maureen Freely
    (London: Faber, 2009), 415.
The landscape thinks itself in me, and I am its consciousness – Maurice
    Merleau-Ponty, 'Cézanne's Doubt', in *Sense and Non-sense,* trans.
    Hubert L. Dreyfus and Patricia Allen Dreyfus (Evanston, IL:
    Northwestern University Press, 1964), 9–25.